Mental Health, Intellectual Disabilities, and the Aging Process

Philip W. Davidson, Vee P. Prasher and Matthew P. Janicki

Blackwell
Publishing

© 2003 by Blackwell Publishing Ltd

Editorial Offices:
9600 Garsington Road, Oxford OX4 2DQ
   Tel: +44 (0) 1865 776868
Blackwell Publishing Inc, 350 Main Street,
Malden, MA 02148-5018, USA
   Tel: +1 781 388 8250
Iowa State Press, a Blackwell Publishing
Company, 2121 State Avenue, Ames, Iowa
50014-8300, USA
   Tel: +1 515 292 0140
Blackwell Munksgaard, 1 Rosenørns Allé,
P.O. Box 227, DK-1502 Copenhagen V,
Denmark
   Tel: +45 77 33 33 33
Blackwell Publishing Asia Pty Ltd,
550 Swanston Street, Carlton South,
Victoria 3053, Australia
   Tel: +61 (0)3 9347 0300
Blackwell Verlag, Kurfürstendamm 57,
10707 Berlin, Germany
   Tel: +49 (0)30 32 79 060
Blackwell Publishing, 10 rue Casimir
Delavigne, 75006 Paris, France
   Tel: +33 1 53 10 33 10

First published 2003

A catalogue record for this title is available
from the British Library

ISBN 1-4051-0164-4

Library of Congress
Cataloging-in-Publication Data
Is available

Set in 10/13pt Palatino
by DP Photosetting, Aylesbury, Bucks
Printed and bound in Great Britain by
MPG Books Ltd, Bodmin, Cornwall

For further information on
Blackwell Publishing, visit our website:
www.blackwellpublishing.com

Contents

Contributors

Nick Bouras MD, PhD, FRCPsych
Professor of Psychiatry, Estia Centre, GKT School of Medicine, York Clinic, Guy's Hospital, London, England

Nancy N. Cain MD, FAPA
Director of MR/DD Psychiatric Programs, Strong Behavioral Health, University of Rochester Medical Center, Department of Psychiatry, Rochester, New York, USA

Christine D. Cea PhD
Associate Director, Development Disabilities Project, Fordham University Center for Ethics Education, Bronx, New York, USA

Philip W. Davidson PhD
Professor of Pediatrics, University of Rochester School of Medicine and Dentistry, Rochester, New York, USA

Philip Dodd MB, BCh
Stewart's Hospital Services Ltd, Palmerstown, Dublin, Republic of Ireland

Sandra Dowling BA(hons) Social Anthropology, MA
Research Assistant, Department of Psychiatry of Disability, St George's Hospital Medical School, London, England

Laura Smith Emmick MD, MA, BA
Physician, Family Physicians of Hopkinton, Hopkinton, New Hampshire, USA

Celia B. Fisher PhD
Professor of Psychology, Fordham University Center for Ethics Education, Bronx, New York, USA

Lynda L. Geller PhD
Associate Professor of Pediatrics, Stony Brook University, Stony Brook, New York, USA

Colin Griffiths RMHN, MSc, RNT, PGDipCHSE
Department of Training and Education, Stewarts Hospital, Palmerstown, Dublin, Republic of Ireland

Anthony Holland BSc, MBBS, MRCP, MRCPsych, MPil, Dip. Hum. & Cl. Genetics
PPP Foundation Professor of Learning Disabilities, Department of Psychiatry, University of Cambridge, England

Sheila Hollins MBBS, FRCPsych, FRCPCH, MIPD
Professor of Psychiatry of Learning Disability, St George's Hospital Medical School, University of London, England

Geraldine Holt FRCPscyh, BSc(hons)
Consultant and Senior Lecturer, Psychiatry of Learning Disability, Estia Centre, Guy's Hospital, London, England

John W. Jacobson PhD, BCBA
Instructor, Sage Colleges Center for Behavior Analysis, Troy, New York, USA

Matthew P. Janicki PhD
Associate Research Professor and Director for Technical Assistance, Department of Developmental Disability and Human Development, College of Health and Human Development Sciences, University of Illinois at Chicago, USA

Stacey R. Kolomer PhD, MSW
Assistant Professor, School of Social Work, University of Georgia, Athens, Giorgia, USA

Mary McCarron RMHN, RGN, BNS
Research Fellow, Department of Psychiatry and School of Nursing and Midwifery Studies, Trinity College, Dublin, Republic of Ireland

Philip McCallion PhD
Director and Associate Professor, Center for Excellence in Aging Services, University at Albany, USA

James C. Mead MD
Medical Director, Inpatient Psychiatry, Via Health of Wayne-Newark Hospital, Newark, New York, USA

Paul J. Patti MA
Research Scientist, George Jervis Clinic, Institute for Basic Research in Developmental Disabilities, Staten Island, New York, USA

John C. Pomeroy MBBS, MRCPsych
Associate Professor of Pediatrics and Psychiatry, State University of New York at Stony Brook, New York, USA

Vee P. Prasher MBChB, MMedSc, MRCPsych, MD, PhD
Associate Professor of Neuro-developmental Psychiatry, Monyhull Hospital, Kings Norton, Birmingham, England

Peter Sturmey PhD
Associate Professor, Department of Psychology, Queens College, Flushing, New York, USA

Stephen B. Sulkes MD
Associate Professor of Pediatrics, Strong Center for Develpmental Disabilities, Golisano Children's Hospital at Strong, University of Rochester School of Medicine and Dentistry, Rochester, New York, USA

John A. Tsiouris MD
Associate Director, Psychological/Psychiatric Services, George A. Jervis Clinic, New York State Institute for Basic Research, Staten Island, New York, USA

Janette Tyrrell MD
Department of Psychiatry, Trinity College, and Consultant Psychiatrist, St. Michael's House, Ballymun, Dublin, Republic of Ireland

Germain Weber PhD
University Professor, Institute of Psychology, University of Vienna, Austria

To the members of IASSID whose ideas, science, and practice contributions
made this book possible

Series Foreword

Mental Health, Intellectual Disabilities, and the Aging Process is the third in an initial series of publications being issued jointly by the International Association for the Scientific Study of Intellectual Disabilities (IASSID) and Blackwell Publishing. This series had its origins in an effort to examine how to increase longevity and promote healthy aging on the part of the World Health Organization (WHO, 2001), from three different perspectives: physical health, mental health, and social and health policy. This third book encompasses a range of biobehavioral issues that need to be taken into account when developing and enhancing community support systems for adults with intellectual and developmental disabilities.

Philip Davidson and his co-editors have produced a highly informative and useful text that explores a variety of biobehavioral issues around how mature adults confront the intersecting challenges of lifelong disabilities and aging. Much of this thinking has its roots in the early efforts to quantify and more expertly research the nuances of development of children and adults with intellectual disabilities following the demise of prevailing institutionalization practices and policies within the developed world. Early leaders, such as Cooke (1993) who in the United States was instrumental in establishing the financial and research policy underpinnings for such efforts, have contributed to a sea change of thinking of how people with intellectual disabilities are seen and positioned within our societies. The growing sophistication of research and the emergence of more nuanced studies show that, as in the general population, factors that affect the mental health of people with lifelong disabilities are highly complex and cannot be viewed simplistically, but must be explored and defined from a variety of perspectives. It is clear that the underlying basis for many behaviors evidenced in day-to-day adult life have a variety of etiologies, with roots in both classic psychopathologies as well as in less understood, albeit more common environmental pressures.

It is anticipated that this book, and its two complementary texts (*Health of Women with Intellectual Disabilities* and *Physical Health of Adults with Intellectual Disabilities*), will provide a sound basis for the understanding of adult health issues among people with intellectual disabilities and will provide the springboard for improvements in both mental and physical health care as well as set the stage for both basic and applications research in these areas. IASSID is proud to have been the vehicle for this effort and is thankful to the editors and contributors of this text for their commitment to the quality of the material presented and for improving our collective state of knowledge.

Matthew P. Janicki, PhD
Series Editor
University of Illinois at Chicago
Department of Disability and Human Development
College of Health and Human Development Sciences
Chicago, Illinois, USA

References

Cooke, R.E. (1993) The origin of the National Institute of Child Health and Human Development. *Pediatrics*, **92**, 868–871.

World Health Organization (2001) Health ageing – adults with intellectual disabilities: Summative Report. *Journal of Applied Research in Intellectual Disabilities*, **14**, 256–275.

Foreword

I would propose to readers that this is a provocative book. It deals with the variable concurrence of three human conditions that call for tough love to accommodate 'mental wellness'. Mental health concerns, accompanying the presence of intellectual disabilities, and compounded with the phenomena of the aging process, represent a redoubtable challenge. To me, an appropriate response is the provision of stewardship – which is to say that the carer must be a steward.

In this sense, a steward has some managerial and administrative responsibilities, but is also an agent, a caretaker, a proxy, and a loyal advocate. It is assumed that a steward will be accurate, intelligent, and resourceful. This is not a paternalistic or controlling mode, but rather a collaboration that is affirmative, audacious, and optimistic. Those latter elements also describe this book. It gives us some insights, but limited security. On a personal note, about two decades ago I had contact with and admired the investment of the book's senior editor (Phil Davidson) in assisting adults who had the disconcerting presence of presenting with a serious self-injurious behavior. Now I find him and his colleagues deep in a broader complex territory, somewhat related. They are at the convergence of three cultures. They want us to follow.

The field of mental health, intellectual disabilities, and aging is an emerging one. There is a plaintive call for enhanced knowledge. The urgency for research-related approaches is acknowledged, but the pathways here, and outcome measures, are perplexing. Clarification of mental health maxims, and assurance about the ranges of aging, are needed before the subtle cortical elements of intellectual disability can be factored in. In a complex formula of exceptionality, counts of prevalence of elements or combinations become a difficult call. One feels some jealousy regarding pediatric workers, who have a reasonable reach to cause and prevention.

It could be noted that for many adults with intellectual disabilities, or involved individuals in this field, the association of special states or stresses is more extensive that just the three primary components featured in the title. The multifactor design can also include poverty, immigrant or ethnic/social disadvantage circumstances, and/or important chronic illness, as well. This is an imposing roster of lineaments. Being late in my eighth decade, I find myself regarding more critically some of the descriptors being used for the 'aging' items. The nature of 'aging in place', 'healthy aging', or even 'successful aging' gives me pause; they may be talking about me! Indeed, Chapter 17 of this book states that 'functional decline occurs in many, if not all, older people with or without ID who do not have DAT'. What did *you* say I did yesterday? In some regards it appears now that there is another naughty age group in the human sequence – not only the adolescent years, but also the old timers. Somehow my heart also goes out to the effects of some of the other strands in the multistressed person. It is not graceful to have cognitive impairment, to be confused about reality, to have been homeless, or to have one's kidneys failing. Stewards are needed. And also books like this one.

The point is made several times about the imprecision that may characterize defining of mental status, particularly when there is also intellectual disability. I remain concerned about our approaches to what might be called idiosyncratic behavior, in any age group, and its true nosology. Strangeness is not a disease. On the other hand, loss and loneliness can be cousins to depression. Building experience with larger numbers of elderly persons will help us to find consensus on mental disorder, and on the boundaries that exist for the helpfulness of behavioral guidance.

What a lively matter is the planning of inclusion for persons with these complex states. There is often a tantalizing dynamic when intellectual and developmental disabilities meet the age care network. Our identification of values gets a fresh exercise, and there can be many winners. The happiness ethic can receive effective promotion for those persons with intellectual disabilities, those who are of advanced age, or those with mental illness – and those who have all three. A holistic spirit can work in each of these settings, and do much for the frequently threatened emotional peace of carers at the same time.

The goals presented in Table 1.1, in Chapter 1, are solid, though intimidating. I urge the reader to make their own personal version of Table 1.1, adding objectives and action steps. Reasonably, we are being asked to chart the behavioral phenotype of humans throughout all ages (probably this is a second book). Against this gradient, the impact of age-related stressors is considered; I would speak to the value as well of listing age-related rewards (the good years!). The goals reflect on the cultural and developmental context of special behaviors, and here we must assure linkage with our colleagues in sociology and social anthropology. Holistic assessment is invited for anxiety and depression; a similar broad vision could take a measure of *joy*. Education in mental health skills and creation of affirmative living environments acknowledges the potential nurturing role of professionals and social organization Stable mental health services, of adequate depth, and communities that love people, are indexes of our vision (national, regional or local government, schools, churches, arts, other leadership). The old-fashioned concepts of banding together for the benefit of people in need plays to each of these troubled areas, and more so for those with multiplex special states. Quality of life discussions should be taking place at the local authority, at the United Nations, and in our research planning symposia.

Like we said, a compassionate and accurate steward is a good steward. This book will help *you* clear your mind, get the facts, create a dedicated scene, and measure what *you* do.

Allen C. Crocker MD
Associate Professor of Pediatrics
Harvard Medical School
Boston, Massachusetts
and Program Director
Institute for Community Inclusion
Children's Hospital
Boston, Massachusetts
USA

Acknowledgements

The editors wish to acknowledge the many members of the IASSID Special Interest Research Groups on Aging and Mental Health who collaborated with us to develop the ideas, concepts and research findings presented in this book. The collaboration began in the mid-1990s and lead first to the highly successful WHO meeting on Aging, Health and ID held in Geneva in 1999. The book project is a direct outgrowth of that meeting and its follow-up activities. We would have had no book if it were not for the support of these groups. We want to also recognize the foresight of the IASSID in commissioning and sponsoring the work.

Our mentors Eric Allitt, Allen Crocker, Don Routh, and Steve and Carolyn Schroeder played a large role in creating the atmosphere for each of us chose this field for our life's work. We are indebted to them for so admirably teaching us the importance of science, and the necessity to connect science to practice.

Each of us gratefully acknowledges the support of our wives, Margaret, Suman, and Bonnie, whose continuous support has permitted our collective efforts to flourish. The senior editor (Phil Davidson) is indebted to Catherine Imhof who assisted in the final editing process. This task easily cost her many gray hairs.

We are all inspired by our consumer colleagues, those to whom we have provided services and supports and their families, and the literally thousands of carers and agency personnel whose day to day struggles with persons with dual diagnosis have simultaneously challenged us and instilled a deep sense of admiration. This book is for them.

Introduction

> 'From each soul a different perspective
> a different way of seeing, doing, achieving
> our strength is in our diversity'
> Anon.

For many years it has been recognized that some adults with intellectual disabilities (ID) are at elevated risk for mental and behavioral health problems. Prevalence rates for psychiatric disorders among persons with ID, while somewhat difficult to estimate accurately, tend to be at least as high as for persons without ID – and behavioral disorders seem to occur much more often than would be expected in the general population. The reasons for these trends are not fully understood, but it seems evident that biological and environmental factors conspire and interact to affect both mental and behavioral health (Burns *et al.*, 2002). Further, although specific risk factors for each outcome are largely not understood, the interplay between health status and mental and behavioral health, well known in general medical and psychiatric practice, seems at least as important in affecting behavioral and psychiatric outcomes in persons with ID. Additionally, it appears that a wide spectrum of challenging behavior and mental illnesses can occur in persons with ID and that these disorders persist to varying degrees into older age, and in some instances are first evident in older age.

From the start of organized societal response to persons with lifelong disabilities, providers and policy makers have concentrated attention on this problem. However, it was not until the beginning of the deinstitutionalization movement that occurred in most developed countries in the latter decades of the twentieth century, that progress was made in understanding causes, treatment and prevention. Since then considerable effort has been expended to devise straightforward and effective intervention methods to permit persons with ID who were affected by behavioral and psychiatric difficulties to live, work, be educated and recreate in inclusive settings. These methods generally fall into one of two categories: psychopharmacologic and behavioral. Progress was made in linking psychiatric diseases to specific neurotransmitters and new medications appeared that were shown to affect neurochemical corrections. Subsequent use of these medications slowly infiltrated the pharmacopeia for persons with ID and replaced older, less effective medications while reducing the likelihood of unacceptable side effects and the problems inherent in polypharmacy. At the same time, behavioral psychology research brought forth treatment approaches for individuals with ID that effectively reduced severe behavioral morbidity that previously would have jeopardized independent living in the community for affected persons (often at a very young age) and relegated them to lifelong institutional care.

These successes have led to a large number of adults living and working successfully in the community. Like their counterparts without ID, these persons are aging. By the year 2040, the number of persons with ID age 65 and older – who now represent about 12% of the ID population – will grow to about 25%. Additionally, about the same proportion of these persons who now have what we may term a 'dual diagnosis' (i.e. both an intellectual and psychiatric impairment) will retain that status into older adulthood and old age. Unfortunately, our scientific and treatment literature has had little information for us to draw upon to make the appropriate decisions about best practices as more elderly individuals with dual diagnosis present for services.

Goals of the book

This book is designed to review the scientific and practice literatures pertinent to dual diagnosis in adults with ID, identify best clinical practices, and suggest models for both community services and professional education in the field. This work grew out of a meeting held at the World Health Organization in 1999 that addressed the health and mental health practice and policy needs of older persons with ID. Eleven recommendations concerning dual diagnosis emerged from that meeting as listed in Table 1.1. The general findings of the meeting regarding the problems people face as a result of dual diagnosis (Thorpe *et al.*, 2000, p. 7) were as follows:

'Most research in the area of mental or behavioral disorders or problems has had treatment as its focus. Much less has been done about the causes and risk factors of such disorders and their prevention. Almost all of the data available come from populations of persons with intellectual disabilities from nations with established market economies, where research funding has been most available and there has been a critical mass of workers who specialized in this field. For instance, prevalence data for psychiatric and behavioral disorders may differ between nations with established market economies and developing

Table 1.1 Goals addressing biobehavioral issues resulting from the 1999 WHO Conference on *Healthy Aging: Adults with Intellectual Disabilities*. (Adapted from Thorpe *et al.*, 2002).

- To improve the understanding of normal psychological functioning throughout the life span
- To improve knowledge and awareness of age-related stressors and their impact
- To understand and appreciate the social, cultural, environmental and developmental context of behaviors and their functions
- To improve the detection and holistic assessment of mental disorders such as depression, anxiety and dementia
- To increase mental health knowledge and skills in professionals, carers and families
- To develop living environments that are responsive to the mental health needs
- To promote mental health and minimize negative outcome of mental health problems
- To increase mental health services and supports in communities
- To collaborate with older people with ID and their support system in developing culturally sensitive, humane and minimally restrictive mental health interventions with an integrated bio-psychosocial orientation.
- To improve the quality of life in older people with ID and mental health problems
- To develop a research agenda that will provide evidence concerning each goal for all nations.

nations and treatment outcomes may vary where the cultural ethos may inhibit referrals and special resources or services are limited. Improved health status and prevention in developing nations, the principal goal of WHO, must depend on identification of special issues pertaining to developing nations and application of techniques that permit information to be gathered free of cultural or other restraints.

'Well-controlled research in mental and behavioral disorders as they occur in persons with intellectual disabilities is limited. Most of the work over the past 30 years addresses treatment issues; fewer focused on diagnosis or etiologic factors, or prevention. Only a small number address basic mechanisms. These disappointing data probably reflect several things, including a well-known lack of a research focus or funding. As a consequence, there are limited numbers of scientists in the field and a lack of programmatic efforts in research centers addressing any relevant issue related to intellectual disabilities. Without specific attention from health planners and ministerial level policy makers, as well as a critical mass of investigators working on a common problem in programmatic ways, little converging data can emerge and, quite likely, few if any major discoveries will appear quickly.

'Promising lines of inquiry relate to both treatment strategies and biological determination and regulation of behavior. Rigorous methodologies are available to undertake controlled or randomized clinical trials for behavioral and pharmacologic interventions. Recent advances in molecular genetics and neuropharmacology provide new opportunities for linking severe behavioral and psychiatric disorders to brain neurochemistry. The field must move toward a research focus that includes a better balance of studies of basic mechanisms, translational and clinical outcome studies.'

One goal of this book is to review what is known in the areas identified by the WHO report from the 1999 meeting. We have organized the book into three broad sections paralleling the WHO goal statements. Part 1 addresses prevalence and diagnosis, Part 2 looks at treatment and interventions, and Part 3 considers service system issues. In Part 1, the chapters by Jacobson (Chapter 2) and Tyrrell and Dodd (Chapter 3) are designed to explore and further pinpoint as best as possible the prevalence of behavioural and mental health disorders and the range of psychopathology that may be seen in older persons with ID. As these authors point out, estimating prevalence is fraught with pitfalls, starting with our lack of any common agreement on what constitutes a behavioral disorder and how competent the diagnosis of psychopathology may be. In Chapter 4 Holland reviews the complexities of recognizing psychopathology, which are often more difficult in adults with ID than in the general population. The remaining three chapters (Chapters 5, 6 and 7) address specific issues rarely discussed at any length in the literature on older adults with ID: depression, emotional health and Down syndrome, and interactions between mental health and health conditions. Each of these topics has been studied too little as yet, and further exploration holds promise for spawning new methods of looking at the intersection of mental health and aging.

Part 2 of this book explores various traditional treatment methods, including psychotherapy (Chapter 8), behavior modification (Chapter 9), and psychopharmacology (Chapter 10). In each case, the authors emphasize unique approaches that have evolved for addressing the needs of adults with ID as they age. To complement these explorations, Fisher *et al.* in Chapter 11 discuss treatment ethics, an issue of growing concern where vulnerable populations are concerned and when the usual medications used to treat persons without ID may not always have the expected result in older adults with ID. Dowling and Hollins' chapter on grief and bereavement (Chapter 12) is particularly important in relation to older adults with or without ID; however, in the case of adults with ID it is even more important, as the lack of typical ability to communicate often coincides with the growing probability of experiencing loss and manifesting problematic behaviors. In extreme instances, unfocused grief may then present as a more complex mental illness. Models for addressing this common and quite treatable outcome are discussed. A chapter by McCallion and Kolomer on the impact of mental illness on carers (Chapter 13) rounds off these explorations. As is the case in persons without ID who have mental or behavioral problems, constant carers may play a crucial role in any treatment or intervention, but often they may be so engaged with their own stresses that participation may be difficult to achieve. A further consideration is that unresolved carer burden and stress may in itself contribute to the behavioral symptomology of the adult under their care.

Rounding off the book, we have a section on system issues. Factors affecting biobehavioral and dual diagnosis issues are very complex, ranging from a lack of understanding of the factors contributing to behavior, to a deficit in well-trained personnel for assessment, treatment and care, and to a lack of available community-based systems of care that are accessible to persons who pose special challenges. Such deficiencies in community care are found worldwide, equally affecting both developed and developing nations. In some instances the deficiencies are the result of a lack of public realization of the need or commitment to specialized services for people with ID; in other instances they may be the result of financial constraints and the paucity or lack of allocation of scarce public resources to these types of services. In other areas they may be the result of the lack of sophistication of mental health professionals and care providers, where the special needs or situations of people with ID go misunderstood and confounded with archaic psychiatric treatment and hospitalization practices. Lastly, they may be due to the confusion around behavioral presentations and the misattribution of the diagnosis of mental illness to rather mundane and treatable maladaptive behaviors.

Chapters in Part 3 describe innovative models for community services for adults with ID (Chapter 14), and address training as a preventive tool (Chapter 15) and the role of nurses in assisting adults to remain in community settings (Chapter 16). By including these chapters we aim to help put the less-noxious individual idiosyncratic behaviors as well as more severe behavioral pathologies in the perspective of community care alternatives.

Final thoughts

Two last thoughts. First, the scope of this book was initially limited to older adults with ID, but as we explored the myriad issues affecting adults in their mature years, it was decided that contributors also needed to address broader age-span issues (when appropriate). We believe that, with the exception of organic age-associated conditions such as dementia and depression, mental or behavioral difficulties occurring in older age may, and almost always do, have origins in earlier years. Second, we have used the term 'intellectual disability' throughout the text, recognizing that in some countries other terms are used (such as mental retardation, learning disability, mental handicap, intellectual handicap, etc.). We consider these terms synonymous. One exception is 'developmental disability', which we recognize encompasses a broader set of impairments, only one of which is intellectual disability. We have asked our contributors to use these two terms with care and within the context of their targeting meaning.

References

Burns, A., Purandare, N. & Craig, S. (2002) *Mental Health in Older People in Practice.* RSM Publishing, London.

Thorpe, L., Davidson, P., Janicki, M.P. & Working Group (2000) Healthy aging – adults with intellectual disabilities: biobehavioral issues. *Journal of Applied Research in Intellectual Disabilities,* **14**, 218–228.

Thorpe, L., Davidson, P. & Janicki, M.P. (2002) *Healthy Aging – Adults with Intellectual Disabilities: Summative Report.* (WHO/MSD/HPS/MDP/00.3). World Health Organization, Geneva, Switzerland.

Part 1
Prevalence and Characteristics

2 Prevalence of Mental and Behavioral Disorders

John W. Jacobson

Many older people with intellectual disabilities (ID) manifest mental disorders and associated severe behavioral problems that may extend into later life. In general, they are at risk of the same conditions as the older general population, in particular various forms of depression and dementia, and impairments of aging. Ascertaining the prevalence of these disorders among older people with ID has been a complex undertaking, partly because there has been research interest in these issues for slightly less than two decades, and partly because of diversity in the developmental and functional characteristics of the aging and aged population of people with ID. Ascertaining the prevalence of mental and behavioral disorders among older people with ID is also slowed by the changing impacts of secular practice on biobehavioral morbidity and cohort effects, and the need to acquire further, prospective longitudinal information regarding onset, offset and persistence of these conditions in this population.

Issues affecting prevalence estimation

Prevalence of a condition or disorder refers to the number of people identified as meeting reporting criteria in a population or other sample. Prevalence is a function of incidence (number of new cases occurring over time) and duration of a condition (its persistence over time). The more cases that occur over time and the longer the duration, the higher the prevalence rate will be for a condition. The number of cases with a condition can be expressed in a number of ways, the most common being *point prevalence* (number of cases on a population basis at a single point in time), *annual prevalence* (cumulative number of cases on a population basis during a year), and *lifetime prevalence* (cumulative number of cases during an average lifetime). Thus there are several components to a prevalence rate: enumerated cases, an identified and verifiable population cohort, and a time period.

Most reports of prevalence of mental or behavioral disorders in adults with ID have been based on convenience samples derived from clinical populations. This practice may result in referral bias secondary to factors affecting whether a person is referred for services, as well as the availability of local alternatives to admission to services provided by that organization or to that setting.

There have been a few examples of prevalence estimates that were based on large service registries. While overcoming some of the issues of referral bias, registry-based studies may lack specificity of information about the disorders of interest, and the degree to which disorders and behaviors are defined in operational terms that encourage reliable and valid reporting. For example, registries typically rely on reported instances of conditions, but when rates are calculated on a population base (e.g. all known instances of older people with ID), these rates include false positives and exclude false negatives. Although it has been suggested that a considerable number of people with ID fall into the category of 'misses' with respect to mental conditions, this seems to be a much less evident issue in terms of behavior disorders or problem behaviors, which are generally simpler in topology and may not entail multiple criteria (e.g. criteria for a syndrome) for reporting.

Studies of the prevalence of mental and behavioral disorders among older people with ID have relied on point prevalence or annual prevalence (for example, in registries that are renewed annually). This component of prevalence estimation is fairly consistent from study to study, and there has been much less focus on incidence estimates than on prevalence estimates.

Nonetheless, when different procedures are used in different registries to report conditions, or the registry samples differ in their level of access to diagnostic services, this may still bias enumeration of cases. Furthermore, aside from registries that have clear criteria for reporting a case and associated diagnostic information, associated with specific state, provincial or other geographic areas with ascertained populations, there is no means of clearly specifying the population cohort to which information gathered from a single organization or setting can be generalized. For example, based on screening findings, it has been suggested that the rates of occurrence of mental and behavioral disorders in many registries are severe underestimates of the 'true' prevalence rates, and the studies that have identified much higher prevalence rates than those reported in registries are generally based on samples that cannot be generalized. Although one cannot generalize from these samples, there is some merit to the notion that, as many small samples have been reviewed, substantial additional numbers of people have been identified with mental disorders, in addition to people previously so classified. But, although research provides some support for the premise of underidentification, it does not permit us to estimate the degree to which underidentification typically occurs, because of problems extrapolating from samples of convenience or that are bounded in various ways.

Respondent characteristics may vary with the sampling frame. Small-scale studies may be conducted in smaller geographic areas, or in single or a few residential or other service contexts. The training and qualifications of practitioners or personnel who report data regarding mental and behavioral disorders are often known, generally quite high or assured by training in use of protocols, and reported by researchers, and the methods and criteria used to assess and classify these conditions can also be ascertained. In registry studies the rates reported might reflect diagnostic decisions made by many practitioners using substantially different local threshold norms or criteria for assignment of a related diagnosis or classification, and who may vary in extent and type of professional training. There seem to be indications that more highly trained practitioners tend to report higher rates of mental disorders. This interpretation may not be well-justified since many of the relevant research studies consist of non-random or referred samples, which could severely bias the rates identified. In a randomly drawn population-based sample, these same practitioners might identify lower rates of mental and behavioral disorders, intermediate to those in narrow samples and registries.

Another major consideration in the estimation of prevalence for mental and behavioral disorders is the method of measurement that contributes to diagnosis or reporting. Some studies determine cases based on clinical assessment, which may be unstructured or practitioner-selected and non-uniform. Other estimates have been based on the results of screening or assessment tools or other measures that are intended to contribute to more objective or robust and consistent diagnostic formulation. Application of research diagnostic criteria (Lund, 1985; Clarke & Gomez, 1999) may represent a practice that is desirable from a research standpoint; it may not mirror actual diagnostic practice in the field extremely well. Researchers are most concerned about sampling, interpractitioner consistency in the criteria used, uniformity of the assessment process, and factors affecting access to skilled assessment services – thus they emphasize the need for large samples. Experience suggests that clinicians, however, may find studies on specific service settings – with smaller samples of people with ID, small numbers of practitioners involved, and particulars of diagnostic practices reported – to be most appealing in addressing questions of prevalence of mental and behavioral disorders among people with ID. This preference may not be justified, as both approaches – as implemented in contemporary research – have weaknesses that hinder drawing firm conclusions regarding prevalence.

The generalization of findings from numerous reports addressing various aspects of prevalence of mental and behavioral disorders among older people with ID is limited by a lack of an appropriate 'gold standard' of diagnostic practice. Since the early 1990s work has begun to develop diagnostic criteria that entail modest alterations to criteria for use with people with mild or moderate ID who communicate well or who can self-report distress effectively, more substantive alterations for criteria for use with people with moderate ID who do not speak or communicate well, and very extensive alterations for use with people with severe or profound ID. Suggested alterations include substitution of behaviors or combinations of behaviors that parallel criteria used with people who can communicate verbally (or could do so prior to onset of a condition). Modified criteria for psychotic and affective disorders have also been suggested (Sovner & Hurley, 1982a,b; Clarke & Gomez, 1999; Einfeld & Tonge, 1999). Modified criteria are also evident in screening measures for mental disorders for use in assessing people with ID (Sturmey & Bertman, 1994; Duncan *et al*, 1999).

Criteria for the identification of behavioral disorders or problem behaviors may not be as clouded as those for mental disorders when applied to people with ID. Although concurrence on their parameters can be readily achieved, the use of terms such as conduct disorder, aggression, property destruction, self-injury or withdrawal refers to classes of behavior, rather than specific behaviors. A given individual may manifest one or more behaviors that are heuristically considered to be aggressive in nature. When prevalence of aggression is ascertained, for example, this may or may not include specification of form, intensity, frequency or clinical significance of the aggressive behavior. In an ideal assessment of prevalence these factors will be distinguished, but they can seldom be addressed in larger population samples because data are collected in registries with limited detail about behaviors or are collected in survey form, where use of very lengthy protocols may adversely affect response rate and population representation. Despite these issues, estimates of behavior disorder or problem behavior prevalence, from adequately specified samples, are probably more robust than those for mental disorders in the same samples.

Prevalence of mental and behavior disorders

Subject to the limitations noted above, numerous studies have reported on the occurrence of mental and behavioral disorders among older people with ID. Many of these studies, however, have aggregated data on such conditions among people age 60 years or older, often as a consequence of sample size. This practice may mask differences among the older and oldest people. In reporting the rates found in various samples and by various investigators, comparable groups can generally be formed only for broad categories of disorder, and comparisons necessarily entail groups defined by somewhat different age ranges. Moreover, studies include varying proportions of people with differing degrees of ID.

Table 2.1 shows rates for the identification of mental and behavioral disorders in a variety of age-defined samples of people with ID. Related studies have been reviewed in detail elsewhere (Jacobson, 1990a; Day & Jancar, 1994). Total rates of mental and behavioral disorders range from about one-fifth to two-fifths of assessed or registered older individuals (Cooper, 1999; Moss *et al.*, 2000). The rates of various disorders are relatively unstable across samples. Day and Jancar (1994) have characterized research findings as showing declines in all conditions except for dementia, which increases with advancing age in some studies. As they note, generally, behavioral disorders account for one-third to one-half of cases in many samples, behavioral problems that arise with advancing age are 'not uncommon', there is a high prevalence of depression and anxiety states that may be reactive to physical illness or social factors, and mental disorders may be underdiagnosed in many instances (Jacobson, 1990b; Day & Jancar, 1994).

Haveman and associates (1994) reported instances of psychological and behavioral problems in a cohort of 1580 people with ID living at 83 group homes and 24 institutions, including 715 people age 50 or older, representing all levels of ID. Psychological problems declined slightly from age 20 through 60 years and older, but problem behavior increased slightly over the same ages, both non-significantly. There was a correlation of 0.52 between psychological problems and problem behaviors in people over age 50. The occurrence of less problem behavior with advanced age was apparent only for people without Down syndrome and severe ID. People with Down syndrome and mild or severe ID had more psychological problems with advancing age, beginning above age 40 years for those with severe ID, and at age 50 years for those with mild ID. Among individuals over 40 years, problems were reported in adapting to minor changes in routines, and they were more often characterized as displaying incoherent or apathetic behavior, and as lacking initiative. A majority over age 60 was drowsy and had higher rates of irritation, fear, restlessness at night, feelings of sadness, suspiciousness and lack of appetite (Haveman *et al.*, 1994).

Haveman and his colleagues (1994) also reported that 34% of those with psychiatric diagnosis showed serious problem behavior compared to 18% of another sample without psychiatric diagnosis. Among 85 people age 50 years and older, 46% were diagnosed with dementia, and many of these were noted to have psychological problems but few behavior problems. The authors suggested that dementia appears to be the main cause of many psychological problems found among older people with Down

Table 2.1 Prevalence (as %) of mental and behavioral disorders among people with intellectual disabilities in six studies.

Citation	Age (Yrs)	Prevalence of mental or behavioral disorder (% of cohort)						
		Overall	Schizophrenia	Affective psychosis	Autism	Neuroses	Dementia	Behavior/personality disorder
Corbett (1979)	≥ 60	36	5	3	4	2	—	23
James (1986)	≥ 60	42	2	8	—	18	—	14
Day (1985)	60–69	25	13	—	—	1	2	9
Day (1985)	≥ 70	17	—	3	—	—	10	4
Day (1987)	≥ 65	20	3	2	1	1	6	5
Lund (1985)	≥ 65	26	4	—	—	—	22	—

Adapted from Day and Jancar (1994) and from the studies cited.

syndrome, but it is not closely related to behavior problems. As Thorpe *et al.*, (2000) have noted, behavioral disorders 'may be related to another mental disorder in the individual, biological vulnerability, longstanding learned behaviors, or mismatch between environmental expectations and resources with the individual's capabilities and wishes' (p. 2). This variety of potential causal or contributory factors may tend to attenuate expected relationships between mental disorders or dementia and behavioral disorders or behavior problems.

Table 2.2 provides an overview of general diagnostic categories of disorders and frequently reported behaviors for three age cohorts, based on a diverse survey sample representing the range of ID levels, including people both with and without Down syndrome living in community and institutional settings, as reported by Jacobson and Harper (1989). These data show that from age 55 about one-fifth of subjects is reported to have mental disorders and about one-sixth has neurological syndromes (see Table 2.2a). Clinically significant rates of tantrums, resisting supervision, verbal abusiveness, hyperactivity, running or wandering away, and withdrawal (reflecting a range of possible impairments of self-regulation) are apparent among 55–59-year-olds, and rates of occurrence remain high even among people age 75 years and older (see Table 2.2b).

Table 2.3 shows a further contrast of other behavior problems among the two older age cohorts reported by Jacobson and Harper (1989). Disrupting activities, inappropriate sex acts, hoarding, stealing, physical assault, obsessions and self-injury occur at rates requiring considerable

Table 2.2 Mental disorders and problem behaviors among older people with intellectual disabilities.

Disorders and Behaviors (%)	Age (Years)		
	55–59 (n = 83)	60–74 (n = 216)	≥ 75 (n = 80)
(a) General conditions or classifications			
Psychiatric diagnosis	19	23	21
Progressive neurological condition	4	12	4
Neurological disease	8	9	10
(b) Primary reported behavior problems			
Tantrums	76	51	21
Resists supervision	25	45	21
Verbally abusive	15	26	27
Hyperactive	28	26	18
Runs/wanders away	37	21	21
Withdrawn	28	53	21

Adapted from Jacobson and Harper (1989)

Table 2.3 Prevalence of behavioral disorders and behavior problems among older people with intellectual disabilities.

	% of age group	
Behavioral disorders or behavior problems	60–74 (n = 216)	≥ 75 (n = 80)
Disrupts activities	34	6
Inappropriate sexual acts	19	6
Hoarding	19	6
Steals	18	8
Physical assaults	18	4
Obsessions	16	4
Self-injury	15	4
Damages property	8	4
Eats inedibles/pica	4	4
Compulsions/rituals	3	3
Suicide threats or attempts	1	1
Fire-setting attempts	1	0

Adapted from Jacobson and Harper (1989)

clinical attention in the age group 60–74 years, but the rates for these behaviors are relatively attenuated in the age group 75 years and older.

Day and Jancar (1994) noted that the linkage between physical illness and mental disorders in the general elderly population has not been demonstrated among older people with ID. However, they also note that with advancing age, people with Down syndrome experience higher-than-expected rates of visual and auditory impairments, osteoporosis, epilepsy, motor impairments, lung disease, hypothyroidism, diabetes mellitus, neurological disorders and strokes. Table 2.4 shows rates for several health conditions among older people with ID, including people with Down syndrome (Janicki & Jacobson, 1986). These data show clear indications of increased rates of musculo-skeletal, sensory and cardio-vascular conditions among successive age cohorts. In addition to the listed conditions, it has been estimated that between 20% (ages 51–60 years) and 30% (ages 61–70 years) of older people with Down syndrome will evidence dementia (principally Alzheimer disease), compared to less than 10% of their peers with other etiologies of ID (Zigman *et al.*, 1996). Some data suggest that onset of behavior problems is associated with occurrence of dementia (Moss & Patel, 1997; Cooper & Prasher, 1998; Prasher *et al*, 1998; Cosgrave *et al.*, 1999), and physical conditions (Cooper, 1999; Davidson *et al.*, in press).

Physical conditions may be associated with psychological impacts and also with changes in behavior that may constitute onset of behavioral

Table 2.4 Physical conditions among older adults with intellectual disabilities.

Health condition (%)	Age (Years)		
	65–69	75–79	> 80
Musculoskeletal	21	23	33
Special issue	23	34	43
Cardiovascular	26	42	55
Respiratory	3	5	8
Neoplastic	2	4	7
Other health conditions	18	24	26

Adapted from Janicki and Jacobson (1986)

disorders. For example, Pary (1993) found that 87% of older adults with ID admitted on an acute basis to a psychiatric service also had at least one medical diagnosis (and 28% had three such diagnoses). Cohen and Eisdorfer (1985) have observed that, within the general population, 'Although the prevalence of the major depressive disorders is about the same in the aged compared with younger and middle-aged adults, the prevalence of significant depressive symptomatology increases in the aged population' (p. 878). They note many causes for depressed affect, including a range of mental disorders, (acute or recurring) physical illness, acute or persisting medication side effects, 'late-life dementia, substance-induced dementia, Cushing syndrome, hypothyroidism, malignancy, vitamin deficiencies, brain lesions, adjustment disorder(s)... or bereavement...' (Cohen & Eisdorfer, 1985, p. 878). Quite plausibly, these conditions and disorders occur at similar rates in the older general population and older population with mild or moderate ID, who represent the majority of older individuals with ID. Changes in physical function or activity may also be associated with onset of paranoia, suspiciousness, social hearing losses, subtle perception of hearing or vision loss, loss of physical (motor) skills or speediness, or memory problems associated with locating objects or environmental relocation (Cohen & Eisdorfer, 1985).

Among older adults with severe or profound ID, some behavioral disorders have also been found to be more pronounced or common than among younger individuals. For example, Cherry *et al.*, (1997) reviewed records on 84 20–29-year-olds and 84 60–79-year-olds who were institutionalized, and found that adults in the older age group had greater severity ratings on assessment protocol subscales for anxiety, stereotyped behavior and impulse control disorders.

Future research needs

Considerable work remains to be done to improve ascertainment of mental and behavioral disorders in this population. Assessment protocols with appropriate prognostic validity and reliability are required, and uniform combined protocol and clinical procedures for ascertainment of positive cases and better and more representative population samples of older people with ID are needed to assure that both the numerators and denominators of epidemiological estimates are accurately constructed and robust. As previously noted, sampling is a particular concern, with many recent studies continuing to include relatively small samples that are not drawn from a broad population with a sampling frame. Larger population samples are needed to stratify samples within the sample studies by intellectual or adaptive level to assure parity in assessment of mental and behavioral disorders, particularly breadth and depth of assessment procedures, for more and less able older people. In recent years selected prospective longitudinal studies have clarified such issues as age of onset of dementias, the relation of dementias to onset of affective and anxiety disorders, and the relations among mental disorders, dementias and occurrence of behavior problems. The existing research consists primarily of cross-sectional studies, but additional prospective studies will be the key to further elucidating issues of prevalence and incidence of disorders and of biobehavioral morbidity among older people with ID during the coming decade. As the segment of the general population that is older continues to grow, interest in research on mental and behavioral disorders among older people with ID, particularly those with mild or moderate ID, or with Down syndrome, should continue to grow and to provide insights into aging effects in the rest of the population.

Summary

Although there are indications that clinically significant behavioral disorders and behavior problems occur at higher rates in the older population with ID than in the general population at age 55 and older, as these people with ID age, rates of many behavior problems and associated behavioral disorders appear to decrease to levels that are consistent with those seen in the general population. For the oldest age cohorts, in both the general and ID population, behavior disorders and alterations in psychosocial functioning tend to be associated with the onset of dementia. In the older population with ID there are indications of some elevated rates of diagnosed mental disorders, but ascertainment of representative rates remains elusive, and populations of older people with ID in some societies may have better access to psychological and psychiatric diagnostic services than do their peers in the general population. This means that the conclusion often drawn that older people with ID without coarse, pre-existing neurological impairment or anomalies are more likely to have a variety of mental or behavioral conditions, is based for the present on rather tenuous grounds. In no way, however, should this factor be considered a rationale by which the social significance and consequences of the occurrence of mental and behavioral disorders can be minimized.

References

Cherry, K.E., Matson, J.L. & Paclawskyj, T.R. (1997) Psychopathology in older adults with severe and profound mental retardation. *American Journal on Mental Retardation*, **101**, 445–458.

Clarke, D.J. & Gomez, G.A. (1999) Utility of modified DCR-10 criteria in the diagnosis of depression associated with intellectual disability. *Journal of Intellectual Disability Research*, **43**, 413–420.

Cohen, D. & Eisdorfer, C. (1985) Major psychiatric and behavioral disorders in the aged. *Principles of Geriatric Medicine* (eds R. Andres, E.L. Bierman, & W.R. Hazzard) pp. 867–908. McGraw-Hill, New York.

Cooper, S.A. (1999) The relationship between psychiatric and physical health in elderly people with intellectual disability. *Journal of Intellectual Disability Research*, **43**, 54–60.

Cooper, S.A. & Prasher, V.P. (1998) Maladaptive behaviors and symptoms of dementia in adults with Down's syndrome compared with adults with intellectual disability of other etiologies. *Journal of Intellectual Disability Research*, **42**, 293–300.

Corbett, J. (1979) Psychiatric morbidity and mental retardation. *Psychiatric Illness and Mental Handicap* (eds F.E. James & R.P. Snaith) pp. 11–25. College of Psychiatrists, Headley Brothers, Ashford Kent, UK.

Cosgrave, M.P., Tyrrell, J., McCarron, M., Gill, M. & Lawlor, B.A. (1999) Determinants of aggression, and adaptive and maladaptive behavior in older people with Down's syndrome with and without dementia. *Journal of Intellectual Disability Research*, **43**, 393–399.

Davidson, P.W., Janicki, M.P., Ladrigan, P., Houser, K., Henderson, C.M. & Cain, N.C. (in press) Association between behavior problems and health status in older adults with intellectual ability. *Journal of Aging and Mental Health*.

Day, K. (1985) Psychiatric disorder in the middle-aged and elderly mentally handicapped. *British Journal of Psychiatry*, **147**, 660–667.

Day, K. (1987) The elderly mentally handicapped in hospital: a clinical study. *Journal of Mental Deficiency Research*, **31**, 131–146.

Day, K. & Jancar, J. (1994) Mental and physical health and ageing in mental handicap: A review. *Journal of Intellectual Disability Research*, **38**, 241–256.

Duncan, D., Matson, J.L., Bamburg, J.W., Cherry, K.E. & Buckley, T. (1999) The relationship of self-injurious behavior and aggression to social skills in persons with severe and profound learning disability. *Research in Developmental Disabilities*, **20**, 441–448.

Einfeld, S.L. & Tonge, B.J. (1999) Observations on the use of the ICD-10 Guide for Mental Retardation. *Journal of Intellectual Disability Research*, **43**, 408–412.

Haveman, M.J., Maaskant, M.A., van Schrojenstein Lantman-de Valk, H.M.J., Urlings, H.F.J. & Kessels, A.G. (1994) Mental health problems in elderly people with and without Down's syndrome. *Journal of Intellectual Disability Research*, **38**, 341–355.

Jacobson, J.W. (1990a) Assessing the prevalence of psychiatric disorders in a developmentally disabled population. *Assessment of Behavior Problems in Persons with Mental Retardation Living in the Community* (eds E. Dibble & D.B. Gray) pp. 19–70. National Institute of Mental Health and National Institute of Child and Human Development, Rockville, MD.

Jacobson, J.W. (1990b) Do some mental disorders occur at lower rates among persons with mental retardation? *American Journal on Mental Retardation*, **94**, 596–602.

Jacobson, J.W. & Harper, M.S. (1989) Mental health status of older persons with mental retardation in residential care settings. *Australia and New Zealand Journal of Developmental Disabilities*, **15**, 301–310.

James, D.H. (1986) Psychiatric and behavioral disorders amongst older severely mentally handicapped adults. *Journal of Mental Deficiency Research*, **30**, 341–345.

Janicki, M.P. & Jacobson, J.W. (1986) Generational trends in sensory, physical, and behavioral abilities among older mentally retarded persons. *American Journal of Mental Deficiency*, **90**, 490–500.

Lund, J. (1985) The prevalence of psychiatric morbidity in mentally retarded adults. *Acta Psychiatrica Scandinavia*, **7**, 563–570.

Moss. S.C., Emerson, E., Kiernan, C., Turner, S., Hatton, C. & Alborz, A. (2000) Psychiatric symptoms in adults with learning disability and challenging behavior. *British Journal of Psychiatry*, **177**, 452–456.

Moss, S., & Patel, P. (1997) Dementia in older people with intellectual disability: Symptoms of physical and mental illness, and levels of adaptive behavior. *Journal of Intellectual Disability Research*, **41**, 60–69.

Pary, R.J. (1993) Acute psychiatric hospital admissions of adults and elderly adults with mental retardation. *American Journal on Mental Retardation*, **98**, 434–436.

Prasher, V.P., Chung, M.C. & Haque, M.S. (1998) Longitudinal changes in adaptive behavior in adults with Down syndrome: Interim findings from a longitudinal study. *American Journal on Mental Retardation*, **103**, 40–46

Sovner, R. & Hurley, A.D. (1982a) Diagnosing mania in the mentally retarded. *Psychiatric Aspects of Mental Retardation Newsletter*, **1**, 10–12.

Sovner, R. & Hurley, A.D. (1982b) Diagnosing depression in the mentally retarded. *Psychiatric Aspects of Mental Retardation Newsletter*, **1**, 1–4.

Sturmey, P. & Bertman, L.J. (1994) Validity of the Reiss Screen for maladaptive behavior. *American Journal on Mental Retardation*, **99**, 201–206.

Thorpe, L., Davidson, P., Janicki, M.P. & Working Group (2000) Healthy aging – adults with intellectual disabilities: biobehavioral issues. *Journal of Applied Research in Intellectual Disabilities*, **14**, 218–228.

Zigman, W.B., Schupf, N., Sersen, E. & Silverman, W. (1996) Prevalence of dementia in adults with and without Down syndrome. *American Journal on Mental Retardation*, **100**, 403–412.

3 Psychopathology in Older Age

Janette Tyrrell and Philip Dodd

In the general population, there is a high prevalence of psychiatric disorder in older people. This is due to the increased prevalence of dementia and the increase in depressive episodes with age. With age the incidence of organic psychiatric disorders increases, as well as complications from physical illness and sensory impairments. There is a need for a specialization in the psychiatry of old age to reflect the need for expertise in this area as presentation of psychiatric illness differs in the older person, particularly in older persons with intellectual disabilities (ID). This chapter will concentrate on psychopathology of common psychiatric disorders of old age.

Prevalence of psychiatric disorder

The prevalence of psychiatric disorder is higher in people with ID than in the general population. Lund (1985) found a prevalence of 27.1% for psychiatric disorder in a population of 302 adults older than 20 years with ID. In the older age-group 45–64 years (n = 67), behavior disorder was present in 10.4%, psychosis in 1.5%, dementia at 6%, autism at 1.5%, neurosis at 1.5%, depression at 6% and schizophrenia at 3.1%.

Pary (1993) looked at the medical records of 247 inpatients with ID or autism with regard to psychiatric disorder and found that elderly adults (age >55 years) with ID had significantly more medical problems than younger adults (age 18–54 years). Patel *et al.*, (1993) used the Psychological Assessment Schedule for Adults with Developmental Disabilities (PAS-ADD) and DSM-III-R criteria to assess 105 people ≥ 50 years and found a prevalence of dementia of 11.4%, mood disorder of 6.7%, and generalized and phobic anxiety 5.8%. Sansom *et al.*, (1994) used DSM-III-R criteria to examine 124 residents over the age of 60 years with ID. They found a prevalence of dementia of 12.9%, mood disorder 8.9% and schizophrenia 6.5%.

Cooper (1997a) in Leicestershire, England, found high rates of psychiatric morbidity in 134 adults aged over 65 years. Using the Present Psychiatric State for Adults with Learning Disability (PPS-LD), a semi-structured psychiatric interview, she found that 61.9% had psychiatric morbidity compared to 43.8% in 73 adults under age 65 years. Cherry *et al.* (1997) compared 168 older adults to 168 younger adults with ID for psychopathology using the Diagnostic Assessment of the Severely Handicapped (DASH) (see Matson *et al.*, 1991). Cherry found that behavior disorders were the most common disorders.

The above studies show that people with ID have a high prevalence of psychiatric disorder that increases with age. Increased frequency of dementia is responsible for a large proportion of psychiatric disorder in later life.

Reasons for increased prevalence of psychiatric disorder in adults with ID

Social

Cooper (1997b) has documented some of the reasons for increased prevalence of psychiatric disorder in later life for people with ID. People with ID have had different life experiences than their peers in the general population, that may lead to secondary disabilities. These may be due to early formative experiences such as lack of education, institutionalization at an early age, loss of close confiding relationships and careers and limited coping strategies to cope with stress. All of these may impact on the development of personality and lead an individual to be more vulnerable in later life to mental ill health.

Biological

These may be the presence of a behavioral phenotype, e.g. Down syndrome may predispose to an increased risk for dementia of the Alzheimer's type (Oliver & Holland, 1995). In addition, people with ID are more likely to have additional physical problems such as epilepsy and cerebral palsy that may increase dependency as the person ages.

Medication

Side effects of medications are more common in the elderly due to slower hepatic metabolism and renal excretion and also in some people with ID due to altered brain anatomy. Secondly, medications such as phenobarbitone and phenytoin for treatment of epilepsy may lead to oversedation and confusion.

Sensory impairments

Sensory impairment may occur as the result of the disability itself, or as a consequence of the syndrome if present, e.g. presbyacousis and cataracts in people with Down syndrome or as a consequence of aging. Hearing loss may cause additional communication difficulties that may in turn lead to behavior disturbance.

Specific disorders of age

Organic disorders that must be also considered in the older general population include dementia of the Alzheimer's type, multi-infarct dementia, cerebrovascular disease and Parkinson's disease. Hypothyroidism is common in people with Down syndrome and increases with age; hypothyroidism may also be associated with depression. Cancer, respiratory and cardiovascular disease and other disorders are more common with age and may predispose to depression and anxiety (Pary, 1992).

Life events

Bereavement is a common experience as one ages and people with ID suffer additional losses if their main carer dies as they may have to move into residential care and move day-center, as well as having to cope with the loss of a loved one. Abuse may present as post-traumatic stress disorder at any time of life.

Psychiatric disorders in older persons with ID may be increased due to a combination of these factors. Potential reasons for psychiatric illness in older adults with intellectual disabilities should be explored along a biopsychosocial model with cognizance taken of these factors. Biological susceptibility coupled with social factors makes older people with ID more vulnerable to the effects of aging than older people in the general population.

Psychiatric assessment scales

There have been attempts to clarify and standardize the diagnosis of psychiatric disorder in people with ID using carer-rated and direct assessment of the individual with rating scales.

Diagnostic Assessment of the Severely Handicapped (DASH) (Matson *et al.*, 1991) is an instrument that measures psychiatric disorders along three behavioral dimensions (frequency, duration and severity in persons with severe and profound ID). The DASH contains 86 items with 13 clinical subscales derived from the Diagnostic and Statistical Manual (DSM-III-R) yielding anxiety, depression, mania; autism; schizophrenia; stereotypies/tics; self-injurious behavior; elimination disorders; eating disorders; sleep disorders; organic syndromes and impulse control and miscellaneous problems.

The Psychiatric Assessment Schedule for Adults with a Developmental Disability (PAS-ADD) (Moss *et al.*, 1993) is a semi-structured clinical interview for use with people with ID, based on items drawn from the Present State Examination. It allows for parallel interviewing of staff and client and allows diagnoses to be made on ICD-10 (WHO, 1992) and DSM-IV (APA, 1994) criteria. There are 13 sections covering areas of physical illness, eating and weight change, sleep, energy, tension, worries and fears, depression, substance abuse, auditory hallucinations, hallucinations of other senses, thought interference, replacement of will and delusions, observational items and retrospective ratings. Possible diagnoses are depression, hypomania, schizophrenia, other psychoses, phobic disorder, panic and generalized anxiety disorder and non-organic hypersomnia. Diagnoses of dementia, obsessive-compulsive disorder or autism cannot be made on this instrument.

The Psychopathology Inventory for Mentally Retarded adults (PIMRA) by Matson (1988) consists of 56 dual-answer items organized over eight separate scales allowing for assessment in the area of psychopathology as well as seven specific disorders defined in accordance with DSM-III.

The Present Psychiatric State for Adults with Learning Disability (PPS-LD) (Cooper, 1997a) is based on the Present State Examination and allows an ICD-10 psychiatric diagnosis to be made by a psychiatrist based on the Diagnostic Research Criteria-10 (DCR-10) (WHO, 1993). The PPS-LD (Cooper, 1997a) is a modified version of the Schedules for Clinical Assessment in Neuropsychiatry (Present State Examination-10) (WHO, 1993). The PPS-LD integrates information collected by interviewing carers and subjects and undertaking a mental state examination, and contains 116 items. The psychopathology elicited by the PPS-LD can be classified using a variety of diagnostic criteria.

Psychiatric diagnoses are usually made in people without ID according to DSM-IV (APA, 1994) criteria or ICD-10 (WHO, 1992) criteria. Authors in the field of ID may modify these criteria for use in ID. The DC-LD is a diagnosis system based on ICD-10 that allows clinicians to make a multiaxial classification of psychiatric disorder based on ICD-10 criteria.

Specific scales for assessment of dementia are discussed in the section on dementia.

Specific psychiatric disorders

Anxiety

As people grow older it appears to be much more difficult to diagnose anxiety. There is a high rate of co-morbidity with depression (Manela *et al.*, 1996), which may mean that anxiety may not be as readily diagnosed in later life, unless it is associated with co-morbid depression. This may be due to clinicians' preconceptions regarding anxiety in the elderly, or it may be that the physical symptoms of anxiety are assessed more readily than the psychological ones, and so the diagnosis may be complicated. In the general population a number of epidemiological studies have attempted to clarify these issues, and conservative estimates put the prevalence of anxiety disorders in older people at between 0.7% and 5.9%, but more recent studies suggest that rates may be as high as 15% (Krasucki *et al.*, 1999).

In all of the anxiety disorders, anxiety is the cardinal symptom; where and how often the symptoms of anxiety occur determines whether the person is suffering from generalized anxiety disorder, panic disorder or phobic anxiety disorders. Diagnostic criteria for these disorders can be found in the ICD-10 (WHO, 1992) manual or the DSM-IV manual (APA, 1994).

The presentation of the symptom of anxiety in elderly people with ID is still being explored. In response to the fact that many people with ID find it very difficult to verbally describe symptoms of anxiety, the DC-LD (Royal College of Psychiatrists, 2001) contains proposed changes to some of the ICD-10 diagnostic criteria for anxiety disorders in adults with ID. In DC-LD, either the person's subjective description of the symptom or its observation by others are included in the criteria, allowing the diagnosis of anxiety disorders in those people with ID who are unable to describe such symptoms because of either limited intellect or limited skills.

Examining some of the limited literature describing anxiety symptoms (Ryan, 1994; Masi *et al.*, 2000), adults and elderly adults with ID may be able to describe persistent generalized anxiety or tension. However, when anxiety is not verbally described, persistent irritability, difficulty getting to sleep and somatic complaints often dominate the clinical picture. In addition, the presentation may be through a behavior disorder with possible violent or disruptive behaviors. Other symptoms in diagnosed anxiety disorders have been described, including obsessive-compulsive phenomena such as self-mutilation, ritualistic behaviors and obsessive fears (Stavrakaki & Mintsioulis, 1997).

Dementia

Dementia is more common in people with Down syndrome than in the general population; there are mixed reports on its prevalence in people with ID other than Down syndrome (Cooper, 1997a; Janicki & Dalton, 2000). In persons with Down syndrome, dementia, particularly that of the Alzheimer's disease (AD) type, has been found to occur at rates of between 15 and 40% (Prasher & Corbett, 1993); in persons with ID not associated with Down syndrome, the rates are more in line with the general population (Janicki & Dalton, 2000). The prevalence of dementia increases with age for all groups.

Due to the possession of an extra copy of chromosome 21, people with Down syndrome are more at risk for AD than the general population. The gene for the amyloid precursor protein is located near to the critical region for Down syndrome on chromosome 21 (Hardy *et al.*, 1991) and people with Down syndrome secrete 1.5 times the amount of amyloid than people without Down syndrome (Rumble *et al.*, 1989). Neuropathological studies (Wisniewski *et al.*, 1985) show the brains of people with Down syndrome to have the classic plaques and tangles of AD after the age of 35 years in almost all cases. Not all people with Down syndrome will demonstrate signs of AD in their lifetime. This suggests that either people with Down syndrome are protected from developing clinical AD by virtue of their altered brain anatomy or biochemistry, or that clinicians find it difficult to recognize dementia due to low pre-morbid cognitive performance.

When Langdon Down first described Down syndrome in 1876, he did not describe the associated dementia. The relationship between Down syndrome and AD was clarified by the description of three clinical cases of dementia in Down syndrome in which there was corresponding neuropathology of AD (Jervis, 1948). The classical neuropathological findings of neuritic plaques and neurofibrillary tangles are present in almost all people with Down syndrome after the age of 35 years (Wisniewski *et al.*, 1985). Clinical findings of AD, however, are generally not present until after the age of 50 years (Prasher & Corbett, 1993).

Clinical studies consisted initially of case-reports on people with both AD and Down syndrome, some of which have been summarized by Oliver and Holland (1986) and Crayton and Oliver (1993). Subsequent studies were conducted in institutions for people with ID in which prevalence data were examined. The instruments utilized consisted of either standard intelligence tests or tests borrowed from the general population. Not surprisingly, there were low-test scores in people without dementia due to the presence of the ID, and therefore discrimination between the demented and non-demented groups was difficult. Secondly, there was inadequate base-line information on previous cognitive function available on test subjects. Finally, the use of case-control studies missed cases of dementia that had occurred prior to the study period.

Later, specific instruments were developed to examine cognitive function such as the Down Syndrome Mental Status Examination (DSMSE) (Haxby, 1989). Informant-based assessment scales were also developed such as the Dementia Scale for Down Syndrome (DSDS) (Gedye, 1995) and the Dementia Questionnaire for Persons with Mental Retardation (DMR) (Evenhuis, 1992). Burt and Aylward (2000) recommended a battery of tests that could be used in the research-based assessment of people with ID on behalf of the International Association for the Scientific Study of Intellectual Disabilities (IASSID).

Dementia in people with ID may not present with the typical memory loss, loss of judgment and loss of discrete cognitive functions, as in the general population; rather it may present as general slowing, personality change, apathy and loss of motivation in the early stages. Holland and his colleagues (1998) have described the early stages of dementia in people with Down syndrome as a frontal lobe type dementia.

In view of the emphasis on cognitive skills loss in DSM-IV (APA, 1994) criteria the IASSID recommend the use of ICD-10 (WHO, 1992) criteria as they rely less on cognitive skills and have a more behavioral focus. The DC-LD (Royal College of Psychiatrists, 2001) includes criteria for dementia that are based on the ICD-10 but are specifically developed for people with ID.

The changes in dementia include:

- Loss of memory for both short term and long term (Burt *et al.*, 1998; Holland *et al.*, 1998)
- Cognitive decline, especially loss of skills of judgment and understanding (Burt *et al.*, 1998; Oliver *et al.*, 1998)
- Change in adaptive behavior which is recognized by loss of skills in self-care (Devenny *et al.*, 1996; Visser *et al.*, 1997; Prasher *et al.*, 1998)
- Language difficulties, both of expressive language and comprehension (Cooper & Collacutt, 1995).

Dementia in Down syndrome has been reported to present with frontal lobe changes of apathy and withdrawal in the early stages of dementia, unlike AD (Holland *et al.*, 2000).

There are a number of associated psychiatric aspects of dementia. In people with Down syndrome, depression may present with loss of cognitive skills and regression of adaptive behavior (Warren *et al.*, 1989; Pary, 1992) and it is recommended that several other diagnoses should be considered in the differential diagnosis of regression in Down syndrome, including depression. Tsiouris and Patti (1997) describe successful treatment of pseudodementia with selective serotonin reuptake inhibitors.

Several studies, however, support an association between depressive illness and dementia (Burt *et al.*, 1992; Collacott & Cooper, 1992; Prasher, 1995a). Burt *et al.* (1992) in an age-matched study of 104 people with ID, found that depression and decline in memory and adaptive skills were strongly correlated in the Down syndrome but not the ID group. Meins (1995) showed an association between age and depressed mood in Down syndrome. These findings suggest that low mood may be a prodromal feature of dementia in Down syndrome.

While behavioral disturbance is a common sequel to AD in the general population, there does not appear to be the same degree of behavioral disturbance in ID. The following behavioral and psychiatric symptoms have been found in people with ID and dementia: low mood, deterioration in communication, incontinence of urine, irritability, inefficient thought, anhedonia, anergia, social withdrawal, sleep disturbance, daytime wandering, loss of concentration, change in appetite, verbal aggression, over-activity and walking difficulties (Prasher & Filer, 1995; Duggan *et al.*, 1996; Cooper & Prasher, 1998; Cosgrave *et al.*, 1999).

Late-onset seizures have been reported to be a common clinical feature of dementia in people with Down syndrome. Prasher and Corbett (1993) and Lai and Williams (1989) found a prevalence of seizures of 82% and 84%, respectively, in people with dementia and Down syndrome. In a comprehensive study of epilepsy in 191 people with Down syndrome (McVicker *et al.*, 1994), late-onset seizures were associated with dementia. Other neurological changes are usually a late feature of dementia and consist of dysarthria (difficulty in articulating speech), dysphasia (difficulty in swallowing), parkinsonian features (cogwheel tremor, muscular rigidity, shuffling gait), spastic paresis of the limbs and finally contractures (Lai & Williams, 1989; Vieregge *et al.*, 1991).

The course of dementia in Down syndrome has been summarized by Lai and Williams (1989) and divided into three stages. In the initial stages in people with mild or moderate intellectual disabilities, there is memory impairment, temporal disorientation and reduced verbal output. In individuals with severe intellectual disabilities, dementia may present initially with apathy, inattention and decreased social interaction. This may correspond to the frontal lobe pattern described by Holland *et al.* (1998). In the middle stages of dementia, there is loss of self-help skills such as dressing, toileting and feeding and gait may be slowed and shuffling. There may be the onset of seizures and decreased work performance. In the final stages of dementia, the person may be non-ambulatory, bedridden with a flexed position and may suffer from sphincteric incontinence and exhibit pathological reflexes. Prasher (1995b) specifically studied end-stage dementia in 20 adults with Down syndrome in the six months prior to death. A terminal phase with severe memory impairment, personality change, cognitive deterioration, incontinence, neurological signs, seizure activity and complete loss of self-care skills was noted.

Depression

In general, depressive symptoms may be divided into cognitive and vegetative/biological. Depression presents with a low mood that is pervasive and associated with feelings of sadness and tearfulness. Anxiety and agitation, loss of concentration and a feeling of slowing down occur. There may be cognitive preoccupation with themes of guilt and regret. Anhedonia, a loss of pleasure in life, is reported. Biological symptoms may be associated with the severity of the depression. The mood is characteristically worse in the morning and lifts as the day progresses, sleep is poor with early morning waking, and appetite is disturbed, with loss of weight. There is also loss of libido and energy. See Chapter 5 for a detailed review of depression in older adults with ID.

Mania

While mania may present for the first time in later life in the general population, it is rare and usually mania in older age is part of a recurrent mood disorder that has presented at an earlier age. Prevalence studies of psychiatric disorders in older adults with ID suggest that new-onset mania in older adults with ID is rare. Specific studies on psychopathology of mania in the older adult with ID are not detailed so it has to be inferred that presentation is similar to younger adults with ID. Cherry *et al.* (1997) found a high prevalence of mania at 11.9% but other studies have not found this and this may reflect the different diagnostic instruments used. Typical symptoms of mania include hyperactivity, overtalkativeness, insomnia, irritability, agitation, anorexia, hypersexuality and grandiosity. Lund (1985) comments that instead of euphoric cheerful mood, the mood in mania in persons with ID is often noisy, vagrant and irritable/aggressive. In severe cases there may also be hallucinations and delusions that are mood-congruent. In people with ID this has to be taken in context (e.g. believing that he or she is now the workshop manager may be a grandiose delusion). In the absence of a mood-disorder in the past and a negative family history of bipolar affective disorder, an organic etiology should always be considered in late-onset mania.

Schizophrenia

Schizophrenia is a severe psychotic illness that usually has its onset in early adulthood and is characterized by auditory hallucinations, bizarre delusions, thought disorder and strange behavior. A progressive deterioration in personal, domestic, occupational and social abilities commonly occurs. All of these clinical features must occur in clear consciousness.

The concept of schizophrenia owes much to the work of Kraepelin (1919), who described cases of dementia praecox; however it was Bleuler (1950) who actually coined the term schizophrenia. Kraepelin believed that auditory hallucinations, delusions, abnormal thought associations, affective flattening and impaired insight were common to hebephrenia, catatonia, paranoia and dementia simplex, and merged these four disorders into the syndrome he called dementia praecox. He believed that some 7% of cases of dementia praecox arose on the basis of 'idiocy' and subsequently suggested an early onset form of psychosis–'pfropfschizophrenia'. This term came to be associated with a particular and distinctive form of schizophrenia grafted on to ID, but as the term's exact definition became unclear, it dropped into disuse. Turner (1989) described the relationship between schizophrenia and ID as having been obscured by historical changes and varying diagnostic criteria. Some argued that 'mental deficiency' was largely caused by the same factors as those responsible for schizophrenia/dementia praecox; however, by the 1950s this argument seems to have been superseded by the impacts of pharmacological treatments, and also the availability of valid tests of intelligence. Schneider (1959) described a number of symptoms that he considered to be of first rank importance in differentiating schizophrenia from similar illnesses, and these were included among the diagnostic criteria for schizophrenia in ICD-10 (WHO, 1992) and DSM-IV (APA, 1994).

The classification of a non-organic, non-affective psychosis with onset in late life is controversial as there has been longstanding uncertainty about the relationship between these disorders and organic or atypical affective disorders as well as delusional disorders. If one adds the diagnosis of ID to this, the classification and diagnosis becomes less clear (Howard & Rabins, 1997). Bleuler's cut-off age of 40 years influenced the German literature, and subsequent reports in the English literature used either 55 or 60 years of age as the dividing line and the adoption of the term 'late paraphrenia'. DSM-III-R (APA, 1987) provided a separate category for adults whose illness emerged after the age of 45; however, neither ICD-10 (WHO, 1992) nor DSM-IV (APA, 1994) contained a separate diagnosis for late onset schizophrenia.

The incidence of late onset psychosis in the general population (i.e. onset after the age of 60) increases with age in both sexes (8.7/100,000 in the 65–74 age group and 14.5/100 000 in the over 75 age group); mean age of onset is 74 years; 50% have third person auditory hallucinations, 20% have visual hallucinations (Howard, 1998). Others, however, have described a different clinical syndrome, which is closer to paranoid schizophrenia in clinical presentation. Against this background, the Late-Onset Schizophrenia Group (Howard *et al.*, 2000) published an international consensus statement in February 2000 that proposed that there is sufficient evidence to recognize two illness classifications. Howard *et al.* (2000) suggest further classification into late onset schizophrenia, in which onset occurs after the age of 40, and very late-onset schizophrenia, in which the clinical onset occurs after the age of 60. This proposal was based on a systematic literature review that included other important points such as:

■ The proportion of schizophrenia patients in the general population whose illness first emerges after the age of 40 has been estimated to be 23.5%
■ Onset of schizophrenia among women is later and there is over-representation of women among late onset cases
■ Description of very late-onset patients (after 60 years) stressed the high prevalence of sensory deficits (especially longstanding deafness)
■ When onset of psychosis is after the age of 60, formal thought disorder and negative symptoms are very rare
■ Late onset patients are more likely than their earlier onset counterparts to complain of visual, tactile and olfactory hallucinations, persecutory delusions, third person, running commentary and accusatory or abusive auditory hallucinations.

Many authors have noted the difficulty in diagnosing schizophrenia (Reid, 1972; Cherry *et al.*, 2000) in those adults with a moderate or more severe ID. The new Diagnostic Criteria for Psychiatric Disorders for use with adults with ID (DC-LD) (Royal College of Psychiatrists, 2001), reflect an effort to rationalize the strict diagnostic criteria of ICD-10. For non-affective psychotic disorders, it is not usually valid or appropriate to subclassify these disorders to the extent described in ICD-10. This is based on the fact that in adults and elderly adults with ID, delusions and hallucinations are often difficult to elicit and are at risk of being obscured by inadvertent interviewer suggestion. In addition, some 'positive symptoms' of schizophrenia such as delusional perception, passivity phenomena, thought echo, and running commentary and auditory hallucinations, are very uncommon in adults with ID. In general, a clear history of change is required with good background history regarding the person's previous linguistic developmental level. The diagnostic notes within the DC-LD text are useful in aiding diagnosis and classification of schizophrenia.

Other disorders

As in the general population, other psychiatric disorders of later life may occur in ID. Delirium may be seen particularly in the context of a febrile illness, cerebral injury or illness or systemic disease. The key symptoms of delirium are fluctuant impairment of consciousness, attention difficulties, confusion, sleep-wake disturbance, psychomotor disturbance and perceptual abnormalities. Delirium may be distinguished from dementia by altered level of consciousness and by a thorough clinical assessment. Obsessive-compulsive disorder may present, characterized by obsessive recurring thoughts and compulsions to perform an action, deed or thought. Personality and behavior disorders may be life-long disturbances in behavior and thought but may be unmasked by physical illness or bereavement. Autistic spectrum disorders and autism may present special challenges in later life also (Nordin & Gillberg, 1998).

Summary

The psychopathology of psychiatric illness in older people with ID shows similarities to the general population, with dementia and depression being common psychiatric disorders. There are important differences, however, in the emphasis of certain symptoms. Non-verbal symptoms such as psychomotor retardation and biological symptoms of depression are of greater importance when the person does not have the verbal skills to communicate adequately. The symptoms of dementia may be difficult to elicit in the early stages of dementia, and behavioral changes may be seen first, such as adaptive skill loss, apathy and social withdrawal prior to cognitive losses. A multidimensional framework in which social and biological factors are considered in addition to psychological factors, is essential in making a psychiatric diagnosis.

References

APA (1987) *Diagnostic and Statistical Manual of Mental Disorders*, 3rd edn (revised). American Psychiatric Association, Washington DC.

APA (1994) *Diagnostic and Statistical Manual of Mental Disorders*, 4th edn. American Psychiatric Association, Washington DC.

Bleuler, E. (1950) *Dementia Praecox or the Group of Schizophrenias* (trans. Zinken from 1911 edn). International Universities Press, New York.

Burt, D.B. & Aylward, E.H. (2000) Test battery for the diagnosis of dementia in individuals with intellectual disability. Working Group for the Establishment of Criteria for the Diagnosis of Dementia in Individuals with Intellectual Disability. *Journal of Intellectual Disability Research*, **44**, 175–180.

Burt, D.B., Loveland, K.A. & Lewis, K.R. (1992) Depression and the onset of dementia in adults with mental retardation. *American Journal on Mental Retardation*, **96**, 502–511.

Burt, D.B., Loveland, K.A., Primeaux S., Chen, Y.W., Phillips, N.B., Cleveland, L.A., Lewis, K.R., Lesser, J. & Cummings, E. (1998) Dementia in people with Down syndrome: Diagnostic challenges. *American Journal on Mental Retardation*, **103**, 130–145.

Cherry, K., Matson, J. & Paclawskyj, T. (1997) Psychopathology in older adults with severe and profound mental retardation. *American Journal on Mental Retardation*, **101**, 445–458.

Cherry, K., Penn D., Matson J. & Bamburg J. (2000) Characteristics of schizophrenia among persons with severe or profound mental retardation. *Psychiatric Services*, **51**, 922–924.

Collacott, R.A. & Cooper, S-A. (1992) Adaptive behavior after depressive illness in Down syndrome. *Journal of Nervous and Mental Disease*, **180**, 468–470.

Cooper, S-A. (1997a) Psychiatry of elderly compared to younger adults with intellectual disability. *Journal of Applied Research in Intellectual Disabilities*, **10**, 303–311.

Cooper, S.A. (1997b) Epidemiology of psychiatric disorders in elderly compared with younger adults with learning disabilities. *British Journal of Psychiatry*, **170**, 375–380.

Cooper, S-A & Collacott, R.A. (1995) The effect of age on language in people with Down's syndrome. *Journal of Intellectual Disability Research*, **30**, 197–200.

Cooper, S-A & Prasher, V.P. (1998) Maladaptive behaviors and symptoms of dementia in adults with Down's syndrome compared to adults with intellectual disability of other etiologies. *Journal of Intellectual Disability Research*, **42**, 293–300.

Cosgrave, M.P., Tyrrell, J., McCarron, M., Gill, M. & Lawlor, B. (1999) Determinants of aggression, and adaptive and maladaptive behavior in older people with Down's syndrome with and without dementia. *Journal of Intellectual Disability Research*, **43**, 393–399.

Crayton, L. & Oliver, O. (1993) Assessment of cognitive functioning in people with Down syndrome who develop Alzheimer Disease. *Alzheimer Disease, Down*

Syndrome and their Relationship (eds J.M. Berg, H. Karlinksky & A.J. Holland) pp. 135–153. Oxford University Press, New York.

Devenny, D., Silverman, W.P., Hill, A.L., Jenkins, E., Sersen, E.A. & Wisniewski, K.E. (1996) Normal ageing in Down's syndrome: a longitudinal study. *Journal of Intellectual Disability Research*, **40**, 208–221.

Duggan, L., Lewis, M. & Morgan, J. (1996) Behavioral changes in people with learning disability and dementia: a descriptive study. *Journal of Intellectual Disability Research*, **40**, 311–321.

Evenhuis, H.M. (1992) Evaluation of a screening instrument for dementia in ageing mentally retarded persons. *Journal of Intellectual Disability Research*, **36**, 337–347.

Gedye, A. (1995) *Dementia Scale for Down syndrome*. Gedye Research and Consulting, Vancouver, BC.

Hardy, J., Mullan, M., Chartier-Harlin, M-C., Brown, J., Goate, A. & Rossor, M. (1991) Molecular classification of Alzheimer's disease. *Lancet*, **337**, 1342–1343.

Haxby, J.V. (1989) Neuropsychological evaluation of adults with Down's syndrome: patterns of selective impairment in non-demented old adults. *Journal of Mental Deficiency Research*, **33**, 193–210.

Holland, A.J., Hon, J., Huppert, F.A., Stevens, F. & Watson P. (1998) Population based study on the prevalence and presentation of dementia in adults with Down's syndrome. *British Journal of Psychiatry*, **172**, 493–498.

Holland, A.J., Hon, J., Huppert, F.A. & Stevens F. (2000) Incidence and course of dementia in people with Down's syndrome: findings from a population-based study. *Journal of Intellectual Disability Research*, **44**, 138–146.

Howard, R. (1998) *Can schizophrenia begin after the age of 60?* Paper presented at the American Psychiatric Association annual meeting, 1 June, Toronto, Canada.

Howard, R. & Rabins, P. (1997) Late paraphrenia revisited. *British Journal of Psychiatry*, **171**, 406–408.

Howard, R., Rabins, P.V., Seeman, M. & Jeste, D. and the International Late-Onset Schizophrenia Group (2000) Late-onset and very late-onset schizophrenia-like psychosis: an international consensus. *American Journal of Psychiatry*, **157**, 172–178.

Janicki, M.P. & Dalton, A.J. (2000) Prevalence of dementia and impact on intellectual disability services. *Mental Retardation*, **38**, 277–289.

Jervis, G.A. (1948) Early senile dementia in mongoloid idiocy. *American Journal of Psychiatry*, **105**, 102–106.

Kraepelin, E. (1919) *Dementia praecox and Paraphrenia* (trans. Barclay and Robertson). Livingstone, Edinburgh.

Krasucki, C., Howard, R. & Mann A. (1999) Anxiety and its treatment in the elderly. *International Psychogeriatrics*, **11**, 25–45.

Lai, F. & Williams, R.S. (1989) A prospective study of Alzheimer's disease in Down's syndrome. *Archives of Neurology*, **46**, 849–853.

Lund, J. (1985) The prevalence of psychiatric morbidity in mentally retarded adults. *Acta Psychiatrica Scandinavica*, **72**, 563–570.

McVicker, R.W., Shanks, O.E.P. & McClelland, R.J. (1994) Prevalence and associated features of epilepsy in adults with Down's syndrome. *British Journal of Psychiatry*, **164**, 528–532.

Manela, M., Katona, C. & Livingston, G. (1996) How common are the anxiety disorders in old age? *International Journal of Geriatric Psychiatry*, **11**, 65–70.

Masi, G., Favilla, L. & Mucci, M. (2000) Generalized anxiety disorder in adolescents and young adults with mild mental retardation. *Psychiatry*, **63**, 54–64.

Matson, J. (1988) *The PIMRA Manual*. International Diagnostic Systems, Orland Park, IL.

Matson, J., Gardner, W., Coe, D. & Sovner R. (1991) A scale for evaluating emotional disorders in severely and profoundly mentally retarded persons: development of the Diagnostic Assessment for the Severely Handicapped (DASH) Scale. *British Journal of Psychiatry*, **159**, 404–409.

Meins, W. (1995) Are depressive mood disturbances in adults with Down syndrome an early sign of dementia? *Journal of Nervous and Mental Disease*, **183**, 663–664.

Moss, S., Patel, P., Prosser, H., Goldberg, D.P., Simpson, N., Rowe, S. & Lucchino, R. (1993) Psychiatric morbidity in older people with moderate and severe learning disability. *British Journal of Psychiatry*, **163**, 471–480.

Nordin, V. & Gillberg, C. (1998) The long-term course of autistic disorders: Update on follow-up studies. *Acta Psychatrica Scandinavia*, **97**, 99–108.

Oliver, C. & Holland, A.J. (1986) Down's syndrome and Alzheimer's disease: a review. *Psychological Medicine*, **16**, 307–322.

Oliver, C. & Holland, A.J. (1995) Down's syndrome and the links with Alzheimer Disease. *Journal of Neurology, Neurosurgery and Psychiatry*, **59**, 111–114.

Oliver, C., Crayton. L., Holland, A., Hall, S. & Bradbury, J. (1998) A four year prospective study of age-related cognitive change in adults with Down's syndrome. *Psychological Medicine*, **28**, 1365–1377.

Pary, R. (1992) Differential diagnosis of functional decline in Down's syndrome. *The Habilitative Mental Healthcare Newsletter*, **11**, 37–41.

Pary, R. (1993) Acute psychiatric hospital admissions of adults and elderly adults with mental retardation. *American Journal on Mental Retardation*, **98**, 434–436.

Patel, P., Goldberg, D. & Moss S. (1993) Psychiatric morbidity in older people with moderate and severe learning disability II: The prevalence study. *British Journal of Psychiatry*, **163**, 481–491.

Prasher, V.P. (1995a) Age-specific prevalence, thyroid dysfunction and depressive symptomatology in adults with Down syndrome and dementia. *International Journal of Geriatric Psychiatry*, **10**, 25–31.

Prasher, V. (1995b) End-stage dementia in adults with Down's syndrome. *International Journal of Geriatric Psychiatry*, **10**, 1067–1069.

Prasher, V.P. & Corbett, J.A. (1993) Onset of seizures as a poor indicator of longevity in people with Down's syndrome and dementia. *International Journal of Geriatric Psychiatry*, **8**, 923–927.

Prasher, V.P. & Filer, A. (1995) Behavioral disturbance in people with Down's syndrome. *Journal of Intellectual Disability Research*, **39**, 432–436.

Prasher, V.P., Cheung Chung, M. & Haque, M.S. (1998) Longitudinal changes in adaptive behavior in adults with Down syndrome: Interim findings from a longitudinal study. *American Journal on Mental Retardation*, **103**, 40–46.

Reid, A. (1972) Psychoses in adult mental defectives: II Schizophrenic and paranoid psychoses. *British Journal of Psychiatry*, **120**, 213–218.

Royal College of Psychiatrists (2001) DC-LD (Diagnostic criteria for psychiatric
disorders for use with adults with learning disabilities/mental retardation)
Gaskell Press, London.

Rumble, B., Retallack, R., Hilbich, C., Simms, G., Multhaup, G., Martins, R.,
Hockey, A., Montgomery, P., Beyreuther, K. & Masters, C.L. (1989) Amyloid A4
protein and its precursor in Down's syndrome and Alzheimer's disease. *New
England Journal of Medicine*, **320**, 1446–1452.

Ryan, R. (1994) Posttraumatic stress disorder in persons with developmental
disabilities. *Networker*, **3**, 1–5.

Sansom, D.T., Singh, I., Jawed, S.H. & Mukherjee, T. (1994) Elderly people with
learning disabilities in hospital: a psychiatric study. *Journal of Intellectual
Disability Research*, **38**, 45–52.

Schneider, K. (1959) *Klinische Psychopathologie* (trans. M.W. Hamilton). Grune and
Stratton, New York.

Stavrakaki, C. & Mintsioulis, G. (1997) Anxiety disorders in persons with mental
retardation: diagnostic, clinical and treatment issues. *Psychiatric Annals*, **27**,
182–189.

Tsiouris, J.A. & Patti, P.J. (1997) Drug treatment of depression associated with
dementia or presenting as pseudodementia in older adults with Down syndrome. *Journal of Applied Research in Intellectual Disabilities*, **10**, 312–322.

Turner, T. (1989) Schizophrenia and mental handicap: an historical review, with
implications for further research. *Psychological Medicine*, **19**, 301–314.

Vieregge, P., Ziemens, G., Freudenberg, M., Piosinski, A., Muysers, A. & Schulze,
B. (1991) Extrapyramidal features in advanced Down's syndrome: clinical
evaluation and family history. *Journal of Neurology, Neurosurgery and Psychiatry*,
54, 34–39.

Visser, F.E., Aldenkamp, A.P., van Huffelen, A.C., Kuilman, M., Overweg, J. & van
Wijk, J. (1997) Prospective study of the prevalence of Alzheimer type dementia
in institutionalized individuals with Down's syndrome. *American Journal on
Mental Retardation*, **101**, 400–412.

Warren, A.C., Holroyd, S. & Folstein, M.F. (1989) Major depression in Down's
syndrome. *British Journal of Psychiatry*, **155**, 202–205.

WHO (1992) *The Tenth Revision of the International Classification of Diseases and
Related Health Problems*, 10th edn (ICD-10). World Health Organization, Geneva.

WHO (1993) *ICD-10 Classification of Mental and Behavioural Disorders – Diagnostic
Criteria for Research*. World Health Organization, Geneva.

Wisniewski, K.E., Wisniewski, H.M. & Wen, G.Y. (1985) Occurrence of neuropathological changes and dementia of Alzheimer's disease in Down's
syndrome. *Annals of Neurology*, **17**, 278–282.

4 Assessment of Behavioral and Psychiatric Disorders

Anthony J. Holland

Sound and theoretically valid assessment is the bedrock of successful intervention and treatment for behavioral and psychiatric disorder affecting older people with intellectual disabilities. This group of people are very heterogeneous with some having a mild intellectual disability, the origins of which are likely to be a combination of polygenic influences and psychosocial disadvantage, whereas others will have genetic or environmentally determined disorders that have had a marked effect on brain development and therefore on intellectual, social and emotional development (Fryers, 2000; Kaski, 2000). Increasing age adds a further complexity as age-related mental and physical disorders become more prevalent, and people affected will have experienced a lifetime of varied and possibly problematic social care support.

This group of people by definition have delayed or abnormal patterns of early development. However, this may also affect the developmental processes of later life. A developmental psychopathological approach to behavioral and psychiatric disorders in older people with intellectual disabilities requires an understanding of how the developmental trajectory of a given individual over his/her life differs from what would be expected, and how this might account for what is observed. For example, are the behaviors (e.g. obsessional and ritualistic behaviors) long-standing and a function of early developmental arrest? Are the failing skills of an older person with Down syndrome best conceptualized as a consequence of normal aging or as a deviation from this process brought about by the onset of Alzheimer's disease (Devenny *et al.*, 1996). For those without intellectual disabilities, deviation from the normal developmental pathways of later life may be obvious. This is less likely to be the case for those whose early development was abnormal and whose predicted developmental trajectory throughout life may be far from clear. For this reason failing memory, for example, is not recognized as indicative of dementia, or behavioral changes following bereavement are not seen as a normal manifestation of grief (Hollins & Esterhuyzen, 1997).

Background

As noted in Chapter 2, epidemiological studies have demonstrated that prevalence rates of both physical and psychiatric disorders associated with old age, such as those of depression and dementia, are high among people with intellectual disabilities (Cooper, 1997). For some, with particular genetic syndromes, the risks of specific adult psychopathology are markedly increased. The best example of this is the early onset of Alzheimer's disease in adults with Down syndrome, where rates of dementia increase from a few per cent in the third and fourth decades of life to over 40% in the fifth decade (Zigman *et al.*, 1997; Holland *et al.*, 1998). What is also now becoming apparent is that rates of psychotic illness are also increased specifically in adults with, for example, the velo-cardio-facial syndrome (Shprintzen *et al.*, 1992) and with the chromosome 15 maternal disomy genetic subtype of Prader-Willi syndrome (Boer *et al.*, 2002). These syndrome specific risks are examples of the complex relationship between developmental processes and the risk for specific psychiatric disorders, which can go beyond childhood and may extend into later life.

Physical disorders are also important. In a survey undertaken in New York of a representative sample of adults known to intellectual disability services aged 40 to 79 years, specific physical illnesses, such as cardio-vascular, respiratory, musculo-skeletal and gastro-intestinal disorders and sensory impairments, were found to increase with age, as did thyroid disorder in people with Down syndrome (Janicki *et al.*, 2002). In a study of 70 people living in community institutions for people with intellectual disabilities in the Netherlands, sensory impairments became increasingly prevalent in the elderly (Evenhuis, 1995a,b). Where a person may have limited spoken language the presentation of such disorders may be in the form of behavioral or mental state changes. The identification of physical and/or psychiatric co-morbidity is crucially important, both because it may provide an explanation for observed changes, and also because the identification of a problem could point to possible treatment.

The purpose of assessment is to identify the developmental, biological, psychological and environmentally determined factors that might be predisposing to, might have precipitated, or might be maintaining the identified maladaptive behaviors or abnormal mental states. These assessments frequently require a multidisciplinary approach as there may be multiple factors at play and no one approach can truly develop the necessary holistic level of understanding. For some people who cannot communicate or whose memory is very poor, little may be known about their pasts, particularly if their family has died or moved away, and information on the individual's past life and emotional experiences is lost forever. Arriving at an understanding of why particular maladaptive behaviors have developed, or establishing whether there has been an apparent change in mood, mental state, or general well-being, may therefore be a considerable challenge as the relevant information may be lacking. However, such an approach is essential as similar behaviors (e.g. aggression) may occur for very different reasons. For example, aggressive outbursts may occur in the context of a developing dementia or of depression, or could occur due to anxiety associated with changes of routine that can affect a person with autism. In another person the aggression may have a communicative function when in situations of boredom or high demand.

Inadequate assessment may often lead to ill-informed intervention. At its best, this is likely to be ineffective and, at its worst, harmful. This is best illustrated by the reported excessive use of major tranquillizing medications for people with intellectual disabilities (Linaker, 1990). The use of such medications for the treatment of serious mental illness would be acceptable and likely to be effective, but when used for the treatment of 'behavior' in the absence of mental illness, it may have little benefit but still has the potential for negative side effects (Brylewski & Duggan, 1999).

Diagnostic classification, labels and definitions

Systems of classification, such as those used in the diagnostic process, are an important way of putting information in order such that the validity of the information can be subsequently tested. In medicine the use of diagnostic classification provides the means whereby the etiology of specific problems and validity of treatments can be investigated. In psychiatric practice the diagnostic criteria have been codified in manuals that set out the clinical criteria that have to be present for the diagnosis of specific psychiatric disorders (WHO, 1993; APA, 1994). In the case of people with intellectual disabilities the presentation of psychiatric disorder may be atypical. For this reason modifications to ICD-10 have been suggested (WHO, 1996) and further revision to this multi-axial system proposed (Einfeld & Tonge, 1999). More recently it has been argued that diagnostic criteria for psychiatric disorders in the case of people with intellectual disabilities should be modified (DC-LD) (Royal College of Psychiatrists, 2001). However, this carries the danger of incorrect diagnosis or overdiagnosis of psychiatric disorders. In most circumstances the core diagnostic characteristics of disorders, such as depression or bipolar disorder, can be elucidated by means of a careful assessment and information from an informant (Tsiouris, 2001; Cain et al., in press). The diagnostic process by itself has its limitations and cannot give a truly comprehensive picture. This is subsequently arrived at through the process of formulation that brings together relevant information of a developmental, biological, psychological and social nature to give a more comprehensive picture.

It is therefore important to be clear about the labels used, and their diagnostic significance. Some are descriptive and imply little about likely etiology. Others imply an understanding as to their possible pathophysiological basis, etiology and treatment. This is best illustrated by contrasting the implications of such terms as 'challenging or maladaptive behavior' with those for 'psychiatric illnesses' such as 'depression' or 'schizophrenia'. For example, in the UK the term 'challenging behavior' has been used to describe behavior of a nature or degree that limits access to mainstream services and appropriate day and social care provision (Emerson, 2001). Such terminology by itself does not indicate any understanding of the likely cause, rather that there is a problem requiring a solution. However, further assessment identifying such a behavior as having a specific 'function', such as being 'attention maintained' or 'demand avoidant', takes the descriptive use of such terms further as it implies some understanding of the underlying mechanism (in this case psychological) that might be etiologically important. From a psychiatric perspective the diagnosis of a particular mental illness such as 'depression' or 'dementia' implies some level of understanding as to pathophysiology and cause, and enables access to a body of knowledge that has tested specific interventions for that particular disorder (e.g. antidepressant medication or cognitive behavior therapy for depression), which have been found to be more effective than placebo. Similarly, the diagnosis of dementia of the Alzheimer's type implies the presence of particular neuropathological changes and a progressive course.

The diagnosis of co-morbid psychiatric disorders depends on evidence of a particular onset and course, and of characteristic cognitive and/or functional changes and/or the presence of abnormal mental experiences. For those with mild intellectual impairments, the presentation and subsequent diagnosis of such disorders may be relatively unproblematic, providing the possibility of their presence is considered in the first place. The same may not be true for those with more severe disabilities and limited language development. The two major problems that can make diagnosis particularly problematic are first, that the person's previous level of functioning and general well-being may be very uncertain and therefore any change from that may be difficult to judge, and second, that assumptions about his/her inner mental state may have to be made on the basis of informant information if he/she is unable to give that information. The assessments of specific psychiatric disorders are considered in more detail later in the chapter.

Psychiatric and psychological assessment models

The purpose of assessment is to arrive at an understanding of an individual. Such assessments are rooted in particular conceptual frameworks, and informed by epidemiological and other research. As described below, the process of assessment moves from the descriptive to the explanatory through the use of different conceptual models that enable the bringing together of information about the person in some sort of order that has established validity. In practice there are two fundamental approaches that are used to inform about psychiatric and behavior disorders: one is based on a *psychiatric diagnostic model* (also referred to as the medical model); the other, the *behavioral model*, is based on *learning theory*. Other theoretical models may also inform, such as a psychoanalytical perspective and an understanding of how systems (for example, staff or family dynamics) might influence behavior. The two main approaches complement each other and should not be seen as mutually exclusive.

The psychiatric diagnostic model

The psychiatric diagnostic approach, at its most basic, explores first whether the observed problems are long-standing and can best be explained as part of the abnormal or arrested developmental profile of that person (e.g. rituals and routines associated with autism) or second, whether they are of recent onset and can be wholly or partly explained by the development of a physical and/or mental health problem. This and other relevant diagnostic information is obtained through history taking, mental and physical state examination, and, where necessary, investigations. Part of this process requires that the information obtained from the history and examination is compared with the diagnostic criteria for specific psychiatric disorders, such as affective disorders, anxiety or dementia, thus establishing a differential diagnosis leading to a psychiatric formulation. The interventions that follow will include the use of established treatments for identified co-morbid disorders.

The behavioral model

The behavioral approach uses both an interview-based and an observational methodology and considers how past and present support strategies and particular environments might have shaped the way a person responds to others and to his/her environment and/or internal states. At its most basic it investigates whether a particular maladaptive behavior has a 'function', such as that of demand avoidance, whether it might be 'attention maintained', and/or whether it occurs preferentially under particular 'setting conditions'. Detailed observations of the antecedents to the maladaptive behavior, and the nature and the consequences of such behavior, can be obtained using ABC charts, that chart the **A**ntecedent stimuli associated with the occurrence of a specific **B**ehavior, and the **C**onsequences of the behavior. This sort of charting helps establish whether there are particular circumstances or responses to the behavior that are positively reinforcing its occurrence. The interventions that might follow could include the use of specific behavioral strategies, or improving the communication skills of that person so that he/she can indicate need, or changing the environment in a manner that increases, for example, its predictable nature, or the use of strategies that facilitate control of anger or improve skills.

The process of assessment

The task of assessment is to undertake the collection of the necessary data through history taking, observation and psychological and medical investigations and to then construct a model of understanding. This in turn guides intervention. Assessment is therefore a process as illustrated in Fig. 4.1.

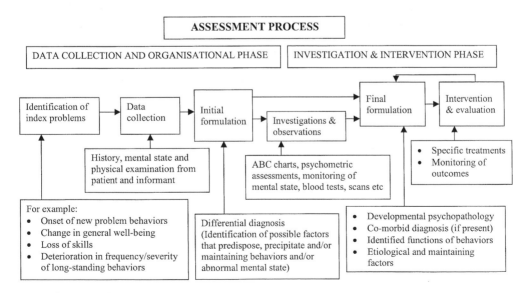

ASSESSMENT PROCESS

DATA COLLECTION AND ORGANISATIONAL PHASE | INVESTIGATION & INTERVENTION PHASE

Identification of index problems → Data collection → Initial formulation → Investigations & observations → Final formulation → Intervention & evaluation

History, mental state and physical examination from patient and informant

ABC charts, psychometric assessments, monitoring of mental state, blood tests, scans etc

- Specific treatments
- Monitoring of outcomes

For example:
- Onset of new problem behaviors
- Change in general well-being
- Loss of skills
- Deterioration in frequency/severity of long-standing behaviors

Differential diagnosis (Identification of possible factors that predispose, precipitate and/or maintaining behaviors and/or abnormal mental state)

- Developmental psychopathology
- Co-morbid diagnosis (if present)
- Identified functions of behaviors
- Etiological and maintaining factors

Fig. 4.1 The assessment process.

Data collection and organization phase

The first stage is to establish the nature of the 'problem' (e.g. loss of skills, aggression, etc.). This is necessary as such information provides the focus for the subsequent enquiry. The problem may be the appearance of new and problematic behaviors, and/or a change in general well-being and mental state, or the loss of abilities, or a deterioration in the frequency and/or severity of existing maladaptive behaviors (e.g. long-standing obsessions have become more intense and pervasive).

The collection of data and the application of particular theoretical models of understanding focus on establishing the information pertinent to understanding the reasons for the index problems that require an explanation. Psychiatric assessment will include a detailed history of the onset, nature and subsequent course of the identified problems, and information on the circumstances surrounding the onset and occurrence of the problems. Detailed developmental, personal and family histories and past medical and psychiatric histories are required, as are physical and mental state examinations.

The mental status examination should be structured. This process may be aided by the use of instruments such as the PAS-ADD checklist or full PAS-ADD (Moss *et al.*, 1993). Where a person cannot give a history him/herself, the use of information from an informant who knows the person well is essential, and the mental states of people with intellectual disabilities unable to communicate for themselves may have to be inferred. Information on change is most important. If a particular behavior is new or an existing behavior has become worse, there has to be an explanation. (The assessment of affective disorder, psychotic illness and dementia are discussed in greater detail below.) At the end of this process it should be possible to construct a preliminary formulation and to identify developmental, biological, psychological and environmentally determined factors that might be predisposing, precipitating or maintaining the behaviors or abnormal mental state. In certain situations the explanation of the problem may be clear and the intervention is obvious. In other situations a period of observation and data collection, or the undertaking of investigations, may be indicated before a final formulation can be arrived at. This might include the use of ABC charts to examine the circumstances surrounding the onset and resolution of particular behaviors, or blood tests to rule out possible physical explanations for the apparent behavioral or mental state changes (e.g. hypothyroidism).

Investigation and intervention phase

The final formulation will include information on the cause and nature and severity of the person's developmental disability, the diagnosis of any suspected co-morbid physical or mental disorder, and the identification of predisposing, precipitating and maintaining factors. These might include, for example, issues relevant to the past or present circumstances (e.g. changing social circumstances, poor quality and unpredictable environment, and inappropriate carer strategies), biological or co-morbid factors (e.g. epilepsy, physical illness, depression, dementia, psychotic illnesses), factors that may have had a significant psychological effect on self-esteem or have resulted in post traumatic stress or depression (e.g. possible past or present abuse, grief), possible internal or external setting circumstances (e.g. behavior occurs only in the context of a depressed mood, or in certain environments), and the relationship between the person's present abilities, which may have declined with age, and the demands of their environment. This is not an exhaustive list, but illustrates the range of factors that might help to explain the occurrence of problem behaviors and thereby the importance of assessment.

Diagnosis of specific psychiatric disorders

Four potential factors have been identified that alter the way that psychiatric illness may present in people with intellectual disabilities, impeding recognition and diagnosis (Sovner & Hurley, 1990). These may be particularly pertinent in the elderly as these factors may be further increased by the effects of age. These four factors are:

(1) The impaired intellectual abilities of the person may limit his/her ability to both conceptualize and describe his/her own mental experiences
(2) Limited life experiences and social skills may limit the psychiatric phenomenology
(3) The impact of cognitive disintegration under stress and/or mental illness
(4) The manifestations of mental illness as a deterioration in pre-existing behaviors – change in behavior may be due to the onset of a mental illness

Affective disorder

There is increasing evidence that within the population of adults with intellectual disabilities affective disorders are common and often chronic (Richards et al., 2001; Cain *et al.*, 2003; Tsiouris *et al.*, 2003), and as with the general population, an increase in prevalence arises in later life. Diagnosis is based on objective and, where possible, subjective evidence of a change in mood (depressed, hypomanic or manic), and the associated characteristic changes in concentration, sleep pattern, appetite and general interest. The biological features of affective disorder, and the fact that internal mental states such as depression may be inferred on the basis of tearfulness and sometimes self-injurious behavior, make the diagnosis relatively straightforward. Depression may also lower the threshold for other specific behaviors (e.g. aggression), and may be associated with irritability and obvious agitation, or result in pre-existing rituals and routines becoming more marked and intrusive (Meins, 1995). Aggression may have occurred if such routines are challenged or interrupted in a manner that would not have been the case if he/she had not been depressed. In this case depression can be seen as an internal setting event that lowers the threshold for such behavior.

Psychotic illness

The diagnosis of psychotic illness depends on evidence of the occurrence of specific mental experiences which may include delusional beliefs, visual, auditory, somatic or olfactory hallucinations, thought disorder, and other abnormalities of thinking, such as thought withdrawal or insertion, passivity feelings, and incongruous or abnormal mood states. For schizophrenia to be diagnosed, very specific mental experiences need to be present that require a certain level of language development in those affected. Where that is the case, the psychopathology of schizophrenia is relatively similar to those without intellectual disabilities (Meadows *et al.*, 1991). For those adults with more severe intellectual disabilities, there will still be some uncertainty as to how best to diagnose psychotic illness, but change in behavior and mental state, the onset of catatonic symptomatology, particularly in those with autism (Wing & Shah, 2000) and a deterioration in functioning and possible associated abnormal mental experiences, such as evidence of hallucinations, for instance responses to noises, may be apparent. A carefully designed trial of antipsychotic medication with good outcome measures may be indicated under such circumstances (see Hess-Rover *et al.*, 1999 for case example).

Dementia and delirium

Much has been written about the problems associated with the diagnosis of dementia in people with intellectual disabilities, especially those with Down syndrome (Aylward *et al.*, 1997). The main problem is the lack of longitudinal information on an individual's functional ability and therefore a failure to recognize decline. Screening assessments such as the Mini Mental State Examination (Foldstein *et al.*, 1975) are unhelpful as low scores do not distinguish between the effects of the developmental intellectual disability and developing dementia. The diagnosis requires evidence of functional decline in five broad areas: memory, general mental functioning (e.g. thinking, planning, etc.), higher cortical functioning including language (evidence of developing dyspraxias, dysphasias, etc.), skills (e.g. living and work skills), and personality (e.g. onset of disinhibited behaviors, stubbornness, apathy, etc.). Memory is the most crucial. Assessment must therefore be through an informant who has known the person for a minimum of six months and must probe into possible functional decline across these different domains. Although repeat neuropsychological assessments can be helpful over time, if the diagnosis is in doubt, so as to demonstrate deterioration in cognitive function, informant-based questionnaires are recommended for the purpose of diagnosis (Deb & Braganza, 1999). Clouding of consciousness should be absent and the disorder should be progressive over time, thereby ruling out delirium. The exclusion of depression and physical explanations for any observed decline is crucial as they may be treatable.

Summary

Assessment is a process that requires the bringing together of information and through this the development of hypotheses as to the causative and maintaining factors giving rise to a particular pattern of maladaptive behavior and/or abnormal mental state. This process is informed by the use of established conceptual models and findings from research studies. A deterioration in the frequency and/or nature of a person's maladaptive behavior, or the recurrence of new behaviors, require that such assessments are undertaken, as similar behaviors may have very different causes in different people. This process maximizes the chance that subsequent interventions will be successful. Assessments are required to be more rigorous as there is an increasing range of potentially valuable interventions ranging from the psychopharmacological to the psychological, to improvements in communication to changes in the social environment. Patient, informed and multidisciplinary assessments guide the intervention and maximize the chance of benefit.

Acknowledgement

My thanks to Robbie Patterson for her help in the preparation of this chapter.

References

APA (1994) *Diagnostic and Statistical Manual of Mental Disorders*, 4th edn. American Psychiatric Association, Washington DC.

Aylward, E.H., Burt, D.B., Thorpe, L.U., Lai, F. & Dalton, A.J. (1997) Diagnosis of dementia in individuals with intellectual disability. *Journal of Intellectual Disability Research*, **41**, 152–164.

Boer, H., Holland, A.J., Whittington, J., Butler, J., Webb, T. & Clarke, D. (2002) Psychotic illness in people with Prader Willi syndrome due to chromosome 15 maternal uniparental disomy. *Lancet*, **359**, 135–136.

Brylewski, J. & Duggan, L. (1999) Antipsychotic mediation for challenging behavior in people with intellectual disability: a systematic review of randomized controlled trials. *Journal of Intellectual Disability Research*, **43**, 360–371.

Cain, N.N., Davidson, P.W., Burhan, A.M., Andolsek, M.E., Baxter, J.T., Sullivan, L., Florescure, H., List, A. & Deutsch, L. (2003) Identifying bipolar disorders in individuals with intellectual disability. *Journal of Intellectual Disability Research*, **47** (Part 1), 31–38.

Cooper, S-A. (1997) Epidemiology of psychiatric disorders in elderly compared with younger adults with learning disabilities. *British Journal of Psychiatry*, **170**, 375–380.

Deb, S. & Braganza, J. (1999) Comparison of rating scales for the diagnosis of dementia in adults with Down's syndrome. *Journal of Intellectual Disability Research*, **43**, 400–407.

Devenny, D.A., Silverman, W.P., Hill, A.L., Jenkins, E., Sersen, E.A. & Wisniewski, K.E. (1996) Normal ageing in adults with Down's syndrome: a longitudinal study. *Journal of Intellectual Disability Research*, **40**, 208–221.

Einfeld, S. & Tonge, B.J. (1999) Observations on the use of the ICD-10 guide for mental retardation. *Journal of Intellectual Disability Research*, **43**, 408–412.

Emerson, E. (2001) *Challenging behavior: Analysis and intervention in people with severe intellectual disabilities*. Cambridge University Press, Cambridge.

Evenhuis, H.M. (1995a) Medical aspects of ageing in a population with intellectual disability: 1. Visual impairment. *Journal of Intellectual Disability Research*, **39**, 19–26.

Evenhuis, H.M. (1995b) Medical aspects of ageing in a population with intellectual disability: II Hearing impairment. *Journal of Intellectual Disability Research*, **39**, 27–34.

Folstein, M.F., Folstein, S.E. & McHugh, P.R. (1975) Mini-mental state. A practical method for grading the cognitive state of patients for the clinician. *Journal of Psychiatry Research*, **12**, 189–198.

Fryers, T. (2000) Epidemiology of mental retardation. *Oxford Textbook of Psychiatry* (eds M.G. Gelder, J.J. Lopez-Ibor & N.C. Andreasen) pp. 1941–1945. Oxford University Press, Oxford.

Hess-Rover, J., Crichton, J., Byrne, K. & Holland, A. (1999) Case report: Diagnosis and treatment of a severe psychotic illness in a man with dual severe sensory impairments caused by the presence of Usher syndrome. *Journal of Intellectual Disability Research*, **43**, 428–434.

Holland, A.J., Hon, J., Huppert, F.A., Steven, F. & Watson, P. (1998) A population-based study of the prevalence and presentation of dementia in adults with Down Syndrome. *British Journal of Psychiatry*, **172**, 493–498.

Hollins, S. & Esterhuyzen, A. (1997) Bereavement and grief in adults with learning disabilities. *British Journal of Psychiatry*, **170**, 497–501.

Janicki, M.P., Davidson, P.W., Henderson, C.M., McCallion, P., Taets, J.D., Forces, L.T., Sulkes, S.B., Frangenberg, E. & Ladrigan, P.M. (2002) Health characteristics and health services utilization in older adults with intellectual disabilities living in community residences. *Journal of Intellectual Disability Research*, **46**, 287–298.

Kaski, M. (2000) Aetiology of mental retardation: general issues and prevention. *New Oxford Textbook of Psychiatry* (eds M.G. Gelder, J.J. Lopez-Ibor & N.N. Andreasen) pp. 1947–1952. Oxford University Press, Oxford.

Linaker, O.M. (1990) Frequency and determinants for psychotropic drug use in an institution for the mentally retarded. *British Journal of Psychiatry*, **156**, 525–530.

Meadows, G., Turner, T., Campbell, L., Lewis, S.W., Reveley, M.A. & Murray, R.M. (1991) Assessing schizophrenia in adults with mental retardation: A comparative study. *British Journal of Psychiatry*, **158**, 103–105.

Meins, W. (1995) Symptoms of major depression in mentally retarded adults. *Journal of Intellectual Disability Research*, **39**, 41–46.

Moss, S., Goldberg, D.P., Simpson, N., Patel, P., Rowe, S., Prosser, H. & Ibbotson, B. (1993) *Psychiatric assessment schedule, modified for use in adults with developmental disabilities (PAS-ADD) ICD-10 version*. Hester Adrian Research Centre, University of Manchester.

Richards, M., Maughan, B.R.H., Hall, I., Strydom, A. & Wadsworth, M. (2001) Long-term affective disorder in people with mild learning disability. *British Journal of Psychiatry*, **179**, 523–527.

Royal College of Psychiatrists (2001) *Diagnostic Criteria – Learning Disability (DC-LD)*. Gaskell, London.

Shprintzen, R.J., Goldberg, R.B., Golding-Kushner, K. & Marion, R. (1992) Late onset psychosis in the velo-cardio-facial syndrome. *American Journal of Medical Genetics*, **42**, 141–142.

Sovner, R. & Hurley, A. (1990) Assessment tools which facilitate psychiatric evaluation of treatment. *Habiliative Mental Health Care Newsletter*, **9**, 11.

Tsiouris, J.A. (2001) The diagnosis of depression in people with severe/profound intellectual disability. *Journal of Intellectual Disability Research*, **45**, 115–120.

Tsiouris, J.A., Mann, R., Patti, P.J. & Sturmey, P. (2003) Challenging behaviors should not be considered as depressive equivalents in individual disability. *Journal of Intellectual Disability Research*, **47**, 14–21.

WHO (1993) *The ICD-10 Classification of Mental and Behavioral Disorders: Diagnostic Criteria for Research*. World Health Organization, Geneva.

WHO (1996) *ICD-10 Guide for Mental Retardation*. World Health Organization, Geneva.

Wing, L. & Shah, A. (2000) Catatonia in autistic spectrum disorder. *British Journal of Psychiatry*, **176**, 357–362.

Zigman, W., Schupf, N., Haveman, M. & Silverman, W. (1997) The epidemiology of Alzheimer disease in intellectual disability: results and recommendations from an international conference. *Journal of Intellectual Disability Research*, **41**, 76–80.

5 Depression in Aging Individuals with Intellectual Disabilities

Vee Prasher

The occurrence of depression in aging adults with intellectual disabilities (ID) has to date been an underinvestigated area of research (Burt *et al.*, 1992; Myers & Pueschel, 1995; McGuire & Chicoine, 1996). This is in contrast to the general population where numerous studies have been published (Copeland *et al.*, 1987, 1999; Beekman *et al.*, 1999). Depression can significantly impair the quality of life but appears to be rarely recognized as a treatable illness in older adults with ID; therefore the appropriate diagnosis, assessment and treatment of depression, and indeed all other forms of mental illness in people with ID, must concern all professionals. This chapter highlights the important clinical and research issues relating to depression in the field of intellectual disability. There remain ongoing arguments over the most appropriate terminology to be used in the field of psychiatry to describe mood-related disorders. In this chapter, 'depression' implies a single major depressive episode irrespective of whether it conforms to any given classification system such as ICD-10 (WHO, 1992) or DSM-IV (APA, 1994).

Prevalence

Depression is one of the most common psychiatric disorders in the general elderly population (Blazer, 1989) and prevalence rates from 0.4–35% have been reported (Beekman *et al.*, 1999). The majority of studies report a point prevalence rate of 3–5%. Many case reports of depression in a person with intellectual disability have been published and reviewed by other researchers (Carlson, 1979; Sovner & Hurley, 1983). A number of large scale studies investigating depressive disorders in adults with ID have been reported (Collacott *et al.*, 1992; Meins, 1993; Prasher, 1995b; Pary *et al.*, 1996), but few studies highlight depression in older adults with ID (Day, 1985; Patel *et al.*, 1993). These studies report a point prevalence rate in the order of 2–7% in adults with ID. Such reported rates of depression are highly influenced by several methodological factors:

- The use of the term depression. The term has been applied to low mood, to a single current depressive episode, to past depressive episodes, and to a bipolar affective disorder
- Errors in sample selection (small sample size, institutional subjects only)
- The study sample does not accurately represent the wider population of adults with intellectual disabilities
- The subjects' levels of intellectual disabilities and age are not controlled
- Instruments with poor validity and reliability are used to detect psychopathology
- Recognized diagnostic criteria are not used
- Errors are made in the application of the diagnostic criteria

These factors particularly apply to determining how common depression is in the people with intellectual disabilities.

Corbett (1979) in a large epidemiological study used clinical information along with information from the modified Social and Physical Incapacity Scale (Kushlick *et al.*, 1973) to make a diagnosis of a psychiatric disorder according to the Glossary of Mental Disorders based on the Eighth Revision of the International Classification of Diseases (The Stationery Office, 1968); of 110 adults over the age of 60 years, two (1.8%) had a diagnosis of depression and three (2.7%) of manic-depressive psychosis.

Day (1985) reported the findings of a retrospective survey of psychiatric disorder in two groups of people with intellectual disabilities aged 40 years and over. The first group was long-stay hospital residents, and the second group was a series of new admissions. Case note reviews were undertaken and each patient categorized according to the definitions in the Ninth Revision of the International Classification for Mental Disorders (WHO, 1978). Of the 357 long-stay residents, 109 (30%) were found to be subject to a psychiatric disorder, with affective psychosis in 19 (5.3%) subjects, and 'reactive depression' in a further four (1.1%). Of the 215 first admissions during the study period, 43 individuals had a psychiatric diagnosis, five (2.3%) had 'affective psychosis' and 14 (6.5%) reactive depression. The majority of adults had a history of recurrent episodes of illness. From the report the overlap between depression and hypomania/mania was unclear.

Patel *et al.* (1993) presented findings from a prevalence study of psychiatric morbidity in 105 people aged 50 years and over with ID using the Psychiatric Assessment Schedule for Adults with a Developmental Disability (PAS-ADD) (Moss *et al.*, 1993). Community and institutional subjects were recruited. The prevalence of psychiatric disorder was 21.0%

and although it is difficult from the report to state the exact prevalence of depression, it appears to be approximately 5%.

Due to limitations of investigating depression in older adults with ID, it is difficult to make reliable statements but, from the information available, it would appear the point prevalence rate for a major depressive illness is in the order of 5–7%. The rate is significantly lower than that for the elderly general population, which averages 13.5% (Beekman *et al.*, 1999). These findings would suggest that the occurrence of depression is less common in aging adults with ID than in the elderly general population. The effects of genetic make-up, gender and severity of intellectual disability on the onset of a depressive episode have not been fully investigated. From the available literature, it is probable that depression is more common in persons with Down syndrome than in other genetic disorders, in females more than males, and in persons with mild/moderate ID than with severe/profound ID.

There is a paucity of information regarding incidence rates of depression in people with intellectual disabilities, life-time prevalence rates of depression, age and sex differences, differential rates of depression as determined by severity of intellectual disability and differential rates as determined by the etiology of the intellectual disability.

Etiological factors

No single factor has been identified as the cause of depression in either people with intellectual disabilities or the general population. It is likely that a combination of biological, psychological and social factors is important. There is very little information available in the literature regarding predisposing factors for depression in older adults with ID.

Genetic factors

It remains uncertain whether individuals with ID associated with particular syndromes are at greater susceptibility to developing depression as compared to other individuals with and without ID. This applies particularly to older adults. Elderly individuals with Down syndrome (Tsiouris & Patti, 1997) and elderly individuals with fragile-X syndrome (Tranebjaerg & Orum, 1991) have been highlighted as two at-risk populations. The role of familial inheritance, which is important in the general population, has not been investigated in older adults with ID.

Organic brain disorders

No research has been published investigating whether persons who already have abnormalities in the structure and function of the brain are predisposed to depression by age-related neurotransmitter changes. Brain damage will increase difficulties in mood, behavior, personality and language. The presence of epilepsy may further increase the risk of a person suffering an affective disorder. Whether premature aging increases the risk for depression requires further investigation.

Physical health

It has been established that for non-disabled elderly people physical illness predisposes to depression, particularly conditions such as carcinomas, thyroid disease, B_{12} deficiency, sensory impairment and infections. Many of these disorders are also common in older adults with ID and therefore are also likely to predispose them to a depressive illness.

Medication

People with ID have a high rate of drug administration (Clarke *et al.*, 1990). Older adults with or without ID are more susceptible to adverse drug reactions stemming from side effects or drug interactions. Drugs of particular concern include steroids, beta-blockers, antihypertensives, anti-arrhythmic drugs and anti-epileptics. Medication should always be reviewed prior to a diagnosis of depression being made.

Social factors

Social factors or life-events as precipitating factors for depression have been described in the general population (Murphy, 1982) and in younger individuals with ID (Reiss & Benson, 1985). Virtually all older people with ID are subject to a significant number of social stresses. These include increased physical and psychiatric health morbidity, stigmatization, low income, few intimate relationships, loss of social support (especially in the recent climate of de-institutionalization) and death of loved ones. There is minimal information in the literature investigating a causal relationship between these factors and a depressive episode in older adults with ID, but it is possible that, for example, resulting loneliness and feelings of isolation are factors in the etiology of reactive depression.

More research is needed to investigate predisposing and precipitating factors for depression in older adults with ID. Research into candidate genes may have a significant impact in investigating whether particular genotypic individuals are susceptible to depression. Greater community provision can enable researchers to investigate the social influence and social consequences of depression.

Clinical presentation

The spectrum of clinical features associated with depression in persons with ID is similar to those seen in the general population (Charlot *et al.*, 1993; Cooper & Collacott, 1996; Prasher & Hall, 1996; Marston *et al.*, 1997), as shown in Table 5.1. For aging individuals with ID, somatic complaints and more neurovegetative features (psychomotor retardation, disturbed sleep, loss of appetite, loss of weight, diurnal variation) may occur more frequently. Further research is required to determine whether disturbance of memory, decrease in concentration, inability to think clearly, recurrent thoughts of death, guilt and suicide and perceptual changes (hallucinations, delusions) do not occur in people with ID or are present but are not elicited. Suicidal behaviour in depressed people with ID remains rare but does occur (Hurley, 1998). The reason for this has not been investigated but is in part due to limited cognitive and behavioral repertoire, the presence of physical disabilities, and the lack of access to lethal means.

The clinical presentation is influenced by the underlying severity of ID. Individuals with borderline and mild ID will present not too dissimilar to

Table 5.1 Common clinical symptoms of major depression.

Very common	Common	Rare
Low mood	Weight loss	Suicidal ideations
Irritability	Guilt feelings	Change in sexual activity
Anhedonia	Somatic complaints	Hallucinations
Decreased appetite	Self-injury	Delusions
Change in motor activity	Destruction of property	Eating disorder
Sleep disturbance	Diurnal variation of mood	Hysterical conversion
Fatigue	Loss of libido	Hypochrondrias
Decreased concentration	Loss of confidence	
Withdrawn	Constipation	
Aggression	Anxiety	
Tearfulness	Obsessions/compulsions	
Loss of interest		
Decline in social skills		

From Prasher (1999).

a person who is not intellectually disabled and may openly say 'I feel depressed', or 'my life is pointless'. Symptoms more marked in individuals with severe ID include psychomotor agitation, irritable mood and disturbed behavior. Symptoms less apparent include subjective depressed mood, reduced energy and complaints of general fatigue.

Assessment and diagnosis of depression

Generally a depressive episode should be diagnosed by a standard psychiatric assessment (Singh *et al.*, 1991; Einfeld, 1992). This should include a patient and/or informant history regarding presenting problem, review of information from other sources (e.g. medical notes) and from other professionals (nurses, psychologists, social workers, general practitioners), a mental state examination (including direct observation and self-reporting) and the exclusion of a primary physical illness by a physical examination and investigations which may include blood tests for thyroid dysfunction, diabetes and anticonvulsant toxicity. More detailed tests such as the dexamethasone suppression test, changes in the sleep or waking electroencephalogram, impaired evoked potential response and abnormalities in functional and structural neuroimaging of the brain have been proposed for the general population, but their validity with population of adults with intellectual disabilities has been contradictory (Wolkowitz, 1990). At present the widespread use of such tests cannot be recommended for adults with intellectual disabilities.

Further information should be sought by the assessment of weight, sleep and behavior by recordings made over time on standard charts. A multidisciplinary assessment (using doctors, nurses, psychologists, social workers, occupational therapists and pharmacists) should, where possible, be undertaken with a diagnosis made according to standard diagnostic guidelines (such as ICD-10 (WHO, 1992) or DSM-IV (APA, 1994)). If need be, a trial of medication may be necessary to aid making a diagnosis of a depressive episode.

The assessment and diagnosis of depression in people with ID and especially in older adults remains problematic (Hurley, 1996). Particular groups include those on high dose neuroleptic medication, individuals with severe/profound ID, persons with autism spectrum disorders, those with underlying physical disorders (epilepsy, diabetes, neurological diseases) and individuals with Down syndrome who are affected by Alzheimer's disease. The underlying reasons for the diagnosis being more difficult than in the general population, are difficulties in the understanding and expression of feelings of sadness by people with ID, misinterpretation of behaviors, low levels of recognition of symptoms by carers and professionals, overlapping symptoms (e.g. sleep disturbance in depression and dementia), and the high rate of misdiagnosis.

Table 5.2 shows that several psychometric assessment instruments have been developed to aid the clinical diagnosis of depression. Such instruments improve detection, reduce diagnostic disagreement, improve management of the illness, allow comparisons within and between research studies, aid planning of services, and aid communication between the doctor and patient/carers. Unmodified and modified rating scales have been proposed but their correlation with the clinical diagnosis remains to be fully established, especially in the aging population with intellectual disabilities. Such scales include the Beck Depression Inventory (Beck et al., 1961), Zung Self-Rating Depression Scale (Zung, 1965), Hamilton Rating Scale for Depression (Hamilton, 1960), Mental Retardation Depression Scale (Meins, 1996) and the Self-Report Depression Questionnaire (Reynolds & Baker, 1988).

Table 5.2 Commonly used instruments to detect depression.

Instrument	Comments
Psychiatric Assessment Scale for Adults with Developmental Disability (PAS-ADD) (Moss *et al.*, 1994)	Interview schedule completed by trained interviewer of patient and informant
Diagnostic Assessment Scale for the Severely Handicapped (DASH) (Matson *et al.*, 1991)	Rating scale assesses severity, frequency and duration of symptoms of 13 psychiatric disorders. Informant based. For severe/profound ID
Reiss Screen for Maladaptive Behavior (Reiss, 1988)	Rating scale detects eight psychiatric disorders. Informant based. For mild/moderate ID
The Psychopathology Inventory for Mentally Retarded Adults (PIMRA) (Matson *et al.*, 1984)	Scaled self-report screening questionnaire. Informant based. For mild-moderate ID

The use of such instruments will enhance their clinical assessment. The use of repeat assessments using such instruments can be a means of measuring response to treatment. However, such instruments should not be solely used to make the diagnosis of depression and indeed should be used with caution. Prior to the application of any given instrument clinicians should always satisfy themselves with the reliability, validity and practicalities of the test.

As there is no definitive biological test for depression, the diagnosis is dependent on the identification and subsequent classification of symptoms and signs. The classification may also be influenced by severity, frequency and the duration of the symptoms. To date, a number of studies have investigated the role of standard diagnostic criteria in their applicability to people with ID (Pawlarcyzk & Beckwith, 1987). The consensus view appears to be that for mild or moderate intellectual disability, DSM-IV criteria (APA, 1994) or ICD-10 criteria (WHO, 1992) are applicable. Difficulties arise for individuals with severe and profound ID where the use of standard diagnostic criteria requires modification to emphasize the biological features and behavioral changes (Marston et al, 1997; Tsiouris, 2001).

Differential diagnoses

The differential diagnosis of depression in a person with an intellectual disability must consider other causes of depressed mood and symptoms associated with depression in the elderly. Aging adults with ID have a high prevalence and incidence of physical illnesses. Distinguishing a primary depressive illness from secondary mood changes due to a general medical illness (e.g. vitamin deficiency, hypo/hyperthyroidism, head injury or cancer) should always be considered. If a physical illness is present clinical features suggestive of the illness are usually present and the features associated with depression do not reach full diagnostic criteria for a depressive disorder. A full and proper history from the adult and informant, through physical examination, laboratory investigations and more specific tests, should highlight that the mood disturbance is secondary to an underlying physiological disorder.

Drug-induced mood disorders are not uncommon in older adults with ID. This can result from the direct physiological effect of the medication in susceptible individuals or can occur as part of the side-effect profile, drug toxicity or drug withdrawal. Again, a detailed assessment will demonstrate that the depressive symptomatology present does not fulfil recognized diagnostic criteria for a depressive disorder. Particular drugs of concern are anticonvulsants, hypnotics, antipsychotics, analgesics, anticholinergic, beta-blockers and steroids.

Older adults with ID can experience a bereavement reaction to change in residence or separation from a loved carer as well as to the death of someone emotionally close. Symptoms characteristic of a depressive illness (low mood, episodes of crying, loss of appetite, insomnia, loss of weight) may be present. However, a detailed history should alert the clinician to a bereavement reaction although the time of onset, duration and severity may vary widely making the differential diagnosis from depression difficult.

A number of researchers (Harper & Wadsworth, 1990; Burt et al., 1992;

Prasher, 1995a; Sung *et al.*, 1997) have highlighted the occurrence of depressive symptoms in dementia of Alzheimer's type and the differential diagnosis between dementia and depression in older adults with Down syndrome. Patients with depression may present with marked cognitive defects termed pseudodementia (Lishman, 1998). However, in particular features such as a fluctuating mood, an anxious rather than a blunting effect, patchy cognitive impairment and prominent biological features of depression would suggest depression rather than primary dementia. Response to treatment and a longitudinal review may be necessary before there is clarification of the situation.

Treatment

The approach to the appropriate management of depression in older adults with ID is principally the same as that for younger intellectually disabled adults and that for the general population. There are several recommended forms of treatment, which may be used individually or in conjunction with each other.

Drug therapy

The mainstay of treatment is antidepressant drug therapy and has been highlighted in the population with intellectual disabilities (Howland, 1992; Tsiouris & Patti, 1997; Bhaumik *et al.*, 2000). Medications of choice are shown in Table 5.3. The rational use of antidepressants for older adults with ID, more than for younger depressed individuals, is dependent on the awareness of their efficacy, side effects, drug interactions and secondary complications. Tricyclic medication, for example, should be used with caution in the elderly as it can commonly cause postural hypotension, which may lead to dizziness or dangerous falls. In individuals with cardiac disease or dementia the risk of experiencing detrimental side effects is high. The selective serotonin reuptake inhibitors (SSRIs) are thought to be as efficacious as the tricyclics, but the side-effect profile (less sedation, less cardiotoxicity, less anticholinergic side effects) is more benign and the risk from overdose much lower. SSRIs may have greater efficacy in adults with self-injurious behaviour and aggressive behavior.

The adage 'start low and go slow' particularly applies to the treatment with medication of depression in elderly adults with intellectual disabilities. Medication should be started at a low dose and increased gradually over the following few weeks to determine an effective dose.

Table 5.3 Antidepressant medications.

Group of antidepressant	Generic names
Tricyclic antidepressants (TCAs)	amitripytline, lofepramine, dothiepin, imipramine, clomipramine, trimipramine, nortriptyline
Monoamine oxidase inhibitors (MAOIs)	phenelzine, tranylcypromine, moclobemide, isocarboxazid
Selective serotonin reuptake inhibitors (SSRIs)	fluoxetine, fluvoxamine, paroxetine, sertraline
Noradrenergic and specific serotonergic Antidepressants (NaSSAs)	citalopram mirtazapine
Selective noradrenaline reuptake inhibitors (NARIs)	reboxetine
Serotonin/noradrenaline reuptake inhibitors (SNRIs)	venlafaxine

This limit may be significantly less than that for younger individuals. If there is no benefit within a three to five-week course of an antidepressant, including at a higher dosage, the diagnosis should be reviewed. An alternative antidepressant can be prescribed but a monoamine oxidase inhibitor (MAOI) should be used with caution and only 10 days after stopping the tricyclic and only when individuals and carers are fully aware of serious interactions with alcohol, cheese and other prohibited foods. Both adults and carers must be advised of the possible side effects and drug interactions and that improvement may not be apparent for 10–14 days. Monitoring of compliance is essential. Serum monitoring of antidepressants is possible and should be considered if there is sudden unexpected behavioral or cognitive change.

Withdrawal symptoms (discontinuation reactions) have been reported for virtually all classes of antidepressants. Symptoms usually start two to three days after stopping medication. They are usually reversible with recommencement of therapy and most are mild and short-lived. Common symptoms include dizziness, nausea, headache, lethargy, sleep disturbance, agitation and restlessness. The likelihood of a discontinuation reaction can be prevented by gradual reduction of the antidepressant over four to six weeks.

Psychological approaches

For the general population, psychotherapy, cognitive therapy and behaviour therapy are established forms of treatment for depression.

Limited information is available regarding their use in people with ID (Lindsay *et al.*, 1993; Mattek & Wierzbicki, 1998). For people with mild ID such therapies may enable underlying psychological factors to be explored. This applies in particular to individuals presenting with self-injurious or suicidal behavior. Such treatments may also require the need for a course of antidepressants. Antidepressants can often lift mood to allow a person to work more effectively in the other treatments. The role of the effectiveness of non-pharmaceutical therapy for older adults with ID and depression requires further evaluation.

Electroconvulsive therapy (ECT)

ECT has remained an effective form of treatment of depression in the general population since it was introduced in 1938, but its application to persons with ID is uncommon. Other than case reports on young individuals (Bates & Smeltzer, 1982; Goldstein & Jensvold, 1989; Lazarus *et al.*, 1990), there are no systematic reviews of the effectiveness of ECT for depressed adults with intellectual disabilities. The indications should not be too dissimilar as for the general population: severe illness with significantly impaired food and fluid intake, psychotic depression resistant to antidepressants, previously responded to ECT and where pharmacotherapy is contraindicated. A good response is expected in depressive episodes where delusions, hallucinations and biological features are present. Maintenance drug treatment is required to prevent relapse soon after treatment.

Social support

The management of depression in older people with ID requires the involvement of both professionals and non-professionals. Carers have a significant role to play. A simple and understandable explanation of the illness to the adult and their carers can aid cooperation and compliance with medication use. Increased physical activity at home or at their day service can reduce feelings of tiredness and apathy and maintain good physical health. Maintaining the daily routine can reduce feelings of helplessness and enable individuals to continue to function in the community. The encouragement of involvement in activities that previously the adult has enjoyed can contribute to improving self-esteem. It is important that carers continue to encourage eating foods and drinking of fluids and the maintenance of appetite and weight.

Prognosis

For the general population a number of different outcome criteria have been used giving a wide range of prognostic results (Baldwin & Jolley, 1986). For older adults with intellectual disabilities there is a total absence in the scientific literature of the prognosis of a depressive episode. Outcome will be dependent on a number of factors: number of previous episodes, previous manic episodes, interval between episodes, cluster of symptoms, response to treatment, social and residential factors, genotype, and possibly severity of intellectual disability. The short-term outlook for the general population is usually good, but for adults with intellectual disabilities prognosis can vary from a full recovery to ongoing chronic difficulties (Langee & Conlon, 1992; Cooper & Collacott, 1993; Prasher & Hall, 1996). The long-term prognosis for the elderly general population suggests that up to one-third will continue to have future problems. No information is available regarding the long-term follow-up of depression in aging people with ID but it is reasonable to assume that a high proportion will have persistent problems.

Further research involving treatment trials is required to asses the benefit of maintenance therapy (antidepressants, lithium, carbamazepine, sodium valproate) used to prevent future depressive illnesses (Naylor *et al.*, 1974; Rivinus & Harmatz, 1979). With use of appropriate caution it is likely that, as per the general population, older adults with ID can benefit from maintenance therapy.

Summary

There is virtually no scientifically-based evidence regarding any aspect of depression in older adults with ID. Epidemiological, clinical, treatment and outcome information is absent. Information from the general population and that from the younger population of adults with intellectual disabilities has had to be extrapolated and applied to the older population of adults with intellectual disabilities. This may be generally reasonable but depression in older adults in the general population does significantly differ from that found in the younger population and therefore professionals working with depressed adults with intellectual disabilities must also expect there to be important differences.

The prevalence of depression is relatively common in adults with ID and of a similar rate to the general population. Genetic abnormalities (for example trisomy 21, fragile-X) or increased intellectual impairment may predispose people with ID to depression. A depressive episode in adults with intellectual disabilities should, if a systematic assessment, appropriate instruments and diagnostic criteria are used, be accurately detected. Subsequent management usually involves a course of antidepressant therapy along with non-pharmaceutical community support.

There remain several areas ripe for future research, which should help answer the many deficiencies in our knowledge of depression in older adults with ID. Detailed case reports and small-scale studies can provide invaluable information, but multicenter large-scale studies are necessary to reliably and with good validity provide accurate information which clinicians can implement to the benefit of their patients.

References

APA (1994) *Diagnostic and Statistical Manual of Mental Disorders*, 4th edn (DSM IV). American Psychiatric Association, Washington, DC.

Baldwin, R.C. & Jolley, D.J. (1986) The prognosis of depression in old age. *British Journal of Psychiatry*, **149**, 574–583.

Bates, W.J. & Smeltzer, D.J. (1982) Electroconvulsive treatment of self-injurious behavior in a patient with severe mental retardation. *American Journal of Psychiatry*, **139**, 1355–1356.

Beck, A.T., Ward, C.H., Mendelson, M. *et al.* (1961) An inventory for depression. *Archives of General Psychiatry*, **4**, 561–585.

Beekman, A.T.F., Copeland, J.R.M. & Prince, M.J. (1999) Review of community prevalence of depression in later life. *British Journal of Psychiatry*, **174**, 307–311.

Bhaumik, S., Branford, D., Naik, B.I. & Biswas, A.B. (2000) A retrospective audit of selective serotonin re-uptake inhibitors (Fluoxetine and Paroxetine) for the treatment of depressive episodes in adults with learning disabilities. *The British Journal of Developmental Disabilities*, **46**, 131–139.

Blazer, D. (1989) Affective disorders in late life. *Geriatric Psychiatry* (eds E. Busse & D. Blazer) pp. 369–401. Cambridge University Press, Cambridge.

Burt, D.B., Loveland, K.A. & Lewis, K.R. (1992) Depression and the onset of dementia in adults with mental retardation. *American Journal on Mental Retardation*, **96**, 502–511.

Carlson, G. (1979) Affective psychoses in mental retardates. *Psychiatric Clinics of North America*, **2**, 499–510.

Charlot, L.R., Doucette, A.C. & Mezzacappa, E. (1993) Affective symptoms of institutionalized adults with mental retardation. *American Journal on Mental Retardation*, **98**, 408–416.

Clarke, D.J., Kelley, S., Thinn, K. & Corbett, J.A. (1990) Disabilities, drugs and mental retardation. 1. Disabilities and the prescription of drugs in three residential settings. *Journal of Mental Deficiency Research*, **34**, 385–395.

Collacott, R.A., Cooper, S.A. & McGrother, C. (1992) Differential rates of psychiatric disorders in adults with Down's syndrome compared with other mentally handicapped adults. *British Journal of Psychiatry*, **161**, 671–674.

Cooper, S-A. & Collacott, R. (1993) The prognosis of depression in Down's syndrome. *Journal of Nervous and Mental Disorders*, **181**, 206–207.

Cooper, S-A. & Collacott, R.A. (1996) Depressive episodes in adults with learning disabilities. *Irish Journal of Psychological Medicine*, **13**, 105–113.

Copeland, J.R.M., Dewey, N.E., Wood, N., Searle, R., Davidson, I.A. & McWilliam, C. (1987) Range of mental illness among the elderly in the community. Prevalence in Liverpool using the GMS-AGECAT. *British Journal of Psychiatry*, **150**, 815–823.

Copeland, J.R.M., Beekman, A.T.F., Dewey, M.E., Hooijer, C., Jordan, A., Lawlor, B.A., Lobo, A., Magnusson, H., Mann, A.H., Meller, I., Prince, M.J., Reichies, F., Turrina, C., deVries, M.W. & Wilson, K.C.M. (1999) Depression in Europe. Geographical distribution in older people. *British Journal of Psychiatry*, **174**. 312–321.

Corbett, J.A. (1979) Psychiatric morbidity and mental retardation. *Psychiatric Illness and Mental Handicap* (eds F.E. James & R.P. Snaith) pp. 11–26. Gaskell Press, London.

Day, K. (1985) Psychiatric disorder in the middle-aged and elderly mentally handicapped. *British Journal of Psychiatry*, **147**, 660–667.

Einfield, S.L. (1992) Clinical assessment of psychiatric symptoms in mentally retarded individuals. *Australian and New Zealand Journal of Psychiatry*, **26**, 48–63.

Goldstein, M.Z. & Jensvold, M.F. (1989) ECT treatment of an elderly mentally retarded man. *Psychosomatics*, 104–106.

Hamilton, M. (1960) A rating scale for depression. *Journal of Neurology, Neurosurgery and Psychiatry*, **23**, 56–62.

Harper, D.C. & Wadsworth, J.S. (1990) Dementia and depression in elders with mental retardation: A pilot study. *Research in Developmental Disabilities*, **11**, 177–198.

Howland, R.H. (1992) Fluoxetine treatment of depression in mentally retarded adults. *The Journal of Nervous and Mental Disease*, **180**, 202–205.

Hurley, A.D. (1996) Identifying psychiatric disorders in persons with mental retardation: A model illustrated by depression in Down syndrome. *Journal of Rehabilitation*, Jan/Feb/Mar, 27–33.

Hurley, A.D. (1998) Two cases of suicide attempt by patients with Down's syndrome. *Psychiatric Services*, **49**, 1618–1619.

Kushlick, A., Blunden, R. & Cox, G. (1973) A method of rating behavior characteristics for use in large scale surveys of mental handicap. *Psychological Medicine*, **3**, 466–478.

Lazarus, A., Jaffe, R.L. & Dubin, W.R. (1990) Electroconvulsive therapy and major depression in Down's syndrome. *Journal of Clinical Psychiatry*, **51**, 422–425.

Langee, H.R. & Conlon, M. (1992) Predictors of response to antidepressant medications. *American Journal on Mental Retardation*, **97**, 65–70.

Lindsay, W.R., Howells, L. & Pitcaithly, D. (1993) Cognitive therapy for depression with individuals with intellectual disabilities. *British Journal of Psychology*, **66**, 135–141.

Lishman, W.A. (1998) *Organic Psychiatry*, 3rd edn. Blackwell, Oxford.

Marston, G.M., Perry, D.M. & Roy, A. (1997) Manifestations of depression in people with intellectual disability. *Journal of Intellectual Disability Research*, **41**, 476–480.

Matson, J.L., Kazdin, A.E. & Senatore, V. (1984) Psychometric properties of the psychopathology instrument for mentally retarded adults. *Applied Research in Mental Retardation*, **5**, 81–89.

Matson, J.L., Gardner, W.I., Coe, D.A. & Sovner. R. (1991) A scale for evaluating emotional disorders in severely and profoundly mentally retarded persons: development of the Diagnostic Assessment for the Severely Handicapped (DASH) scale. *British Journal of Psychiatry*, **159**, 404–409.

Mattek, P.W. & Wierzbicki, M. (1998) Cognitive and behavioral correlates of depression in learning-disabled and nonlearning-disabled adult students. *Journal of Clinical Psychology*, **54**, 831–837.

McGuire, D.E. & Chicoine, B.A. (1996) Depressive disorders in adults with Down syndrome. *The Habilitative Mental Healthcare Newsletter*, **15**, (1).

Meins, W. (1993) Prevalence and risk factors for depressive disorders in adults with intellectual disability. *Australia and New Zealand Journal of Developmental Disabilities*, **18**, 147–156.

Meins, W. (1996) A new depression scale designed for use with adults with mental retardation. *Journal of Intellectual Disability Research*, **40**, 222–226.

Moss, S.C., Patel, P., Prosser, H., Goldberg, D.P., Simpson, N., Rowe, S. & Lucchino, R. (1993) Psychiatric morbidity in older people with moderate and severe learning disability (mental retardation). Part I: Development and reliability of the patient interview (the PASS-ADD). *British Journal of Psychiatry*, **168**, 471–480.

Moss, S.C., Ibbotson, B. & Prosser, H. (1994) *The Psychiatric Assessment Schedule for Adults with Developmental Disability (The PAS-ADD); Interview development and compilation of the clinical glossary.* Hester Adrian Research Centre, University of Manchester, Manchester.

Murphy, E. (1982) Social origins of depression in old age. *British Journal of Psychiatry*, **141**, 135–142.

Myers, B.A. & Pueschel, S.M. (1995) Major depression in a small group of adults with Downs syndrome. *Research in Developmental Disabilities*, **16**, 285–299.

Naylor, G.J., Donald, J.M., LePoidevin D. & Reid, A.H. (1974) A double-blind trial of long-term lithium therapy in mental defectives. *British Journal of Psychiatry*, **124**, 52–57.

Pary, R.J., Strauss, D. & White, J.F. (1996) A population survey of bipolar disorder in persons with and without Down syndrome. *Down Syndrome Quarterly*, **1**, 1–4.

Patel, P., Goldsberg, D. & Moss, S. (1993) Psychiatric morbidity in older people with moderate and severe learning disability II: The prevalence study. *British Journal of Psychiatry*, **163**, 481–491.

Pawlarcyzk D. & Beckwith, B.E. (1987) Depressive symptoms displayed by persons with mental retardation: A review. *Mental Retardation*, **25**, 325–330.

Prasher, V.P. (1995a) Age-specific prevalence, thyroid dysfunction and depressive symptomatology in adults with Down syndrome and dementia. *International Journal of Geriatric Psychiatry*, **10**, 25–31.

Prasher, V.P. (1995b) Prevalence of psychiatric disorders in adults with Down syndrome. *European Journal of Psychiatry*, **9**, 77–82.

Prasher, V.P. (1999) Presentation and management of depression in people with learning disability. *Advances in Psychiatric Treatment*, **5**, 447–454.

Prasher, V.P. & Hall, W. (1996) Short-term prognosis of depression in adults with Down syndrome: Association with thyroid status and effects on adaptive behaviour. *Journal of Intellectual Disability Research*, **40**, 32–38.

Reiss, S. (1988) *Test manual for the Reiss Screen for Maladaptive Behavior*. International Diagnostic Systems, Columbus, Ohio.

Reiss, S. & Benson, B.A. (1985) Psychosocial correlates of depression in mentally retarded adults: I. Minimal social support and stigmatization. *American Journal of Mental Deficiency*, **89**, 331–337.

Reynolds, W.M. & Baker, J.A. (1988) Assessment of depression in persons with mental retardation. *American Journal on Mental Retardation*, **93**, 93–103.

Rivinus, T.M. & Harmatz, J.S. (1979) Diagnosis and lithium treatment of affective disorder in the retarded: Five case studies. *American Journal of Psychiatry*, **36**, 551–554.

Singh, N.N., Sood, A., Sonenklar, N. & Ellis, C.R. (1991) Assessment and diagnosis of mental illness in persons with mental retardation. *Behaviour Modification*, **15**, 419–443.

Sovner, R. & Hurley, A.D. (1983) Do the mentally retarded suffer from affective illness? *Archives of General Psychiatry*, **40**, 61–67.

The Stationery Office (1968) *A Glossary of Mental Disorders*. Based on the International Statistical Classification of Disease, Injuries and Cancer of Death. The Stationery Office, London.

Sung H., Hawkins, B.A., Eklund, S.J., Kim K.A., Foose, A., May, M.E. & Brattain Rogers, N. (1997) Depression and dementia in aging adults with Down syndrome: A case study approach. *Archives of Behavioral Psychiatry*, **35**, 27–28.

Tranebjaerg, L. & Orum, A. (1991) Major depressive disorder as a prominent but underestimated feature of Fragile X syndrome. *Comprehensive Psychiatry*, **32**, 83–87.

Tsiouris, J.A. (2001) Diagnosis of depression in people with severe/profound intellectual disability. *Journal of Intellectual Disability Research*, **45**, 115–120.

Tsiouris J.A. & Patti, P.J. (1997) Drug treatment of depression associated with dementia or presented as 'pseudodementia' in older adults with Down syndrome. *Journal of Applied Research in Intellectual Disabilities*, **10**, 312–322.

WHO (1978) *Mental Disorders; Glossary and Guide to their Classification in Accordance with the Ninth Revision of the International Classification of Disease (ICD-9)*. World Health Organization, Geneva.

WHO (1992) *The ICD-10 Classification of Mental and Behavioural Disorders. Clinical Descriptions and Diagnostic Guidelines*. World Health Organization, Geneva.

Wolkowitz, O.M. (1990) Use of the dexamethasone suppression test with mentally retarded persons: review and recommendations. *American Journal on Mental Retardation*, **94**, 509–514.

Zung, W.W.K. (1965) A self-rating depression scale. *Archives of General Psychiatry*, **12**, 63–70.

6 Behavioral Manifestations of Medical Conditions

Stephen Sulkes and Laura Smith Emmick

As adults with intellectual disabilities (ID) age, they are subject to the same array of health problems to which older individuals without ID are subject. Many of these conditions are known to result in emotional disorders and behavioral symptoms in persons of all ages, while some are more commonly seen in people as they age and still others are more frequently seen in conjunction with ID. This chapter provides an overview of some medical conditions that commonly present with behavioral manifestations in older individuals with ID, and provides a framework for cost-effective medical evaluations when such conditions are being considered.

It has been recognized for decades that physical illness can present as psychiatric disease. In 1978, Hall and associates reported that 9% of people in their series of 658 outpatient psychiatric evaluations had identifiable medical causes, and 46% of these had not had their medical conditions previously recognized. Presenting psychiatric complaints were of depression, anxiety, confusion and speech. In a meta-analysis of 21 studies looking at over 9000 adults presenting with chiefly psychiatric complaints, Koranyi and Potoczny (1992) found an average of 42.2% (17–80%) of such people had unrecognized medical complaints, with 17% contributing directly to the psychiatric condition. Pinquart (2001) also conducted a meta-analysis of the relationship between physical and mental health and found that subjective health was strongly associated with mental health, and especially so in the oldest of people. Another illustrative study comes from Beekman *et al.* (1995) who examined the relationship between physical health and depression in 224 older adults living in community settings. They found strong associations between subjective measures of health, such as pain and subjective health, and depression. This relationship was stronger than for objective measures of health and disability.

Several studies have examined the relationship between physical and mental health in older adults with intellectual disabilities. Moss and Patel (1997) compared the physical health and disability of 12 adults aged over 50 years with dementia and a group of 89 similarly aged peers without dementia. Those participants with dementia had more physical health conditions and greater disabilities than their peers. Also, they had less self-directed activity, less enjoyment of activities and more irritable and violent behavior. In a larger-scale study, Cooper (1999) examined the relationship between physical and mental health in a group of 134 older adults with intellectual disabilities aged over 65 years. Separate analyses were conducted for dementia and other mental disorders. In a multiple regression model the number of physical health problems, degree of intellectual disability, and smoking predicted dementia. The regression model for other mental disorders only included level of intellectual disability as a predictor of mental disorder; physical health was not a predictor.

Recently Davidson and colleagues (in press) reported a cross-sectional study that examined the association between health status and behavior disorders with increasing age in a cohort of 60752 adults with ID clustered into four age groupings (21–44, 45–57, 60–74 and >74). Age grouping data suggested an association between morbidity and increased likelihood of behavior symptoms in all but the oldest age grouping. The magnitude of the association and trend varied by specific disease across age groupings compared to that found in healthy cohorts. About 25% of the adults with ID had psychiatric diagnoses and the frequency of such diagnoses did not decrease with age grouping. These results suggested that health status might increase the likelihood of persistent behavioral disturbances in older persons with ID. The authors suggested that behavioral disorders might be sentinels for occult medical morbidity, which in turn may be responsive to intervention.

Many conditions causing ID have associated behavioral features that evolve from childhood onward (e.g. the activity level and language patterns of individuals with fragile-X and Williams syndromes, or the self-injury of individuals with Lesch-Nyhan syndrome). However, the following discussion will focus on behavioral manifestations that are not life-long, but recent in onset when seen in adults with ID.

Types of specific psychiatric and behavioral manifestations

Depression

The most common presentation of behavioral significance in the older individual with intellectual disability is depression. As described in Chapter 5, the typical manifestations of depression include withdrawal, sleep disturbance, decreased appetite, changes in activity level, lethargy, changes in sexual performance, and self-injurious or suicidal behavior. However, these manifestations, evident in people without ID, are not the only features seen in people with cognitive limitations. In this population, aggression, agitation, and stereotypic behavior can also be seen. Before assuming that such behavioral outcomes are the result of depression, however, evaluation to rule out underlying medical conditions must occur.

The symptoms of depression can be manifestations of a myriad of medical conditions. Pathology in virtually any organ system can cause pain that might result in depressive symptoms in a person with limited communication skills or other intellectual disability. Similarly, chronic functional failure of virtually any organ system can present with fatigue, sleep and appetite changes, and affective changes that can mimic depression.

Depression has been specifically associated with overactive bladder (Brown *et al.*, 2000), chronic obstructive pulmonary disease (Gift & McCrone, 1993; van Ede *et al.*, 1999), Parkinson's disease (Slaughter *et al.*, 2001), fractures caused by osteoporosis (Gold, 2001), end-stage renal disease requiring dialysis (Finkelstein & Finkelstein, 2000), malignancies including pancreatic carcinoma (and most other organ systems) (Passik & Breitbart, 1996; Cleeland, 2000), folate deficiency (Alpert & Fava, 1997; Alpert *et al.*, 2000), sleep apnea (Yantis, 1999), infections including hepatitis and HIV (Barroso, 1999), arthritis (Zautra *et al.*, 1999), diabetic neuropathy (Godil *et al.*, 1996), gluten enteropathy (Holmes, 1996), gynecologic conditions including antiphospholipid antibody syndrome (Brey & Escalante, 1978) and normal menopause (Coleman, 1993; Khastgir & Studd, 1998), and post-operative states (Gardner & Worwood, 1997).

As noted in Chapter 4, an excellent history is crucial in identifying associated health problems. This becomes even more critical when the ability of the individual to provide historical information is limited, when there are multiple carers and observers, and when old records must serve as the primary source of information.

Sleep disturbance

Like depression, sleep is a life activity in which disruptions are highly noticeable to the individual experiencing them, and especially so to an individual living in a supervised environment. An accurate history of the individual's sleep and wake times is essential to identify precipitating factors. A search for the underlying cause of a new-onset sleep change is very valuable, helping to avoid the use of sedatives or other sleep aids that may complicate the individual's medical situation as well as impact daytime function.

Sleep disruption is a common expression of a variety of medical concerns, and can manifest as inadequate night-time sleep or daytime drowsiness. Depression can affect sleep quality, and disrupted sleep can mimic depression; a detailed sleep history is therefore always an essential piece of the evaluation of behavior disturbance.

Sateia *et al.*, (2000) divided sleep-related problems into six areas: insomnia, sleep-wake cycle (circadian rhythm) disorders, hypersomnia, sleep-related breathing disorders, motor disturbances in sleep, and parasomnias. Chronobiology (circadian rhythms and their regulation) changes with age. Van Someren (2000) and Vitiello (1997) have outlined some useful approaches to evaluation and treatment in older individuals. Periodic limb movements in sleep (also known as 'restless legs syndrome') may awaken the individual, as might obstructive sleep apnea (Ancoli-Israel, 1997).

Obstructive sleep apnea commonly causes inadequacy of sleep cycles. The airway obstructs during deep sleep, resulting in snoring, thrashing and multiple brief interruptions of the sleep. The individual may not completely awaken, but incomplete sleep cycling results in daytime drowsiness, irritability and apparent disinterest. Because of their craniofacial structure and differences in lymphoid systems, persons with Down syndrome are particularly susceptible to obstructive sleep apnea, leading to concerns about early Alzheimer's-like dementia. This phenomenon is commonly associated with obesity, and weight loss can help to reduce its severity. Other treatments include nasal expansion appliances, surgical removal of obstructing lymphoid tissue, continuous positive airway pressure (CPAP), and tracheostomy to bypass upper airway obstruction. In addition to dietary sources of caffeine, numerous medications can also disrupt sleep. Notorious among these are anticonvulsants, neuroleptics, stimulants, systemic bronchodilators, and others.

Some medical conditions known to affect sleep include menopausal changes (Shaver & Zenk, 2000; Polo-Kantola *et al.*, 2001), endocrine changes (Touitou & Haus, 2000; Van Someren, 2000), and underlying neurological disease including seizures. Visual impairment has a profound impact on sleep, at least in part through impaired regulation of melatonin production (Stores & Ramchandani, 1999), and this can be problematic in older individuals with associated sensory disabilities. Many older individuals suffer from other conditions that, by affecting respiration, also impact sleep quality. Congestive heart failure can be associated with orthopnea (difficulty breathing when supine), a symptom responsive to elevation of the head (Obenza Nishime *et al.*, 2000). Chronic obstructive pulmonary disease and asthma (Lewis, 2001) and aspiration also affect respiration and, in turn, sleep quality. Gastroesophageal reflux and associated painful esophagitis are common causes of discomfort when supine, and can also result in sleep disturbance by exacerbating obstructive apnea (Senior *et al.*, 2001) and reactive airway disease (Cibella & Cuttitta, 2001).

Appetite and weight changes

Appetite changes are common in endocrine disorders such as diabetes (increased, along with thirst), hyperthyroidism (increased), hypothyroidism (decreased), and possibly hypoparathyroidism. Malignancies, both gastrointestinal and of other organ systems, are well known to decrease appetite, with associated weight loss. Weight changes can result from any condition that affects caloric intake (e.g. hypothalamic appetite disorders), retention (e.g. gastroesophageal reflux, diarrheal diseases, bowel obstructions), absorption (e.g. lactose intolerance, gluten enteropathy), or metabolism (e.g. diabetes mellitus). A quality dietary history is essential in evaluating anyone who is failing to maintain body weight.

Self-injurious behavior

Self-injury can be a behavioral manifestation of pain or discomfort anywhere, or it may reflect specific discomfort in the body area toward which the self-injury is directed (e.g. head banging in response to headache). Bosch *et al.* (1997) found that 28% of their study population had previously undiagnosed medical conditions that could be expected to cause pain or discomfort, and most of these decreased self-injury when these conditions were treated. Self-injury is known to be associated with some syndromes of intellectual disability that have other health problems as well, such as Lesch-Nyhan syndrome (Breese *et al.*, 1990) and Prader-Willi syndrome (obesity, diabetes) (Schepis *et al.*, 1994). Self-injurious eye-poking can be associated with visual disability, as the pressure creates a photic equivalent stimulus, and can also be associated with other causes of eye discomfort, like glaucoma (Jan *et al.*, 1994).

Aggression and agitation

Aggression is often a non-specific behavioral symptom, associated with agitation, triggered by environmental stimuli as well as medical concerns. A few specific medical causes associated with aggression include hypothalamic tumors (Arita *et al.*, 1999) and Lesch-Nyhan syndrome (Breese *et al.*, 1990). Agitation can be secondary to endocrinopathies such as hyperthyroidism, parathyroid abnormalities and hypoglycemia. Increasing intracranial pressure, due to malfunctioning ventriculoperitoneal shunts and brain tumors, can also cause agitation. Agitation can also be a side effect of many medications.

Pain

Acute and chronic pain may precipitate behavior change in people with ID and functional communication limitation. Researchers in geriatric care have recognized that individuals with communication barriers may manifest pain in different ways from other people. However, no generally accepted assessment tools are yet available (Huffman & Kunik, 2000; Epps, 2001). One study (Feldt, 2000) offered a checklist of six non-verbal pain indicators that correlates well with self-reporting in cognitively intact individuals. McGrath and colleagues (1998) have also reported on a carer interview approach to determine pain in individuals with cognitive impairment. Pain may be produced by psychological states and may also be a cause for psychological disturbance; treatment approaches may need to be multipronged (Merskey, 1996; Ruoff, 1996). Empiric use of non-sedating analgesics (acetaminophen, ibuprofen) can help to differentiate behavior due to pain when it is suspected.

Known behavioral associations with specific medical conditions

Nutritional factors

Nutritional issues are often anecdotally associated with behavioral problems. Since nutrition in older individuals is more often associated with identifiable disease and disruption of physical well-being, a review of nutritional factors in this population is more likely than in other groups to reveal identifiable and treatable conditions that might affect behavioral outcomes. As in pain syndromes, nutritional disorders can be both cause and effect of behavioral conditions (Markson, 1997; Clarke *et al.*, 1999). As can be easily imagined, individuals suffering from chronic protein-calorie malnutrition will appear depressed, with decreased activity level, increased sleep, withdrawal and decreased self-directedness (Brozek, 1990). Folate deficiency has been studied recently, noting its association with depression (Alpert & Fava, 1997; Alpert *et al.*, 2000).

Skin

A number of skin diseases are associated with anxiety, depression and sleep disorders. Some of these include alopecia areata (Liakopoulou *et al.*, 1997), atopic dermatitis (Dahl *et al.*, 1995; Hashiro & Okomura, 1997), chronic urticaria (Hashiro & Okumura, 1994) and scleroderma (Muller *et al.*, 1992).

Eyes and ears

Ophthalmologic conditions affecting behavior can be grouped into those affecting functional vision and those associated with optic or periorbital discomfort. Rubbing of eyes may be in response to discomfort (pain, itching, photophobia). Functional vision testing and more detailed eye examination may require the skills of an ophthalmologist. Similarly, otological conditions can be grouped into those affecting hearing (either decreased hearing or undesired sound perception), those associated with otologic discomfort, and those associated with acute vestibular disorders. Simple ear examination may reveal impacted cerumen affecting hearing and causing pain, and functionally-based audiologic assessment may reveal hearing loss that may affect behavior.

Throat

Weight loss and apparent associated depression may be the result of swallowing disorders or oral-pharyngeal discomfort. Dental examination for decay, infection, gum disease, and plaque build-up may identify sources of discomfort that, when treated, will result in decreased agitation and improved eating and sleep.

Cardiac and respiratory disorder

Cardiac and respiratory disorders, as mentioned above, have their effects through fatigue and respiratory distress. Respiratory or cardiac failure can both present with symptoms of depression (van Ede *et al.*, 1999) and sleep disturbance. Pulmonary rehabilitation has been reported to improve fear and depression and improve self-esteem in intellectually normal persons (Schoo, 1997). Recently, increased attention is also being paid to the psychological sequelae of cardiac surgery.

Gastrointestinal disorders

Some sources of abdominal pain and nutritional disorders have been discussed above. In individuals with cognitive disability, two frequent problems are gastroesophageal reflux disease (GERD) and constipation. Both are more common in individuals with low muscle tone and decreased mobility. GERD is well established to have negative effects on quality of life in people without disabilities, where associated heartburn symptoms reduce work productivity and activities of daily living (Wahlqvist, 2001; Wiklund, 2001). Quality of life measures reportedly improve markedly after fundoplication (Lochegnies *et al.*, 2001). In individuals with intellectual disabilities, rumination, dental erosions and hematemesis, GERD should be suspected (Bohmer *et al.*, 2000). Rumination is a self-injurious form of gastroesophageal reflux in which gastric contents are voluntarily regurgitated into the esophagus and into the mouth. Whether this is viewed as a self-stimulating behavior that results in a medical problem or the converse, a combination of antacid and antireflux treatments, psychotropic medication and behavioral intervention is often required to bring it under control (Malcolm *et al.*, 1997). Psychological disorders are frequently associated with GERD in the general population, with increased depression, somatization and anxiety (Clouse, 1991; Baker *et al.*, 1995).

Many individuals with cognitive disabilities suffer from constipation and this leads to a wide range of behavioral manifestations. Dietary differences in people living in residential settings (lower fluid and fiber intake), lack of mobility, and concurrent use of medications that slow gut transit time, all combine to make this a particularly compelling problem (Bishop & Nowicki, 1999; Guerrero & Cavender, 1999). Meiring & Joubert (1998) found constipation to be a particularly prevalent problem in elderly individuals, present in 29% of elderly individuals in their South African cohorts, independent of race or dietary factors. Decreased transit times were found in elderly individuals by Towers *et al.* (1994), again independent of diet, but with an increased association with psychiatric symptoms such as obsessive-compulsiveness, depression and anxiety. Community-living seniors report similar symptoms, and in one study most used laxatives when available (Wolfsen *et al.*, 1993). Even in the general population, constipation is often associated with anxiety, depression and social dysfunction (Mason *et al.*, 2000; Dykes *et al.*, 2001). Dumitrascu and colleagues (1998) noted an association between hostility and functional bowel complaints, especially constipation.

An often-overlooked source of abdominal pain in individuals with ID is the pancreas. Pancreatitis is a well-known complication of therapy with the anticonvulsant valproate (up to 7% of cases of individuals on this medication), and when abdominal pain or vomiting is noted in an individual with ID taking this medication, serum amylase and lipase levels should be obtained (Buzan *et al.*, 1995).

Gynecological

Cyclic behavior changes in women may reflect hormonal cycling with menstruations, especially in women with other neurological disorders (Kaminer *et al.*, 1988; Quint *et al.*, 1999).

Thyroid disease

Thyroid disease is well known to be associated with Down syndrome, both in the hyper- and hypo-thyroid conditions. Pop *et al.*, (1998) suggest that there may be a joint relationship between autoimmune hypothyroidism and depression, while Haggerty *et al.* (1990) note cognitive and mood disturbances appearing in statistically significant numbers of people with otherwise clinically asymptomatic thyroid dysfunction. Hendrick *et al.* (1998) noted that thyroid hormone supplementation may help to treat certain mood disorders, and Cleare and colleagues (1995) noted an effect of hypothyroidism on 5-hydroxytryptamine function. An association has also been made between hypothyroidism and seasonal affective disorder (Ratiere, 1992).

Summary

Individuals with ID who manifest behavioral changes should be reviewed and evaluated for underlying physical disorders. History and physical examinations, combined with judicious use of laboratory studies based on initial findings, will often uncover unrecognized associated medical problems. In addition to disease states, medication side effects often include behavioral symptoms, and medication changes should be considered as initial interventions.

References

Alpert, J.E. & Fava, M. (1997) Nutrition and depression: the role of folate. *Nutrition Reviews*, **55**, 145–149.

Alpert, J.E., Mischoulon D., Nierenberg, A.A. & Fava, M. (2000) Nutrition and depression: focus on folate. *Nutrition*, **16**, 544–546.

Ancoli-Israel, S. (1997) Sleep problems in older adults: putting myths to bed. *Geriatrics*, **52**, 20–30.

Arita K., Ikawa, F., Kurisu, K., Sumida, M., Harada, K., Uozumi, T., Monden, S., Yoshida, J. & Nishi, Y. (1999) The relationship between magnetic resonance imaging findings and clinical manifestations of hypothalamic hamartoma. *Journal of Neurosurgery*, **91**, 212–220.

Baker, L.H., Lieberman, D. & Oehlke, M. (1995) Psychological distress in patients with gastroesophageal reflux disease. *American Journal of Gastroenterology*, **90**, 1797–1803.

Barroso, J. (1999) A review of fatigue in people with HIV infection. *Journal of the Association of Nurses in AIDS Care*, **10**, 42–49.

Beekman, A.T., Kriesgman, D.M., Deeg, D.J., & van Tilburg, W. (1995) The association of physical health and depressive symptoms in the older population: age and sex differences. *Social Psychiatry and Psychiatric Epidemiology*, **30**, 32–38.

Bishop, P.R. & Nowicki, M.J. (1999) Defecation disorders in the neurologically impaired child. *Pediatric Annals*, **28**, 322–329.

Bohmer, C.J., Klinkenberg-Knol, E.C., Niezen-de Boer, M.C. & Meuwissen, S.G. (2000) Gastroesophageal reflux disease in intellectually disabled individuals: how often, how serious, how manageable? *American Journal of Gastroenterology*, **95**, 1868–1872.

Bosch, J., Van Dyke, C., Smith, S.M. & Poulton, S. (1997) Role of medical conditions in the exacerbation of self-injurious behavior: an exploratory study. *Mental Retardation*, **35**, 124–130.

Breese, G.R., Criswell, H.E. & Mueller, R.A. (1990) Evidence that lack of brain dopamine during development can increase the susceptibility for aggression and self-injurious behavior by influencing D1-dopamine receptor function. *Progress in Neuro-Psychopharmacology & Biological Psychiatry*, **14**, Suppl, S65–80.

Brey, R.L. & Escalante, A. (1978) Neurological manifestations of antiphospholipid antibody syndrome. *Lupus*, **7**, Suppl 2, S67–74.

Brown, J.S., McGhan, W.F. & Chokroverty S. (2000) Comorbidities associated with overactive bladder. *American Journal of Managed Care*, **6**, Suppl, S574–9.

Brozek, J. (1990) Effects of generalized malnutrition on personality. *Nutrition*, **6**, 389–395.

Buzan, R.D., Firestone, D., Thomas, M. & Dubovsky, S.L. (1995) Valproate-associated pancreatitis and cholecystitis in six mentally retarded adults. *Journal of Clinical Psychiatry*, **56**, 529–532.

Cibella, F. & Cuttitta, G. (2001) Nocturnal asthma and gastroesophageal reflux. *American Journal of Medicine*, **111**, Suppl 8A, 31S–36S.

Clarke, D.M., Wahlqvist, M.L., Rassias, C.R. & Strauss, B.J. (1999) Psychological factors in nutritional disorders of the elderly: part of the spectrum of eating disorders. *International Journal of Eating Disorders*, **25**, 345–348.

Cleare, A.J., McGregor, A. & O'Keane, V. (1995) Neuroendocrine evidence for an association between hypothyroidism, reduced central 5-HT activity and depression. *Clinical Endocrinology*, **43**, 713–719.

Cleeland, C.S. (2000) Cancer-related symptoms. *Seminars in Radiation Oncology*, **10**, 175–190.

Clouse, R.E. (1991) Psychiatric disorders in patients with esophageal disease. *Medical Clinics of North America*, **75**, 1081–1096.

Coleman, P.M. (1993) Depression during the female climacteric period. *Journal of Advanced Nursing*, **18**, 1540–1546.

Cooper, S.A. (1999) The relationship between psychiatric and physical health in elderly people with intellectual disability. *Journal of Intellectual Disability Research*, **43**, 54–60.

Dahl, R.E., Bernhisel-Broadbent, J., Scanlon-Holdford, S., Sampson, H.A. & Lupo, M. (1995) Sleep disturbances in children with atopic dermatitis. *Archives of Pediatrics & Adolescent Medicine*, **149**, 856–860.

Davidson, P.W., Janicki, M.P., Ladrigan, P., Houser, K., Henderson, C.M. & Cain, N.C. (in press) Association between behavior problems and health status in older adults with intellectual disability. *Journal of Aging and Mental Health*.

Dumitrascu, D.L., Acalovschi, M. & Pascu, O. (1998) Hostility in patients with chronic constipation. *Romanian Journal of Internal Medicine*, **36**, 239–243.

Dykes, S., Smilgin-Humphreys, S. & Bass, C. (2001) Chronic idiopathic constipation: a psychological enquiry. *European Journal of Gastroenterology & Hepatology*, **13**, 39–44.

Epps, C.D. (2001) Recognizing pain in the institutionalized elder with dementia. *Geriatric Nursing*, **22**, 71–77.

Feldt, K.S. (2000) The checklist of nonverbal pain indicators (CNPI). *Pain Management Nursing*, **1**, 13–21.

Finkelstein, F.O. & Finkelstein, S.H. (2000) Depression in chronic dialysis patients: assessment and treatment. *Nephrology Dialysis Transplantation*, **15**, 1911–1913.

Gardner, F.V. & Worwood, E.V. (1997) Psychological effects of cardiac surgery: a review of the literature. *Journal of the Royal Society of Health*, **117**, 245–249.

Gift, A.G. & McCrone, S.H. (1993) Depression in patients with COPD. *Heart & Lung*, **22**, 289–297.

Godil, A., Berriman, D., Knapik, S., Norman, M., Godil, F. & Firek, A.F. (1996) Diabetic neuropathic cachexia. *Western Journal of Medicine*, **165**, 382–385.

Gold, D.T. (2001) The nonskeletal consequences of osteoporotic fractures. Psychologic and social outcomes. *Rheumatic Diseases Clinics of North America*, **27**, 255–262.

Guerrero, R.A. & Cavender, C.P. (1999) Constipation: physical and psychological sequelae. *Pediatric Annals*, **28**, 312–316.

Haggerty, J.J., Jr., Garbutt, J.C., Evans, D.L., Golden, R.N., Pedersen, C., Simon, J.S. & Nemeroff, C.B. (1990) Subclinical hypothyroidism: a review of neuropsychiatric aspects. *International Journal of Psychiatry in Medicine*, **20**, 193–208.

Hall, R.C., Popkin, M.K., Devaul, R.A., Faillace, L.A. & Stickney, S.K. (1978) Physical illness presenting as psychiatric disease. *Archives of General Psychiatry*, **35**, 1315–1320.

Hashiro, M. & Okumura, M. (1994) Anxiety, depression, psychosomatic symptoms and autonomic nervous function in patients with chronic urticaria. *Journal of Dermatological Science*, **8**, 129–135.

Hashiro, M. & Okumura, M. (1997) Anxiety, depression and psychosomatic symptoms in patients with atopic dermatitis: comparison with normal controls and among groups of different degrees of severity. *Journal of Dermatological Science*, **14**, 63–67.

Hendrick, V., Altshuler, L. & Whybrow, P. (1998) Psychoneuroendocrinology of mood disorders. The hypothalamic-pituitary-thyroid axis. *Psychiatric Clinics of North America*, **21**, 277–292.

Holmes, G.K. (1996) Non-malignant complications of coeliac disease. *Acta Paediatrica*, **412**, Suppl, 68–75.

Huffman, J.C. & Kunik, M.E. (2000) Assessment and understanding of pain in patients with dementia. *Gerontologist*, **40**, 574–581.

Jan, J.E., Good, W.V., Freeman, R.D. & Espezel, H. (1994) Eye-poking. *Developmental Medicine & Child Neurology*, **36**, 321–325.

Kaminer, Y., Feinstein, C., Barrett, R.P., Tylenda, B. & Hole, W. (1988) Menstrually related mood disorder in developmentally disabled adolescents: review and current status. *Child Psychiatry & Human Development*, **18**, 239–249.

Khastgir, G. & Studd, J. (1998) Hysterectomy, ovarian failure, and depression. *Menopause*, **5**, 113–122.

Koranyi, E.K. & Potoczny, W.M. (1992) Physical illness underlying psychiatric symptoms. *Psychotherapy & Psychosomatics*, **58**, 155–160.

Lewis, D.A. (2001) Sleep in patients with asthma and chronic obstructive pulmonary disease. *Current Opinion in Pulmonary Medicine*, **7**, 105–112.

Liakopoulou, M., Alifieraki, T., Katideniou, A., Kakourou, T., Tselalidou, E., Tsiantis, J. & Stratigos, J. (1997) Children with alopecia areata: psychiatric symptomatology and life events. *Journal of the American Academy of Child & Adolescent Psychiatry*, **36**, 678–684.

Lochegnies, A., Hauters, P., Janssen, P., Nakad, A., Farchack, E. & Defrennes, M. (2001) Quality of life assessment after Nissen fundoplication. *Acta Chirurgica Belgica*, **101**, 20–24.

Malcolm, A., Thumshirn, M.B., Camilleri, M. & Williams, D.E. (1997) Rumination syndrome. *Mayo Clinic Proceedings*, **72**, 646–652.

Markson, E.W. (1997) Functional, social, and psychological disability as causes of loss of weight and independence in older community-living people. *Clinics in Geriatric Medicine*, **13**, 639–652.

Mason, H.J., Serrano-Ikkos, E. & Kamm, M.A. (2000) Psychological morbidity in women with idiopathic constipation. *American Journal of Gastroenterology*, **95**, 2852–2857.

McGrath, P.J., Rosmus, C., Canfield, C., Campbell, M.A. & Hennigar, A. (1998) Behaviors caregivers use to determine pain in non-verbal, cognitively impaired individuals. *Developmental Medicine & Child Neurology*, **40**, 340–343.

Meiring, P.J. & Joubert, G. (1998) Constipation in elderly patients attending a polyclinic. *South African Medical Journal*, **88**, 888–890.

Merskey, H. (1996) Psychological medicine, pain, and musculoskeletal disorders. *Rheumatic Diseases Clinics of North America*, **22**, 623–637.

Moss, S. & Patel, P. (1997) Dementia in older people with intellectual disability: symptoms of physical and mental illness, and levels of adaptive behavior. *Journal of Intellectual Disability Research*, **41**, 60–69.

Muller, N., Gizycki-Nienhaus, B., Gunther, W. & Meurer, M. (1992) Depression as a cerebral manifestation of scleroderma: immunological findings in serum and cerebrospinal fluid. *Biological Psychiatry*, **31**, 1151–1156.

Obenza Nishime, E., Liu, L.C., Coulter, T.D., Gassler, J.P., Dinner, D.S. & Mills,

R.M. (2000) Heart failure and sleep-related breathing disorders. *Cardiology in Review*, **8**, 191–201.

Passik, S.D. & Breitbart, W.S. (1996) Depression in patients with pancreatic carcinoma. Diagnostic and treatment issues. *Cancer*, **78**, Suppl, 615–626.

Pinquart, M. (2001) Correlates of subjective health in older adults: a meta-analysis. *Psychology and Aging*, **16**, 414–426.

Polo-Kantola, P., Saaresranta, T. & Polo, O. (2001) Etiology and treatment of sleep disturbances during perimenopause and postmenopause. *CNS Drugs*, **15**, 445–452.

Pop, V.J., Maartens, L.H., Leusink, G., van Son, M.J., Knottnerus, A.A., Ward, A.M., Metcalfe, R. & Weetman, A.P. (1998) Are autoimmune thyroid dysfunction and depression related? *Journal of Clinical Endocrinology & Metabolism*, **83**, 3194–3197.

Quint, E.H., Elkins, T.E., Sorg, C.A. & Kope, S. (1999) The treatment of cyclical behavioral changes in women with mental disabilities. *Journal of Pediatric & Adolescent Gynecology*, **12**, 139–142.

Raitiere, M.N. (1992) Clinical evidence for thyroid dysfunction in patients with seasonal affective disorder. *Psychoneuroendocrinology*, **17**, 231–241.

Ruoff, G.E. (1996) Depression in the patient with chronic pain. *Journal of Family Practice*, **43**, Suppl, S25–33.

Sateia, M.J., Greenough, G. & Nowell, P. (2000) Sleep in neuropsychiatric disorders. *Seminars in Clinical Neuropsychiatry*, **5**, 227–237.

Schepis, C., Failla, P., Siragusa, M. & Romano, C. (1994) Skin-picking: the best cutaneous feature in the recognization of Prader-Willi syndrome. *International Journal of Dermatology*, **33**, 866–867.

Schoo, A.M. (1997) A literature review of rehabilitative intervention for chronic obstructive pulmonary disease patients. *Australian Health Review*, **20**, 120–132.

Senior, B.A., Khan, M., Schwimmer, C., Rosenthal, L. & Benninger, M. (2001) Gastroesophageal reflux and obstructive sleep apnea. *Laryngoscope*, **111**, 2144–2146.

Shaver, J.L. & Zenk, S.N. (2000) Sleep disturbance in menopause. *Journal of Womens Health & Gender-Based Medicine*, **9**, 109–118.

Slaughter, J.R., Slaughter, K.A., Nichols, D., Holmes, S.E. & Martens, M.P. (2001) Prevalence, clinical manifestations, etiology, and treatment of depression in Parkinson's disease. *Journal of Neuropsychiatry & Clinical Neurosciences*, **13**, 187–196.

Stores, G. & Ramchandani, P. (1999) Sleep disorders in visually impaired children. *Developmental Medicine & Child Neurology*, **41**, 348–352.

Touitou, Y. & Haus, E. (2000) Alterations with aging of the endocrine and neuroendocrine circadian system in humans. *Chronobiology International*, **17**, 369–390.

Towers, A.L., Burgio, K.L., Locher, J.L., Merkel, I.S., Safaeian, M. & Wald, A. (1994) Constipation in the elderly: influence of dietary, psychological, and physiological factors. *Journal of the American Geriatrics Society*, **42**, 701–706.

van Ede, L., Yzermans, C.J. & Brouwer, H.J. (1999) Prevalence of depression in patients with chronic obstructive pulmonary disease: a systematic review. *Thorax*, **54**, 688–692.

Van Someren, E.J. (2000) Circadian rhythms and sleep in human aging. *Chronobiology International*, **17**, 233–243.

Vitiello, M.V. (1997) Sleep disorders and aging: understanding the causes. *Journals of Gerontology. Series A, Biological Sciences & Medical Sciences*, **52**, M189–191.

Wahlqvist, P. (2001) Symptoms of gastroesophageal reflux disease, perceived productivity, and health-related quality of life. *American Journal of Gastroenterology*, **96**, Suppl, S57–61.

Wiklund, I. (2001) Quality of life in patients with gastroesophageal reflux disease. *American Journal of Gastroenterology*, **96**, Suppl, S46–53.

Wolfsen, C.R., Barker, J.C. & Mitteness, L.S. (1993) Constipation in the daily lives of frail elderly people. *Archives of Family Medicine*, **2**, 853–858.

Yantis, M.A. (1999) Identifying depression as a symptom of sleep apnea. *Journal of Psychosocial Nursing & Mental Health Services*, **37**, 28–34.

Zautra, A.J., Hamilton, N.A., Potter, P. & Smith, B. (1999) Field research on the relationship between stress and disease activity in rheumatoid arthritis. *Annals of the New York Academy of Sciences*, **876**, 397–412.

7 Emotional and Behavioral Disturbances in Adults with Down Syndrome

Paul Patti and John Tsiouris

The prevalence of psychiatric disorders in people with intellectual disabilities (ID) has been reported to be higher than in the general population (Russell & Tanguay, 1981; Eaton & Menolascino, 1982; Benson, 1985; Reiss, 1990). Proposed explanations for this greater incidence are the higher frequency of behavioral disturbances in the ID population when compared to the general population (Day, 1985), and the lack of differentiation between psychiatric disorders and challenging behaviors in the ID population (Day & Jancar, 1994).

A major subgroup of the ID population are people with Down syndrome (DS) who were reported to experience different age-specific physical and mental health problems in comparison to people with ID but without DS. A variety of illnesses are more likely to occur in persons with DS, including thyroid disease (hyperthyroidism), diabetes, depression, obsessive-compulsive disorder, hearing loss, atlantoaxial subluxation and Alzheimer disease (Smith, 2001). Vision and hearing problems along with respiratory infections were identified as the most common health problems affecting children with DS (Turner *et al.*, 1990). In addition, when compared with their non-DS counterparts, older persons with DS were found to have higher rates of visual and hearing deficits, osteoporosis, epilepsy and motor handicaps (Haveman & Maaskant, 1989) suggesting a genetic predisposition to these problems. As noted in Chapter 6, these medical illnesses and sensory deficits may contribute to the display of certain challenging behaviors and psychiatric disorders seen in people with DS.

People with DS have a longer life span than in the past (Baird & Sadovnick, 1987). As people with DS continue to live longer, there is a greater risk for them to develop Alzheimer disease (Wisniewski *et al.*, 1985; Dalton & Crapper-McLachlan, 1986; Oliver & Holland, 1986; Visser *et al.*, 1997). Haveman and colleagues (1994) found that people with DS had more psychological problems with advancing age and attributed many of these problems to an association with dementia. They also found that people with DS have much lower prevalence rates of diagnosed psychiatric disorders than people without DS, even when their ID level was taken into account.

Persons with DS appear to display a susceptibility to a different pattern of psychiatric disorders when compared to the general ID population. Collacott and colleagues (1992) reported that older adults with DS were more likely to be diagnosed with dementia and depressive disorders, but were in some way protected against the development of schizophrenia, paranoid states, conduct and personality disorders. Depression and dementia of Alzheimer type (DAT) in adults with DS had similar presentations (Burt *et al.*, 1992). Difficulties in making a differential diagnosis arise when clinicians confuse depression with dementia and/or over-diagnose DAT in people with DS. For some individuals with DS, a reported decline in functioning associated with depression was labeled as 'pseudo-dementia' and treated accordingly, with favorable results (Tsiouris & Patti, 1997).

The literature has mostly focused on the areas of depression and DAT when addressing mental health issues in older adults with DS. There has been less attention on studying challenging behaviors and the presentation of psychiatric signs and symptoms associated with a reported change or decline in behavior. This chapter highlights challenging behaviors, the presenting psychiatric signs and symptoms, and the types of psychiatric disorders found in adults with DS. Six case examples are presented to highlight some important behavioral and psychiatric issues that can present challenges to clinicians in arriving at a proper psychiatric diagnosis.

Challenging and maladaptive behaviors

Haveman and colleagues (1994) found that people with DS had similar challenging behaviors in comparison with other persons with ID. They did, however, find that people with DS appear to display more mood disturbances (which they called psychological problems) with advancing age starting around age 40. Recent findings revealed that adults with DS exhibit a lower incidence of some types of challenging and maladaptive behaviors compared to other adults with ID (Collacott *et al.*, 1998; Cooper, & Prasher, 1998; Chapman & Hesketh, 2000). A recent study found no evidence that challenging behaviors are depressive equivalents in persons with ID, and stressed that clinicians should look to the presenting psychiatric signs and symptoms to arrive at the proper diagnosis (Tsiouris *et al.*, 2003). Cooper & Prasher (1998) reported 'being excessively unco-operative' as occurring more commonly in a group with DS who also displayed a significantly lower prevalence of aggression but higher incidences of restlessness, low mood and disturbed sleep, than controls.

A diagnosis of dementia with DS was a predictive factor for increased maladaptive behavior (Prasher & Chung, 1996). Behavioral disorders are a common feature of individuals suffering from dementia in the general population, especially those in the later stages of the illness. The difficulties in dealing with behavioral disorders (e.g. agitation, aggression and screaming) rather than cognitive decline, in the general population, were found to be the main reasons why carers seek placement in nursing homes (Stoppe et al., 1999). This is less of an issue for people with ID, as many of them are in supervised group homes where the level of care and supervision is greater than care provided by only one or two carers in the person's home.

People with DS living at home may have better functional abilities, particularly with respect to in-home activities such as dressing and self-care, than do other adults with ID but without DS (Seltzer et al., 1993). This may explain why a greater proportion of people with DS live outside of institutions and function well in the community without a high incidence of challenging behaviors. It is therefore important in any future studies on challenging behaviors to take into account the ages of the individuals studied. Both the frequency and type of challenging behavior displayed in people with DS can vary according to their age, residential setting and psychiatric disorder (if any), and can thereby lead to different conclusions being made.

Common psychiatric signs and symptoms

As noted in Chapter 4, in order to arrive at the proper psychiatric diagnosis according to DSM IV (APA, 1994) or ICD-10 (WHO, 1992) nomenclature, it is important to identify the characteristic signs and symptoms for a specific disorder or condition. Across all age groups, disturbances in sleep and mood were the most prevalent psychiatric signs and increased with advancing age (Haveman et al., 1994). This coincides with the expected age range when dementia is first reported in people with DS. Myers and Pueschel (1995a) reported on a small group of adults with DS and major depression under age 45 who presented with episodes of crying, sad affect and/or mood lability. There were few verbal expressions of guilt or self-deprecation made by these depressed individuals. The vegetative symptoms of severe withdrawal, mutism, psychomotor retardation, decreased appetite, weight loss and insomnia were found to be the prominent features in this group.

Hallucinations and delusions seem to be an infrequent phenomenon in people with DS. In a review of 86 published cases of dementia in adults with DS, none reported the presence of delusions and only one report suggested the possible presence of hallucinations (Prasher, 1997). This differed from Myers and Pueschel (1995a) who reported hallucinations to be a prominent feature (46%) in 22 individuals with DS and major depression. Their case selections, however, were from a biased group. High incidences of hallucinations and delusions have not been reported in any other study. With only a limited number of case descriptions of psychotic disorders reported in people with DS, it appears that the prevalence of hallucinations and delusions remains low (Prasher, 1995, 1997).

A common behavioral feature observed in many people with DS was talking to self. Self-talk was recently studied in younger people with DS (ages 17–24) and was seen as an adaptive behavior rather than an indication of pathology (Glenn & Cunningham, 2000). In a cohort of 206 persons with DS (mean age 47.4 years) who were seen in a diagnostic clinic, 23% engaged in self-talk; however only 5% were diagnosed with psychotic disorder (Patti & Tsiouris, 2002). It is likely that the individuals in the report by Myers & Pueschel (1995a) were engaged in self-talk, which was taken as the individual responding to an internal dialogue and therefore was classified as a hallucination. It is important for clinicians to observe the individual for any change in the quality of their self-talk such as an increase or decrease in the volume or any expressions of fear or anger displayed. It is these types of changes, rather than merely the presence of self-talk, that can indicate psychopathology.

Evans and Gray (2000) suggested that repetitive behaviors might be a part of the behavioral phenotype of individuals with DS. Behavior rituals which commonly involved compulsive hoarding of objects or food, obsessions with clothing, and bathroom rituals can be motivated by anxiety or stress, as seen in obsessive-compulsive disorder. These rituals, especially compulsive hoarding, may be displayed for a specific function or purpose. The hoarding of objects is a common behavior in many persons with Alzheimer disease (Stoppe *et al.* 1999) and may be an adaptive way to minimize forgetting where personal effects are in the environment.

Tics/involuntary movements (exclusive of tremors or myoclonus) have been reported in some persons with DS. Myers and Pueschel (1995b) and Kerbeshian and Burd (2000) reported a small number of cases (1.2% and 2% respectively) with tic disorders in their cohorts of persons with DS. Since both studies only cited Tourette's disorder, it was not clear if they also looked for or included chronic tic disorder in their groups. In a sample of 206 persons with DS seen by Patti and Tsiouris (2002), 12% were observed to exhibit vocal or motor tics as part of their behavioral repertoire. Myers and Pueschel (1995b) proposed that some persons with DS might have tardive or atypical Tourette's disorder due to the exposure to neuroleptics. Holtmann *et al.* (2000) reported a case example of a medication-induced tic in a boy with DS.

Suicidal ideation appears to be extremely low in people with DS. In a large population survey on suicide attempts, individuals with DS had significantly fewer incidences of suicidal behavior compared to the ID control group without DS (Pary *et al.*, 1997).

Psychiatric diagnoses

People with DS present with a different spectrum of psychiatric disorders compared to people with ID without DS (Collacott *et al.*, 1992). A low prevalence of schizophrenia and other psychotic disorders were found in the DS population when compared to other people with ID but without DS (Myers & Pueschel, 1991, 1994; Collacott *et al.*, 1992; Day & Jancar, 1994; Cooper *et al.*, 1995; Prasher, 1995). Collacott and colleagues reported that people with DS have higher prevalence rates of depression than other psychiatric disorders. Indeed, depression along with dementia and hypothyroidism were reported as the primary conditions that can distinguish the adult DS population from age-matched or developmentally-matched control groups (Chapman & Hesketh, 2000). Hypothyroidism can bring about behavioral symptoms suggesting major depression (Haggerty & Prange, 1995) but normalization of subclinical hypothyroidism has been noted with the successful reversal of depression after treatment (Jackson, 1998).

Mania has been reported to be less common in people with DS than in the ID or general populations (Craddock & Owen, 1994). In a large population-based survey, a diagnosis of bipolar disorder was not reported among persons with DS and there was a significantly low prevalence of overactivity in persons with DS when compared to controls (Pary *et al.*, 1996). This suggests that bipolar disorder with mania is uncommon in the DS population. Also noteworthy, a review of the literature did not reveal any study or report as to the presence or incidence of impulse control disorders in people with DS.

Obsessive-compulsive disorder (OCD) has been reported to be more common in persons with DS (Prasher, 1995; Prasher & Day, 1995). Behavior rituals and hoarding are commonly seen in many persons with DS; however, there are no large-scale studies in the literature for any firm conclusions to be made as to the prevalence of OCD in the DS population.

Illustrative case examples

Decline in functioning misdiagnosed as dementia

MM was a 40-year-old female with mild ID who lived in a community residence. Referral was made for a second opinion to rule out dementia. Prior to evaluation, a diagnosis of DAT was made and donepezil was prescribed based on the reports of withdrawal, an inability to focus on tasks and a decline in adaptive functioning.

The reported regression in MM's behavior occurred within a 10-month period. The presenting complaints included an increase in anxiety, irritability and avoidance behaviors, insomnia, weight loss, withdrawal, non-compliance, loss of interest in self-care, becoming confused and forgetful, and talking to herself. A number of life events occurred prior to MM's decline in behavior. In 1993 the death of her father, with whom she had been living, resulted in a series of changes in her day program and living situation over four years until her eventual placement in a group home at age 38.

Cognitive testing revealed the absence of memory impairment, agnosia or apraxia. A mental status exam found depressed mood and constricted effect with some evidence of psychotic features (e.g. talking to objects, fabricating stories). A diagnosis of major depression, single episode with possible psychotic features, and anxiety disorder NOS (not otherwise specified) was made. No clinical findings to support a diagnosis of dementia were evident. Olanzapine and sertraline were prescribed and an improvement in MM's behavior and condition was reported on the 6-month follow-up. Two subsequent follow-ups revealed MM to be active and doing well with major depression in remission.

Delusional disorder and onset of dementia

DL was a 50-year-old male with mild ID who lived in a community residence. Referral was made due to the onset of paranoid ideation and possible auditory hallucinations. Other presenting complaints included periods of agitation, suspiciousness, mental confusion, memory deficits, clothing compulsions and an altered time concept. After the death of his aunt (his only remaining relative), DL fabricated the delusion that he was married and had a wife and an older son.

Initial evaluation found cognitive impairment, confabulation, poor insight and paranoid ideation. A diagnosis of delusional disorder, mixed type was initially given; the diagnosis of dementia was added on 6-month follow-up when a further decline in memory and general functioning was observed. Continued follow-up over a 5-year period noted a gradual loss of cognitive and adaptive skills in all areas. As mental confusion and disorientation increased, delusions and paranoid ideations decreased and were no longer expressed by age 54. Late onset seizures developed at age 54 and a loss of ambulation resulted in DL being relocated to another community residence that provided increased care and supervision. A loss of all self-care skills and total dependence in all areas by age 55 led to his eventual placement in a nursing home where DL died at age 56.

Major depression, single episode with selective mutism

SC was a 28-year-old female with moderate ID who lived at home with her parents. Referral was made due to a significant regression in behavior, which occurred over a one-year period. The presenting complaints included selective mutism, a lack of energy, non-compliance, social avoidance, insomnia, changes in appetite and weight, lability of mood and behavior rituals (e.g. excessive hand washing, tooth brushing). The reported changes in behavior occurred after the birth of her married sister's baby. This event caused a change in focus of the family's attention from SC, especially by her parents, directed to the new baby in the family. Behaviorally, SC closed herself off from her surroundings choosing not to speak; she insisted on sleeping in her parent's bedroom at night and displayed a fear and general lack of interest in previously enjoyable activities.

Initial evaluation found SC anxious and mildly depressed with flat affect. Speech was minimal and nearly inaudible, with frequent throat clearing and complaints that her throat hurt. When not engaged she was detached and withdrawn. Some evidence of auditory hallucinations was suspected; however on subsequent follow-ups this was found to be self-talk. Memory was intact and although functioning had declined, there were no signs of dementia. The start of fluoxetine resulted in improvement with an increase in expressive language and energy levels within a few months and a gradual return in functioning after one year. Follow-up was maintained over a 17-month period with good results.

Tourette's disorder

RC was a 36-year-old male with severe ID who lived at home with his family. Referral was made for his obsessive, compulsive and other maladaptive behaviors. The presenting complaints included checking/

touching compulsions, hesitation in executing motor actions (e.g. descending a staircase), insomnia, and weight loss due to restricted dietary preferences (he ate only puréed foods). Evaluation of RC revealed depressed mood, short attention span, disruptive behavior rituals and the presence of vocal and motor tics. Memory was intact with no signs of psychosis. The initial diagnosis of anxiety disorder with obsessive-compulsive traits was made. A trial of paroxetine was ineffective in altering RC's behavior. On follow-up, a diagnosis of Tourette's disorder was made after it was clear that motor and vocal tics were part of RC's daily repertoire, which waxed or waned along with ritualistic behavior depending on his level of discomfort in different settings. Treatment with clonidine was effective in reducing the intensity and duration of his behavior rituals and tics. The clinical impression was that the compulsive and repetitive behaviors displayed were complex tics and not a function of obsessive-compulsive disorder. The positive response from the use of clonidine appeared to support this impression. Follow-up was maintained over a 5-year period with continued good results.

Anxiety disorder (not otherwise specified) with stereotypic movement disorder

AB was a 48-year-old female with mild ID who lives in a community residence. Referral was made due to an increase in the behavior rituals of impulsive stealing and hoarding of objects. By history, AB was reported to take and hoard objects (e.g. towels, cups, straws and audiotapes) in her bedroom. Mild self-injurious skin picking behavior to her hands and arms was also reported, which appeared motivated by anxiety. Initial evaluation found AB to be mildly anxious and in a state of psychomotor excitation. Memory was intact; insight and judgment were fair. A diagnosis of anxiety disorder (not otherwise specified) and stereotypic movement disorder was made. Follow-up at six-month intervals over a 6-year period revealed some reduction in stealing, hoarding and skin picking behaviors with behavioral programs and the introduction of buspirone. At age 55, reports of forgetfulness in daily routines and getting lost in the community were first reported, and updated cognitive testing revealed a decline in memory-recall scores from baseline. Increasing difficulties in memory, recall and general orientation on follow-up led to a diagnosis of dementia (DAT) at age 56. Stealing and hoarding of objects decreased in frequency; however, skin-picking behavior continued to be displayed. On the most recent follow-up, vitamin E and paroxetine were added.

Major depression with catatonic features; Obsessive-compulsive disorder

CM was a 31-year-old male with moderate ID who lived at home with his family. Referral was made due to a significant decline in his behavior and adaptive functioning. Presenting complaints occurred within a 12-month period and included extreme lethargy, apathy and extreme hesitation in approaching objects and initiating simple motor actions (e.g. standing up, feeding and dressing self). There was also an increase in previous existing behavioral rituals that included touching/checking compulsions and obsessive behavior (e.g. counting). A history of self-talk had been present with no evidence of psychotic features. Medical treatment for varicose veins, dermatitis and hyperthyroidism, and a number of social losses and environmental life events occurred prior to the change in behavior. These events appeared to have precipitated the change in behavior. A suspected diagnosis of dementia and parkinsonism was made prior to his being seen in our clinic; however the parents sought a second opinion.

Initial evaluation noted depressed mood, behavior rituals and social withdrawal. There was a marked rigidity in posture and movements connected with his compulsive behavior, anxiety and ambivalence. The diagnoses of major depression, single episode with catatonic features and OCD were made. Treatment initially with fluoxetine and then with fluvoxamine and risperidone resulted in stabilization of mood, a return in general functioning and a gradual decrease in behavior rituals and obsessions. Follow-up and treatment for OCD was maintained over two years and his parents reported CM to be doing well with fluvoxamine and clonazepam.

Summary

In reviewing the published reports, a number of findings were reported:

(1) The incidence of challenging and maladaptive behaviors (i.e. aggression) was reported to be lower in the DS population when compared to other people with ID. The frequency and types of challenging behaviors were found to differ and decreased in occurrence with advancing age.

(2) When mood disturbances, physical aggression, the loss of self-care skills and other maladaptive behaviors were displayed in persons with DS, they were found to vary as a function of age.

(3) Hallucinations and delusions were found extremely low in people with DS supporting the reported low incidence of psychotic dis-

orders in this population. A very low incidence of suicidal ideation was also reported in people with DS.

(4) Self-talk was found a common behavioral feature in many people with DS. In most cases, engaging in self-talk was not a sign of an underlying psychiatric disorder.

(5) The presence of repetitive behaviors was another common behavioral feature in people with DS. Behavior rituals including hoarding are commonly seen in many persons with DS; however, few studies have been completed to establish their prevalence or association with obsessive-compulsive disorder in the DS population.

(6) Tics/involuntary movements have been reported in some people with DS; however, more studies need to be done in both the ID and DS populations before any firm conclusions can be made regarding their etiology or prevalence rates.

(7) Depression and mood disorders were the predominant psychiatric diagnoses in people with DS across all age groups. The prevalence of schizophrenia and other psychotic disorders conversely was found low in the DS population when compared to other people with ID but without DS.

(8) Bipolar disorder with mania was found to be uncommon in the DS population and no reported studies were found in the literature as to the presence or incidence of impulse control disorders in people with DS.

People with DS display a different behavioral phenotype from people with ID but without DS. The types of challenging behaviors, the presence or absence of psychiatric signs and symptoms, and the accompanying psychiatric disorders seem to differ from the general ID population. It is important that clinicians be made aware of the differing behavioral characteristics that people with DS display so a proper psychiatric diagnosis can be made for treatment.

References

APA (1994) *Diagnostic and Statistical Manual of Mental Disorders*, 4th edn. American Psychiatric Association, Washington, DC.

Baird, P.A. & Sadovnick, A.D. (1987) Life expectancy in Down syndrome. *Journal of Pediatrics*, **110**, 849–854.

Benson, B. (1985) Behavioural disorders and mental retardation. *Applied Research in Mental Retardation*, **84**, 465–469.

Burt, D.B., Loveland, K.A., & Lewis, K.R. (1992) Depression and the onset of dementia in adults with mental retardation. *American Journal of Mental Retardation*, **96**, 502–511.

Chapman, R.S. & Hesketh, L.J. (2000) Behavioral phenotype of individuals with Down syndrome. *Mental Retardation and Developmental Disabilities*, **6**, 84–95.

Collacott, R.A., Cooper, S.A. & McGrother, C. (1992) Differential rates of psychiatric disorders in adults with Down's syndrome compared with other mentally handicapped adults. *British Journal of Psychiatry*, **161**, 671–674.

Collacott, R.A., Cooper, S-A, Brandford, D. & McGrother, C. (1998) Behaviour phenotype for Down's syndrome. *British Journal of Psychiatry*, **172**, 85–89.

Cooper, S.-A. & Prasher, V.P. (1998) Maladaptive behaviours and symptoms of dementia in adults with Down's syndrome compared with adults with intellectual disability of other aetiologies. *Journal of Intellectual Disability Research*, **42**, 293–300.

Cooper, S.-A., Duggirala, C. & Collacott, R.A. (1995) Adaptive behaviour after schizophrenia in people with Down's syndrome. *Journal of Intellectual Disability Research*, **39**, 201–204.

Craddock, N. & Owen, M. (1994) Is there an inverse relationship between Down's syndrome and bipolar affective disorder? Literature review and genetic implications. *Journal of Intellectual Disability Research*, **38**, 613–620.

Dalton, A.J. & Crapper-McLachlan, D.R. (1986) Clinical expression of Alzheimer's disease in Down syndrome. *Psychiatric Clinic of North America*, **9**, 659–670.

Day, K. (1985) Psychiatric disorder in the middle-aged and elderly mentally handicapped. *British Journal of Psychiatry*, **147**, 660–667.

Day, K. & Jancar, J. (1994) Mental and physical health and ageing in mental handicap: A review. *Journal of Intellectual Disability Research*, **38**, 241–256.

Eaton, L. & Menolascino, F. (1982) Psychiatric disorders in the mentally retarded: Types, problems, and challenges. *American Journal of Psychiatry*, **139**, 1297–1303.

Evans, D.W. & Gray, F.L. (2000) Compulsive-like behavior in individuals with Down syndrome: Its relation to mental age level, adaptive and maladaptive behavior. *Child Development*, **71**, 288–300.

Glenn, S.M. & Cunningham, C.C. (2000) Parents' reports of young people with Down syndrome talking out loud to themselves. *Mental Retardation*, **38**, 498–505.

Haggerty, J.J., Jr. & Prange, A.J. (1995) Borderline hypothyroidism and depression. *Annual Review of Medicine*, **46**, 37–46.

Haveman, M.J. & Maaskant, M.A. (1989) Defining fragility of the elderly severely mentally handicapped according to mortality risk, morbidity, motor handicaps and social functioning. *Journal of Mental Deficiency Research*, **33**, 389–397.

Haveman, M.J., Maaskant, M.A., van Schrojenstein Lantman, H.M., Urlings, H.F.J. & Kessels, A.G.H. (1994) Mental health problems in elderly people with and without Down's syndrome. *Journal of Intellectual Disability Research*, **38**, 341–355.

Holtmann, M., Korn-Merker, E. & Boenigk, H.E. (2000) Carbamazepine-induced combined phonic and motor tic in a boy with Down's syndrome. *Epileptic Disorders*, **2**, 39–40.

Jackson, I.M. (1998) The thyroid axis and depression. *Thyroid*, **8**, 951–956.

Kerbeshian, J. & Burd, L. (2000) Comorbid Down's syndrome, Tourette syndrome and intellectual disability: Registry prevalence and developmental course. *Journal of Intellectual Disability Research*, **44**, 60–67.

McGuire, D. & Chicoine, B.A. (1996) Depressive disorders in adults with Down syndrome. *The Habilitative Mental Healthcare Newsletter*, **15**, 1–7.

Myers, B.A. & Pueschel, S.M. (1991) Psychiatric disorders in a population with Down syndrome. *Journal of Nervous and Mental Disease*, **179**, 609–613.

Myers, B.A. & Pueschel, S.M. (1994) Brief report: A case of schizophrenia in a population with Down syndrome. *Journal of Autism and Developmental Disorders*, **24**, 95–98.

Myers, B.A. & Pueschel, S.M. (1995a) Major depression in a small group of adults with Down syndrome. *Research in Developmental Disabilities*, **16**, 285–299.

Myers, B.A. & Pueschel, S.M. (1995b) Tardive or atypical Tourette's disorder in a population with Down syndrome? *Research in Developmental Disabilities*, **16**, 1–9.

Oliver, C. & Holland, A.J. (1986) Down's syndrome and Alzheimer's disease: A review. *Psychological Medicine*, **16**, 307–322.

Patti, P.J. & Tsiouris, J.A. (2002) *Percentages of psychiatric signs and symptoms in a clinic sample with Down syndrome.* New York State Institute for Basic Research on Mental Retardation and Developmental Disabilities, Staten Island, NY.

Pary, R.J., Strauss, D., & White, J.F. (1996) A population survey of bipolar disorder in persons with and without Down syndrome. *Down Syndrome Quarterly*, **1**, 1–4.

Pary, R.J., Strauss, D. & White, J.F. (1997) A population survey of suicide attempts in persons with and without Down syndrome. *Down Syndrome Quarterly*, **2**, 12–13.

Prasher, V.P. (1995) Prevalence of psychiatric disorders in adults with Down syndrome. *European Journal of Psychiatry*, **9**, 77–82.

Prasher, V.P. (1997) Psychotic features and effect of severity of learning disability on dementia in adults with Down syndrome: Review of literature. *British Journal of Developmental Disabilities*, **43**, 85–92.

Prasher, V.P. & Chung, M.C. (1996) Causes of age-related decline in adaptive behavior of adults with Down syndrome: Differential diagnoses of dementia. *American Journal of Mental Retardation*, **101**, 175–183.

Prasher, V.P. & Day, S. (1995) Brief Report: Obsessive-compulsive disorder in adults with Down syndrome. *Journal of Autism and Developmental Disorders*, **25**, 453–458.

Reiss, S. (1990) Prevalence of dual diagnosis in community based day programs in the Chicago metropolitan area. *American Journal of Mental Retardation*, **94**, 578–585.

Russell, A. & Tanguay, P. (1981) Mental illness and mental retardation: Cause or coincidence? *American Journal of Mental Deficiency*, **85**, 570–574.

Seltzer, M.M., Krauss, M.W. & Tsunematsu, N. (1993) Adults with Down syndrome and their aging mothers: Diagnostic group differences. *American Journal of Mental Retardation*, **97**, 496–508.

Smith, D.S. (2001) Health care management of adults with Down syndrome. *American Family Physician*, **64**, 1031–1038.

Stoppe, G., Brandt, C.A. & Staedt, J.H. (1999) Behavioural problems associated with dementia: The role of newer antipsychotics. *Drugs & Aging*, **14**, 41–54.

Tsiouris, J.A. & Patti, P.J. (1997) Drug treatment of depression associated with dementia or presented as 'pseudodementia' in older adults with Down syndrome. *Journal of Applied Research in Intellectual Disabilities*, **10**, 312–322.

Tsiouris, J.A., Mann, R., Patti, P.J. & Sturmey, P. (2003) Challenging behaviors should not be considered as depressive equivalents in individuals with intellectual disabilities. *Journal of Intellectual Disability Research*, **47**, 14–21.

Turner, S., Sloper, P., Cunningham, C. & Knussen, C. (1990) Health problems in children with Down's syndrome. *Child Care Health Development*, **16**, 83–97.

Visser, F.E., Adenkamp, A.P., van Huffelen, A.C., Kuliman, M., Overweg, J. & van Wijk, J. (1997) Prospective study of the prevalence of Alzheimer-type dementia in institutionalized individuals with Down syndrome. *American Journal on Mental Retardation*, **101**, 400–412.

WHO (1992) *The International Classification of Mental and Behaviour Disorders – Clinical Descriptions and Diagnostic Guidelines*, 10th revision (ICD-10). World Health Organization, Geneva.

Wisniewski, K.E., Dalton, A.J., McLaachlan, D.R.C., Wen. G.Y. & Wisniewski, H.M. (1985) Alzheimer's disease in Down's syndrome: Clinicopathologic studies. *Neurology*, **35**, 957–961.

Part 2
Diagnosis and Treatment

8 Psychological Interventions and Psychotherapy

Germain Weber

In this chapter the term 'psychotherapy' is used to mean classical psychotherapeutic methods, reaching from psychoanalysis, humanistic therapies to behavior therapy and cognitive therapy. However, the term 'psychological interventions' is used as a generic term for various psychologically founded interventions, including classical psychotherapies, as well as general psychological counseling and specific psychological interventions aiming at support for defined groups.

Psychological interventions and psychotherapy in older people with intellectual disabilities (ID) are topics largely neglected both in systematic research and general practice. On the one hand this can be explained by the fact that psychotherapists and clinical psychologists show in general a reserve toward therapeutical interventions for older people, and on the other hand, very often psychotherapeutic techniques are thought not to be indicated for people with ID, as these people might lack language capabilities required for verbally-focused psychotherapies, or their capacities for insight are thought to be reduced.

Availability and access to psychotherapy and other psychological interventions remain very limited for adult people with ID, with those 50 and over and those with profound and multiple disabilities experiencing the greatest barriers of access to psychological interventions (Vlaskamp & Nakken, 1999). However, mental health needs and mental disorders show clearly higher prevalence figures for younger adults with ID as compared to their peers without disabilities, and these numbers are reported to be quasi invariant while people with ID are growing older. With increasing age, behavior problems like aggression and self-mutilation show dropping prevalence figures; however, mental disorders like depression, anxiety and sleep disorders might increase in frequency. In addition, new mental health needs related primarily to declines in cognitive functions and frequently related to neurodegenerative processes and other conditions, provide a challenge for psychological interventions with older adults with ID. A good overview for the state of research in mental health and ID in general can be found in Bouras (1999). In addition, the different interactions between psychotherapeutic and psychopharmacological interventions, including the potential for facilitative or inhibitory effects of one treatment modality to the other, should be considered while treating dually diagnosed individuals (Sevin *et al.*, 2001).

This chapter offers an overview of the research and reported experiences related to psychological interventions in the adult population with ID, and especially with respect to the older segment of this population. In addition, emerging models of psychological interventions for older people with ID will be outlined, and psychological interventions as successfully developed for the general older population or people with Alzheimer's disease will be reflected on to look at their appropriateness and usefulness toward an application in elderly persons with ID. To start, the chapter introduces two distinctive markers specific to psychotherapy in ID and old age.

Characteristics affecting psychotherapeutic interventions

Focusing on psychotherapy in older people with ID requires the consideration of main characteristics for psychotherapy and psychological interventions in the population of ID, and characteristics of therapists, as well as main characteristics for psychological interventions related to old age. These specifications should be considered within a general framework for psychotherapy and psychological interventions for older people with ID. Standards for psychotherapeutic interventions for various therapeutic orientations can easily be derived from a general geronto-psychotherapeutic model. ID and old age can, in many ways, be an issue for and during psychological interventions. Major issues linked to ID have been forwarded by Hurley (1989) and supplemented by Weber (1997a).

Limitations in communication

A limited basis for communication, typical for people with ID, will first be addressed. Communications competencies depend on multiple factors, such as the person's intellectual-cognitive level, the verbal and non-verbal expressiveness, and the general developmental level of the person. The etiological background of the disability might be considered for additional understanding of specific communicative features. In general, the therapist should use plain syntax when addressing his or her client. In adult and especially older people with ID, initiating communication can take longer (i.e. several sessions might be needed for developing a relationship between therapist and client for assuring a solid therapeutic basis). Further, non-verbal communication signs, like quality of eye contacts, have to be prominently considered. When explaining something or inquiring, it is important to make use of simple examples that are understandable and meaningful to the client. The therapist is advised not only to make sure and to inquire about the client's understanding within the session but also to refer in later sessions to options, intentions and objectives formerly discussed or defined.

Lack of goal-orientation

The 'rehearsal' strategy points to a second characteristic common in people with ID, which is the lack of goal-orientation. Many adults with ID and especially older adults with ID show difficulties in remembering the reason why they are meeting the therapist, or the reason remains unclear to them from session to session. This very often calls for a directive approach by the psychologist, in order to get the adult re-informed about the course and the objectives of the therapy plan, when addressing the client according to his or her perceptive and intellectual grasp. In addition, it will be important to point to the rules of the therapy, stick to them, and make sure the client 'plays the game'. Aggressive behavior as well as behavior of extreme attachment, which are both reported in older people with ID, can best be handled when addressed directly, pointing clearly to the limits of such behavior.

Lack of self-initiating communication

A more directive approach might also be adopted to face the lack of self-initiative in communication reported to be especially common in older adults with ID. The therapist might encourage such adults to think about questions, or evoke their attention by stimulating some relevant events. Once the client raises questions it is imperative to respond to these immediately by answering in a clear and simple way. One can proceed on the assumption that older people with ID have little experience with this kind of very personal communication, engaging however with ongoing therapy in this mode. As the therapy advances, adult clients can more frequently be asked about their coping with specific situations and problems. This helps to strengthen the client's competences in problem solving (e.g. his/her coping strategies in stressful events and situations with high emotional loads).

Alternative approaches

Adaptations in therapeutic techniques

Often the therapy is at risk of getting paralyzed. Rigidity in the therapy can be overcome by adaptations of therapeutic techniques. A greater flexibility in techniques, methods and settings, without changing the objectives of the therapy, is recommended in such a situation. However, it should be considered whether the selected methods and techniques are conforming both to the mental and chronological age of the adult. Length and frequency of sessions are largely determined by the adult's endurance and attention. In general, psychotherapeutic sessions for people with ID are of shorter duration and are more compactly scheduled as compared to sessions with adults without ID. For older people with ID sessions of 20–25 minutes might be sufficient.

Use of third-party informants

In contrast to most persons without ID, adults with ID frequently rely on information of third parties. As people grow older, the need for information from third parties – such as family members, staff or other carers – might increase, due to memory losses associated with Alzheimer's dementia or other cognitive dysfunctions. A rule of thumb is not to assign an informant in order to achieve the therapy objective. However, if an informant is required in order to keep the therapy process going, it should be assured that the confidential and trustful relation between client and therapist is not violated. As a matter of fact, therapies conducted in an isolated form (i.e. without indirect contacts to a client's environment) have been shown often to be not effective (Hurley, 1989).

Disability as a reality in therapy

Independent of the clinical symptoms that might have led the older individual with ID to enter psychotherapy, for most of the older adults their disabilities remain an issue. A number will raise this issue during psychotherapeutic intervention. Hurley (1989), for instance, recommends that the adult first develop an awareness of his or her disability, thus making the understanding of the disability a prerequisite for a therapeutical intervention. An awareness of the disability might be especially important for people with limited needs of support (such as mild ID)

(Hurley, 1989). This virtually requires special guidance and counseling related to the issue of disability. In the case of older adults with ID this guidance often might be a reflection across the individual's life-span and his or her experiences as a person with a disability. In this case, counseling should not only focus on areas of personal weakness linked to disability but should also point strongly to the personal strengths developed during the life span and relate to the disability. Besides raising issues of disability, older people with mild to moderate ID might experience further difficulties with advancing age. Besides age-related morbidity and co-morbidity they might express concerns over anticipating additional experiences of social rejection and non-acceptance as they grow older. For the psychologist and therapist it is good to remember the high sensibility of people with ID toward social non-acceptance as reported in literature (Reiss & Benson, 1984).

Therapists' attitudes

Distorted attitudes either toward disabilities and/or toward old age might be an additional reason for undesirable effects during therapy. A therapist's personal attitudes and views often influence the relation between client and therapist, and hence can affect the course of the therapy. A typical distortion in a therapist's attitudes might be his or her overprotective or patronizing views. Additional sources for dissonances in the relation between client and therapist might be a therapist's state of general not feeling well while working with the client. Though signs of dissonance might only be present in very subtle forms, clients are generally highly sensitive in capturing these. Therapists should avoid over-estimating the clinical symptoms, and are recommended to focus more on progresses, even the smallest, which contribute to the establishment, the strengthening or the re-establishment of behavior and attitudes promoting relative independence in old age. The therapist, in general, being younger than the older patient with ID, patronizing attitudes might play a crucial role, especially for an older client with ID, in them losing motivation and abandoning therapy.

Therapists' orientation

For psychotherapeutic interventions with people with ID to become a success, Menolascino and McGee (1983) have emphasized the importance of moving from personal disconnectedness to human engagement. Especially when conducting behavioral interventions, a sensitive orientation toward the client that emerges from attachment theory should be maintained during the process. This is particularly important when dealing with adults with autistic symptoms, and older persons with ID. Promoting and maintaining a mutual relationship that is based on the principle of empathy is crucial for the intervention. In general, the recommended approach is human engagement, with the goal of establishing attachment, also referred to as the gentle teaching program. While opting for this orientation, the adult is taught that human presence signifies safety, consistency and positive interaction or reward.

Motivational issues in old age

In addition to the characteristics mentioned for ID, older people with ID, just like their age-peers without ID, are often indifferent or even reluctant toward psychotherapeutical interventions, though they may show symptoms which according to experts definitely require treatment. However, some adults might not be ready for a 'traditional' psychological intervention if they are not fully aware of their mental health state or if they are not motivated for psychological treatment (that is, if they have negative expectations with respect to the effects of treatment on their lives or just reject or quit therapy on the basis that it is not worthwhile), or they experience therapy to be too exhausting and hard for their age (Weber & Fritsch, 1999). This motivational gap is well documented for the general older population, showing an ongoing motivational decline as people are growing older (Peters, 2000). Designing strategies for enhancing motivation toward psychological interventions in old age is a major challenge for improving quality of life in life's last stage. However, successful motivational strategies might need age-adjusted adaptations in 'traditional' therapeutical techniques as well tuning the contents of psychological support toward those subjective needs that the individual expresses in old age. For example, instead of approaching an anxiety disorder with the traditional classical behavioral or cognitive-behavioral setting, an older person might be highly motivated for reviewing his of her most meaningful episodes of life in a systematic way. This intervention alone might be a more appropriate approach for raising the adult's readiness to engage in a therapy. Deducing a general framework for psychotherapy in old age, independent of the psychotherapy 'school', might help raise the motivation for psychological support especially in older people with ID.

A general model for psychotherapy in old age

The founders of classical psychotherapies largely concentrated their attention on young to middle-aged adults, later focusing also on childhood and youth. The theoretical models and intervention techniques often neglected older people, with some schools (e.g. classical psychoanalysis) directly stating the therapy not to be appropriate for older people. Behavior therapy and cognitive therapy though extensively developed in an evidence-based way for applications with people with intellectual and developmental disabilities, were nevertheless mainly aimed at children, adolescents and young adults. In general, the purpose of psychotherapy is modifying or removing existing symptoms and promoting personality growth. With most schools of psychotherapy assuming the roots for major psychological processes to be located in the development of early childhood, and in the family history, or that behavior is largely based on learning processes and can be environmentally controlled, the schools in their early years did not, in general, focus on older people. Rather, old age was seen as a period with declining and ending development, with learning processes becoming more and more irrelevant while growing older. This view is best expressed in some of the early aging theories, still receiving attention at the beginning of the twenty-first century.

Emerging geronto-psychotherapeutic model

A first psychological developmental model considering old age was proposed by Erikson (1963). His eight-phased model relates from infancy to old age. In old age, developmental processes are assumed to be competing between two contrasting outcomes – integrity versus despair. Erikson's model suggested major developmental stages after youth, as outlined in his later work (Erikson *et al.*, 1986).

Cohort-based, context, maturity, specific challenge (CCMSC) model

In modern gerontology there is a broad agreement for research on lifespan approaches. Only recently a framework based on a life-span approach has been proposed in psychotherapy by Knight (1996a). Knight's CCMSC model offers a framework for adapting psychotherapy to the work with older people. The model is based on methods, concepts and recent findings in psychology and on research outcomes from the gerontology life span approach. The model is designed to be trans-theoretical, i.e. it allows implications for various theories and schools of psychotherapy.

The model outlines four 'factors':

(1) the cohort factor considers, besides an individual's cognitive performance, verbal fluency and his education career, the person's normative course of life and life-experiences from a social-historical point of view

(2) Context effects refer mainly to current environmental characteristics such as age-adapted accommodations, residential facilities for senior citizens and spare time options for older persons, as well as to general health and longtime care provisions and to old-age specific acts like regulations related to social or health insurance

(3) Maturity, deals with gathering information on the person's cognitive and emotional complexity, his or her post-formal reasoning, including the areas of expertise and competencies, including experiences in family life and the person's accumulated inter-personal competencies

(4) Dealing with specific challenges, includes areas such as chronic diseases, disabilities, and grieving while experiencing deaths of relatives and friends, as well as the person dealing with their own end-of-life, including preparation for death

Up to now the CCMSC model has generated old age specific therapeutic principles for various schools of psychotherapy, like behavior therapy (Knight & Fox, 1999), cognitive therapy (Knight & Fox, 1999), systemic family therapy (Knight & McCallum, 1998) and psychodynamic therapy (Knight, 1996b).

Model adaptations for older people with ID

The model offers a common basis for defining requirements related to change and adaptation in old age. However, applying the CCMSC-model in the field of ID requires specific complementation.

Maturity effects

Referring to the element of maturity it seems that many psychological variables show a high level of continuity and stability during adulthood of people with ID (e.g. personality, crystallized intelligence), whereas other areas are declining in their functioning similarly to the general population (e.g. fluid intelligence, capacity of working memory, audition, and vision (Weber & Rett, 1991)). However, opportunities for extensive vocational and family experiences are in general limited during the adulthood of people with ID. Accumulated expertise and competences may just be limited in the same way, thus giving a clear disadvantage for older people with ID for effective coping in their later years. Thus, in old age, people with ID might show similar difficulties when coping with a depression as in younger age.

Cohort effects

Cohort effects might be different to those of the general population. Many people of 50 years and older at the beginning have a record of living many of their adult years either in institutions or in their family of origin. The personal identity might be more imprinted by these circumstances than by typical identity cohort effects like marriage, fatherhood and mother-hood, in the general older population. Requirements for a therapist will be – besides the understanding of verbal codes typical for specific cohorts – the understanding of differences between cohorts, and acceptance of the adults' accounts related to important events in their lives. Cohort effects are important for understanding onset, development and maintenance of a depression.

Environmental effects

For older people with ID the effects of the circumstances and environ-ments they are living in as older people (i.e. the effect of context) might not be that important, as for older-age peers in the general population. People with ID in general live in supported and assisted accommodation settings of various community-based degrees for most of their lives. However, when living in larger old-age residential facilities, adults might have been imprinted by institutional characteristics. Permanent or ongoing confrontation with their peers' chronic diseases or multiple disabilities might play a role for triggering condition, such as depression. After moving to new accommodations, syndromes related to relocation in old age and behavioral and/or mood adaptation might be present for more than a year.

Co-morbidity effects

Depression might be a common co-morbidity when there are major health problems, or long-term hospitalization is required, or if the adult suffers from chronic diseases. Older people with ID, who may develop dementia, might show increases in behavior disorders or abnormal behavioral signs like aggressiveness, and delusions or hallucinations, and if relocated to nursing homes these signs might increase. In general, consideration of the clinical record is needed during the first assessment, as for older people with ID it might be that high blood pressure, diseases of the cardiac system or diabetes can go along with co-morbidities of mental disorders (Johnson & Grant, 1985). In general, in old age various reasons may play a role when the emotional balance for people with ID gets disturbed (e.g. chronic disease, personal loss, neurodegenerative processes, additional disabilities, age-related attitudes, attitudes related to the original or primary disability).

Considerations for psychological interventions

When determining and selecting the therapeutic approach, the cognitive functioning of the older person has to be considered first. For some methods good functioning of short-term memory is needed, as information has to be integrated during the session. When opting for a group therapy, the group should be homogeneous with respect to the level of cognitive functioning and communicative skills, as more capable adults might feel they are not being taken seriously.

Institutional-based therapists

When working as a therapist in a residential facility for older people with ID (for example, residential homes or nursing homes), a certain flexibility within the professional's role should be the norm. In many cases, the professional might be obliged to act on behalf of his/her client's interest without forgetting the needs of staff supporting the adult. Cognitive and behavioral modification techniques have been reported to be quite effective within residential settings. However, the success of such interventions is highly dependent on staff compliance to the therapeutic process. Hence, discussing and designing a plan with activities agreeable for the older person and the staff should be the first step before starting a therapy. Next might be preparing staff with respect to the therapy process, thus assuring coherence between professional acts of staff and therapist. Next would be recording a baseline, expressed in the frequency of agreeable and non-agreeable activities, as well as of behavior problems. This will be followed by the determination of priorities for areas of change. These areas might in addition be processed by functional analysis, thus getting first information on possible contingencies related to target behavior. Finally, a realistic plan for change has to be developed, including a concept for evaluating the intended therapy. These steps largely follow a traditional behavioral intervention strategy.

Combining therapeutic approaches

It has been reported that using behaviorally-based therapies mixed with so-called 'simulated presence therapy', and/or 'individualized music therapy', with older people in general resulted in higher ratings for efficacy (Thompson & Gallagher-Thompson, 1997). During individualized music therapy the client actively listens to his preferred pieces of music; in simulated presence therapy, the client listens to prepared audio sequences offering him or her selected segments of his memory which are known for their calming and comforting effects on the individual, thus raising the client's participation for stimulating activities and allowing him or her an uplift in affect. It is thus assumed that combined and integrated therapies might show similar effects when applied to select older people with ID, as some are reported to have high affinities to rhythm and music (Duffy & Fuller, 2000).

Behavioral interventions and specific disorders

As reviewed in Chapter 9, therapies and interventions based on behavioral concepts have been tested and applied to a large variety of disorders found in adults; however, these have been applied mostly to younger adults with ID. Conditions cited in the literature include anxiety disorders, schizophrenia, stress disorders and sleep disorders. For people with severe and profound ID, interventions are reported for stereotypic behavior, problem behavior, self-destructive behavior, aggressive and destructive behavior and challenging behavior as well fits of rage or tantrums (Harris, 1995; Weber, 1997b). Behavior therapies either use positive reinforcement techniques for stimulating desirable social behavior, or/and aim at reducing problem behavior by referring to aversive behavior modification techniques. Since the mid-1980s, the emphasis has clearly shifted to positive reinforcement techniques, primarily using proactive and ecological strategies to prevent behavior problems (Griffiths et al., 1998).

Behavior modification procedures can be grouped in several types of differential reinforcement techniques, with the differential reinforcement of other behavior (DRO) being one of the most popular strategies for decreasing maladaptive and aberrant behavior and improving more socially acceptable behavior. As part of this, functional assessment is a central part of the management of behavior problems, as it aims at determining the multiple conditions that maintain aberrant behavior (Horner, 1994).

Functional communication training

Results, generated through functional assessment, indicate self-injurious behavior, for instance, to be an aberrant form of communication. Based on these findings, Carr and Durand (1985) developed functional communication training and applied it successfully to adults with ID (Bird *et al.*, 1989; Carr *et al.*, 1994), as well as to people with severe disabilities (Durand, 1999).

Anger management training

Through anger management training as proposed by Benson (1986, 1992), adults with ID are taught through self-control techniques better management of their tantrums and aggressive behaviors. This training refers to – besides techniques such as self-instruction – relaxation techniques, identification of emotions and problem-solving strategies. Well-designed studies revealed relaxation techniques and self-monitoring to be highly effective strategies for anger control (Whitaker, 2001). Behaviorally-based interventions and positive behavior support are known to be highly effective, with outcome effectiveness rates varying between 40% and 75% among various behavior problems (Bregman & Harris, 1995; Carr *et al.*, 1999).

Severe communication disabilities

When therapeutically approaching adults with ID who are non-verbal or have severe communication impairments, behavioral techniques (as described above) are highly popular. Further, a therapist might first screen for other modes of communication of the adult, adapting the communication to the individual's full communication capabilities before starting therapy. Known as Augmentative and Alternative Communication (AAC), this approach screens for any residual speech or vocalizations, gestures, signs and areas for aided communication (Beukelman & Mirenda, 1998). This means that AAC techniques act as a gate to communicate with people with severe to profound ID (people requiring pervasive support), thus enabling additional opportunities for psychological interventions. Communication with gestures and other natural modes is known to be helpful for interacting and building relationships. Additional alternative therapies, such as Snoezelen and active therapy, have been employed with people with profound ID, showing increases in positive communication (Lindsay *et al.*, 2001).

Pre-therapy

A further asset in psychological interventions is Prouty's pre-therapy. Derived from the person-centered approach, and originally developed for interventions with schizophrenic patients (Prouty, 1994), it has been applied for treating emotional disorders in non-verbal adults with ID or with severe contact disturbances, thus making the client accessible to more regular kinds of therapy (Pörtner, 1996; Peters, 1999). Essentially, the therapist sets up contact by repeating gestures, vocalizations and body postures of the adult, thus offering reflections. Pre-therapy aims at restoring or developing an adult's contact functions (that is, either his contact to reality, his affective contact or his communicative contact). The effects of reflection on contact functions can be observed and measured. Changes in an adult's behavior are interpreted in terms of increases in interpersonal communication. Referring on the one hand to techniques definitely related to AAC, while on the other hand following the principles of client-centered therapies, pre-therapy is shown to be a highly promising approach for building a therapeutic communicative basis in adults with ID showing mute behavior.

Interventions related to specific situations in old age

Techniques which appear to be effective in older adults include relaxation training, featuring pleasant events, behavior modification based on reinforcement plans, and cognitive restructuring, as well as emotional processing based on expressing and naming emotions (Knight *et al.*, 2002). Whereas emotional processing is recommended for improving the general emotional well-being, the other techniques are applied to specific states. Most of the techniques reported in this section require a minimum of verbal communication skills, present in general in people with mild to moderate ID.

Relaxation techniques

Relaxation training, especially progressive muscle relaxation, is indicated for anxiety symptoms related to chronic diseases and related anxiety symptoms to other therapeutic interventions (Jacobson, 1938; Kohl, 2002). Instructions for muscle relaxation have to be adapted for those muscle groups that might be involved in the adult's present clinical pain record. A script for old-age adapted relaxation training can be found in Knight (1996a). In addition, relaxation techniques can be used as additional treatment for memory impairment and controlling pain.

Behavioral and cognitive reshaping

Behavioral reinforcement or cognitive restructuring procedures are recommended in older age, especially for improving the emotional and affective state following diseases or loss of functional competences. In cases of disease and additional disability, older people with ID, just as peers in the general aging population, show depressive reactions and depressions. These symptoms diminish in frequency and gravity as these people participate in pleasant and/or meaningful activities. During the therapeutic process, areas of activities meaningful to the person prior to the disease or functional loss should be explored, and adaptations for activities to be maintained or replacement activities outlined and defined with the adult. This would be followed by a step-wise implementation plan. For a good understanding of depression in situations of specific challenge, a therapist needs, in addition to his/her knowledge about various therapeutic techniques, a sound knowledge about the adult's condition and the relation between the condition and his or her age.

Grief therapy

Grief therapy is reviewed in detail in Chapter 12. It aims to offer emotional support to adults after the loss of close family members and friends. Though mourning after death of a loved one is a normal reaction, people with ID often show prolonged mourning reactions. Mourning is characterized by depressive and anxiety symptoms and/or by a mixed affective state combined with behavior problems, with major depressions occurring occasionally. After loss of several close persons within a short time, mourning reactions are shown to be especially intense. Older persons with ID who continued to live with their parents are generally confronted with a change of residence in the case of death of their parents.

This extra life-event brings an additional load to the mourning process and has to be considered during grief therapy. Adults and older people with ID may over years show repeated depressive reactions related to the death of a loved one (Weber & Rett, 1991). Such reactions point either to the fact that the mourning process has not been successfully completed and/or to a lack of adequate coping mechanisms in cases of loss of a close person. Besides expressing emotions, grief therapy also focuses on developing an understanding for viewing the loss in a longer perspective, and on offering support and active encouragement for the development of perspectives for life without the loved person.

Life-review therapy

In general, gerontological life-review therapies have been applied since the early 1960s (Butler, 1963; Haight & Webster, 1995). Life-review therapy is offered in either a structured or an unstructured way, and life-review therapy is referred to when applied in the context of a mental disorder. In the general population of older adults, life-review therapy has been shown to be effective in the treatment of depressions, and of special effectiveness when dealing with post-traumatic stress disorders. Reasons for this effectiveness are thought to be related to the fact that the traumatic event often overshadows other positive life-events, thus preventing a balanced review for an older person. Memories related to a traumatic event often lack consistency and appear in a fragmentary form. This indicates incomplete coping processes. From memory research it is known that pending affairs are better remembered then settled matters. In addition, traumatic events are often not following the way autobiographic memory traces are processed and structured. Life-review as a therapy aids in more successful coping and adjusts autobiographic memory, and thus contributes to a differentiated self-assessment of a person's life.

Psychotherapeutic interventions for persons with Alzheimer's disease

People with ID while growing older have a higher risk than their age peers of being affected by Alzheimer's disease. This process goes along with changes in emotional functioning (Nelson *et al.*, 2001), among others. In the early phase, psychological interventions aim at stabilizing the person's decline of independence in various areas. A structured daily activity plan might be required, and the use of external memory supports might help the person to better perform activities of everyday life.

Further, the expression of emotions related to the changes the person is experiencing might help to balance the affective state.

As the neurodegenerative process is progressing, emotion-centered therapies, such as validation therapy (Feil, 1992), enjoy widespread application. As one of the core techniques in validation therapy, highly confused verbal production or behavior is understood as emotional communication and messages, with the factual content being given no major relevance. The fact that the messages of many patients with Alzheimer's disease refer to their parents is interpreted as a special need for affection and attachment. The gap between the propagation of validation therapy and the missing empirical evaluation is noteworthy. The few well-designed studies revealed non-uniform results. However, in the field of intellectual disabilities validation therapy might receive growing attention as professionals see more reasons for emotional-centered assistance, as compared with ameliorating cognitive functioning, with the knowledge that there is no remedy for stopping cognitive decline in patients with dementia (Weber, 1997c).

Supporting mental health

Maintaining mental health in balance is one of the key issues for a high quality of life in older age. Supporting quality of life in older age for people with intellectual disabilities might start years before the individual gets in his or her fifties. Factors such as former lifestyle or former episodes with mental health problems are known to affect a person's quality of life in later years. However, for people with intellectual disabilities a preparation on aging issues might beneficially contribute for their later years.

Late-life planning programs

As people with ID in general show low degrees of self-initiated anticipatory analysis related to their future, or rarely reflect on upcoming events and their effects on their life, a systematic discussion of situations to be expected and an examination of the personal wishes and goals might contribute to entering older age with good prospects from a mental health perspective. Increasing adults' awareness of retirement issues and of later life is the aim of programs as outlined in the Person-Centered Later Life Planning Project (Sutton et al., 1994). This program offers training in goal planning, choice and decision-making, and it aims at increasing awareness of options for sound health and wellness. Further, issues such as leisure activities, work after retirement, living arrangements, accommodation and friendships can be discussed in a systematic way in this training designed for groups. A study on the program's effectiveness showed increased knowledge of later-life options and increased participation for individuals who were living at home (Heller *et al.*, 1996; Reijnders *et al.*, 2000). In addition, the program includes training components for staff and families on later-life planning issues.

Retirement programs

Though often there are few policies or supports that permit people with ID to officially retire from their 'work', people with ID do retire from those programs that they used to be in over many years. Preparing people with ID for retirement and offering adequate retirement programs is a central issue (Heller, 1999). During the transition to retirement people with ID are at risk for decreased social integration, with decline in self-esteem and a reduced range of activities. Changes in these factors might have an impact on the mental health status of aging adults.

Recreational leisure programs

Recreational leisure programs adapted to old age might offer older individuals with ID additional protective effects for their mental health while aging. Such programs generally aim to increase community inclusion, while providing support for those interests and activities that are meaningful to the individual. Recreational programs vary from group programs to more individualized forms, including the person's informal network (Hogg, 1993).

Biography projects

Some older people with ID show interest or have the need to share those moments and events of their life which have been meaningful to them. Reviewing with an individual his or her life might help the person develop integrity and well-balanced attitudes with respect to his past life and experiences. The importance of this approach for the field of ID has been emphasized by Bruckmüller (2002). Life-review can contribute to maintaining the well-being of the person, as opposed to re-establishing mental health when life-review is used as therapy in mental disorders. For effectively conducting a life-review program or a biography project, information and biographic material related to the person's life is very useful. Unfortunately, often staff members have little information about an older person's earlier life episodes. Thus, for future use, in particular with applications to successfully reconstructing autobiographic memory traces, adults with ID and their families should be encouraged to keep a biographic or autobiographic record, including happy and less-happy moments and valued and less-valued episodes of their lives. The record might include notes, letters, cards, photos, short videos and personal items, thus offering material outreaching the information of traditional medical or institutional records. The availability of such a biographic record might be a useful resource for maintaining an individual's well-being in old age.

Carers' emotional well-being

Caring for an older person with ID, especially when that person suffers in addition from dementia, can be a high burden for the staff members and other carers. This topic is reviewed in depth in Chapter 13. The carer's burden (perceived or real) often results in depression, anxiety, irritation and frustration. Changes in carers' emotional well-being might be accompanied with various effects on their environment, including the quality of life of the older person with ID. Therefore, special techniques should be used by frontline staff and carers to prevent distortions in their own emotional well-being. Techniques that staff might use include collecting information of the process specific to the disease, enhancing one's capabilities to cope with stress (i.e. making appropriate use of relaxation techniques, getting emotional support in supervision sessions, and allowing oneself more frequently agreeable events (Kryspin-Exner, 1997)). Caring family members might additionally have recourse to regular family reunions, which permit the family to get a better understanding of the carer's stressors (Olshevski et al., 1999). Considering the special needs of the carer may contribute positively to the emotional well-being of the person for whom care is provided.

Summary

Psychological interventions and/or psychotherapy offer a wide variety of techniques with promising use in aging and older people with intellectual disabilities. However, while reviewing recent developments from the field of geronto-psychotherapy, and considering advances of psychotherapy in ID, a clear need for combined research between these two areas is evident. Substantial advances in research might require a general model for psychological interventions in people with ID. The observations of a tendency for convergence between the techniques of different schools of psychotherapy when applied in the field of ID (Weber, 1997b, p. 86), as well as the growing agreement on a common basic attitude for such interventions, might be a suitable starting point for shaping such a theoretical model. Indeed, besides major contributions from behavior and cognitive therapy, additional schools of psychotherapy show since the 1980s an increasing number of reports focusing on therapies with adults with ID (Weber, 1997b; Bütz *et al.*, 2000). The convergence hypotheses between therapeutic techniques of different schools find support when observing psychoanalytic and humanistic approaches to integrate more directive techniques in their settings, so getting very close to or even directly referring to behavior techniques (e.g. Fuller & Faulkner, 2000). As for successful behavior therapy in people with ID, the relation between therapist and client should be based on human attachment.

In addition, recent advances for a framework for geronto-psychotherapy in the general population might be considered to specify psychological interventions for older people with ID. Based on these outcomes therapeutic techniques should be defined or redefined and adapted, and later followed by well-designed evaluation studies.

References

Benson, B.A. (1986) Anger management training. *Psychiatric Aspects of Mental Retardation Reviews*, **5**, 51–55.

Benson, B.A. (1992) *Teaching anger management to persons with mental retardation*. International Diagnostic System, Inc., University of Illinois, Chicago.

Beukelman, D.R. & Mirenda, P. (1998) *Augmentative and Alternative Communication. Management of severe communication disorders in children and adults*. Paul Brookes, Baltimore, MD.

Bird, F., Dores, P., Moniz, D. & Robinson, J. (1989) Reducing severe aggressive and self-injurious behavior with functional communication training. *American Journal on Mental Retardation*, **94**, 37–48.

Bouras, N. (1999) *Psychiatric and Behavioural Disorders in Developmental Disabilities and Mental Retardation*. Cambridge University Press, Cambridge.

Bregman, J., & Harris, J. (1995) *Mental Retardation: Comprehensive Textbook on Psychiatry*, 6th edn (eds H. Kaplan & B. Saock) pp. 345-383. Williams & Wilkins, Baltimore, MD.

Bruckmüller, M. (2002) Lebensgeschichte und Identität – Meine Biographie. Unterstützung durch Erinnerung – Die Zusammenfassung der Lebensgeschichte (Life history and identity – My biography. Supporting through memory – A summary of life's history). *Kiscsoportos – lakóothonol (Small living*

groups – institutional homes) ed. SOROS Foundation, pp. 141–147. SOROS Ala-
pítvány (SOROS Foundation), Budapest.

Butler, R.N. (1963) The life review: An interpretation of reminiscence in the aged.
Psychiatry, **26**, 65–76.

Bütz, M.R., Bowling, J.B. & Bliss, C.A. (2000) Psychotherapy with the mentally
retarded: A review of the literature and the implications. *Professional Psychology:
Research and Practice*, **31**, 42–47.

Carr, E.G. & Durand, V.M. (1985) Reducing behaviour problems through
functional communication training. *Journal of Applied Behavior Analysis*, **18**,
111–126.

Carr, E.G., Horner, R.H. & Turnbull, A.P. (1999) *Positive Behavior Support for People
with Developmental Disabilities. A research synthesis.* American Association on
Mental Retardation, Washington, DC.

Carr, E.G., Levin, L., McConnachie, G., Carlson, J.I., Kemp, D.C. & Smith, C.E.
(1994) *Communication-based Intervention for Problem Behaviour. A user's guide for
producing positive change.* Paul Brookes Publishing Co, Baltimore, MD.

Duffy, B. & Fuller, R. (2000) Role of music therapy in social skills development in
children with moderate intellectual disability. *Journal of Applied Research in
Intellectual Disabilities*, **13**, 77–89.

Durand, V.M. (1999) Functional communication training using assistive devices:
Recruiting natural communities of reinforcement. *Journal of Applied Behavior
Analysis*, **32**, 247–267.

Erikson, E.H. (1963) *Childhood and Society*, 2nd edn. Norton, New York.

Erikson, E.H., Erikson, J. & Kivnick, H.Q. (1986) *Vital Involvements in Old Age.*
Norton, New York.

Feil, N. (1992) *Validation. Ein neuer Weg zum Verständnis alter Menschen (A new way
for understanding older people)*, 3rd edn. Verlag Altern und Kultur, Vienna,
Austria.

Fuller, A. & Faulkner, K. (2000) Psychodynamically informed individual psychotherapy techniques for managing aggressive behaviour in people with
developmental disabilities. *Journal of Intellectual Disability Research*, **44**, 290.

Griffiths, D.M., Gardner, W.I. & Nugent, J.A. (1998) *Behavioral Supports: Individual
Centered Interventions. A Multimodal Functional Approach. A clinical manual for
practitioners in dual diagnosis.* NADD Press, Kingston, NY.

Haight, K.W. & Webster, J.D. (1995) *The Art and Science of Reminiscing: Theory,
Research, Methods and Applications.* Taylor & Francis, Washington, DC.

Harris, J.C. (1995) *Developmental neuropsychiatry. Volume II: Assessment, diagnosis,
and treatment of developmental disorders.* Oxford University Press, New York.

Heller, T. (1999) Emerging models. *Aging, Rights, and Quality of Life. Prospects for
Older People with Developmental Disabilities* (eds S.S. Herr & G. Weber) pp.
149–165. Paul Brookes, Baltimore, MD.

Heller, T., Sterns, H., Sutton, E. & Factor, A.R. (1996) Impact of person-centered
later-life planning program for older adults with mental retardation. *Journal of
Rehabilitation*, **62**, 77–83.

Hogg, J. (1993) Creative, personal and social engagement in the later years: Rea-
lisation through leisure. *The Irish Journal of Psychology*, **14**, 204–218.

Horner, R.H. (1994) Functional assessment: Contributions and future directions. *Journal of Applied Behavior Analysis*, **27**, 401–404.

Hurley, A.D. (1989) Individual psychotherapy with mentally retarded individuals: A review and call for research. *Research in Developmental Disabilities*, **10**, 261–275.

Jacobson, E. (1938) *Progressive Relaxation*. University of Chicago Press, Chicago.

Johnson, C.L. & Grant, L.A. (1985) *The Nursing Home in American Society*. John Hopkins University Press, Baltimore, MD.

Knight, B.G. (1996a) *Psychotherapy with Older Adults*, 2nd edn. Sage, Thousand Oaks, CA.

Knight, B.G. (1996b) Psychodynamic therapy with older adults: Lessons from scientific gerontology. *Handbook of Clinical Psychology and Aging*, (ed. R. Wood) pp. 545–560. Wiley & Sons, London.

Knight, B.G. & Fox, L.S. (1999) La practica de la terapia conductual (The practice of behavior modification). *Intervencion psicologica in la vejez (Psychological Interventions in Old Age)* (eds I. Montorio & M. Ezal) pp. 85–103. Sintesis, Madrid, Spain.

Knight, B.G. & McCallum, T.J. (1998) Family therapy with older clients: The contextual, cohort-based, maturity, specific challenge model. *Clinical Geropsychology* (eds I.H. Nordhus, G. VandenBos, S. Berg & P. Fromholt) pp. 313–328. American Psychological Association, Washington, DC.

Knight, B.G., Robinson, G.S. & Satre, D.D. (2002) Ein lebensspannenpsychologischer Ansatz der Alterspsychotherapie (A psychological life-span approach for gerontopsychotherapy). *Alterspsychotherapie und klinische Gerontopsychologie (Geronto-psychotherapy and Clinical Gerontopsychology)* (ed A. Maercker) pp. 87–123. Springer, Berlin, Germany.

Kohl, F. (2002) Progressive muscle relaxation according to E. Jacobson. A modern relaxation technique. *Medizinische Monatsschrift für Pharmazeuten*, **25**(3), 77–87.

Kryspin-Exner, I. (1997) Information, Schulung und emotionale Unterstützung für Angehörige und Betreuungspersonal – Mögliche Anwendungen im Umfeld von alten verwirrten Personen mit geistiger Behinderung (Information, training and emotional support for family members and staff members caring for older confused persons with mental retardation). *Psychische Störungen bei älteren Menschen mit geistiger Behinderung (Mental Disorders in Older People with Mental Retardation)* (ed. G. Weber) pp.251–264. Verlag Hans Huber, Bern, Switzerland.

Lindsay, W.R., Black, E., Broxhole, S. & Pitcaithly, D. (2001) The effects of four therapy procedures on communication in people with profound intellectual disabilities. *Journal of Applied Research in Intellectual Disabilities*, **14**, 110–119.

Menolascino, F.J. & McGee, J.J. (1983) Persons with severe mental retardation and behavioral challenges: From disconnectedness to human engagement. *Journal of Psychiatric Treatment and Evaluation*, **5**, 187–193.

Nelson, L.D., Orme, D., Osann, K. & Lott, I.T. (2001) Neurological changes and emotional functioning in adults with Down Syndrome. *Journal of Intellectual Disability Research*, **45**, 450–456.

Olshevski, J., Katz, A. & Knight, B.G. (1999) *Stress reduction for caregivers*. Brunner & Mazel, Philadelphia, PA.

Peters, H. (1999) Pretherapy: A client-centered/experiential approach to mentally handicapped people. *Journal of Humanistic Psychology*, **39**, 8–29.

Peters, M. (2000) Aspekte der Psychotherapiemotivation Älterer und Möglichkeiten ihrer Förderung (Issues of motivation in psychotherapy for the elderly and potential stimulations). *Klinische Psychotherapie mit älteren Menschen (Clinical Psychotherapy in Older People)* (eds P. Bäurle, H. Radebold, R.D. Hirsch, K. Studer, U. Schmid-Furstoss & B. Struwe) pp. 25–33. Verlag Hans Huber, Bern, Switzerland.

Pörtner, M. (1996) Working with the mentally handicapped in a person-centered way – is it possible, is it appropriate and what does it mean in practice? *Client-centered and Experiential Psychotherapy. A Paradigm in Motion.* (eds R. Hutterer, G. Pawlowsky, P.F. Schmid & R. Stipsits) pp. 513–527. Peter Lang Verlag, Frankfurt/M, Germany.

Prouty, G. (1994) *Theoretical Evolutions in Person-centered/Experiential Therapy. Applications to Schizophrenic and Retarded Psychosis.* Praeger, New York.

Reijnders, R., Haveman, M., Michalek, S. & van Laake-Theunissen, M. (2000) Person-centered planning for older adults with intellectual disability: long-term results and the impact on daily choice making. *Journal of Intellectual Disability Research*, **44**, 437–438.

Reiss, S. & Benson, B. (1984) Awareness of negative social conditions among mentally retarded, emotionally disturbed outpatients. *American Journal of Psychiatry*, **141**, 1–12.

Sevin, J.A., Bowers-Stephens, C., Hamilton, M. & Ford, A. (2001) Integrating behavioural and pharmacological interventions in treating clients with psychiatric disorders and mental retardation. *Research in Developmental Disabilities*, **22**, 463–485.

Sutton, E., Heller, T., Sterns, H.L., Factor, A. & Miklos, S. (1994) *Person-centered planning for later life: A curriculum for adults with mental retardation.* University of Akron, Akron, OH.

Thompson, L.W. & Gallagher-Thompson, D. (1997) Psychotherapeutic interventions with older adults in outpatient and extended care settings. *Depression in Long Term and Residential Care: Advances in Research and Treatment.* (eds R.L. Rubinstein & M.P. Lawton) pp. 169–184. Springer Verlag, Berlin, Germany.

Vlaskamp, C. & Nakken, H. (1999) Missing in execution: Therapies and activities for individuals with profound multiple disorders. *British Journal of Developmental Disabilities*, **45**, 99–109.

Weber, G. (1997a) *Intellektuelle Behinderung. Grundlagen, klinisch-psychologische Diagnostik und Therapie im Erwachsenenalter (Intellectual disabilities. Foundations, clinical-psychological diagnostics, and therapy in adulthood).* WUV – Universitätsverlag, Vienna, Austria.

Weber, G. (1997b) Therapeutische Interventionen und Maßnahmen: Möglichkeiten und Grenzen (Therapeutic interventions and provisions). *Psychische Störungen bei älteren Menschen mit geistiger Behinderung (Mental Disorders in Older People with Mental Retardation)* (ed. G. Weber) pp. 68–117. Verlag Hans Huber, Bern, Switzerland.

Weber, G. (1997c) Morbus Alzheimer bei Menschen mit geistiger Behinderung

(Alzheimer's disease in people with mental retardation). *Handbuch Morbus Alzheimer – Neurobiologie, Diagnose und Therapie (Handbook of Alzheimer's Disease – Neurobiology, Diagnosis, Therapy)* (eds S. Weiss & G. Weber) pp. 1311–1335. Beltz – Psychologie Verlags Union, Weinheim, Germany.

Weber, G. & Fritsch, A. (1999) Challenges for residential facilities. *Aging, Rights and Quality of Life. Prospects for Older People with Developmental Disabilities* (eds S.S. Herr & G. Weber) pp. 253–275. Paul Brookes, Baltimore, MD.

Weber, G. & Rett, A. (1991) *Down Syndrom im Erwachsenenalter (Down Syndrome in Adulthood)*. Verlag Hans Huber, Bern, Switzerland.

Whitaker, S. (2001). Anger control for people with learning disabilities. *Behavioral & Cognitive Psychotherapy*, **29**, 277–293.

9 Aging-Related Behavioral Interventions

Peter Sturmey

Applied Behavior Analysis (ABA) is a natural science approach to changing socially significant behaviors to an important degree, understanding the natural processes that lead to the development and maintenance of normal and pathological behavior, and understanding the learning mechanisms that underlie the process of behavior changes. ABA grew out of the earlier science of the *Experimental Analysis of Behavior* (EAB). EAB studies the basic processes of learning such as classical and operant conditioning. (See Fig. 9.1 for illustrations of operant and classical conditioning.) EAB is thus unconcerned about the social importance of the behaviors studied. Rather than study behaviors such as drug addiction, littering or dangerous driving, EAB studies bar pressing in rats and pecking disks in pigeons because it is easy to measure these behaviors and helpful to be able to control the subject's learning history. Because ABA is concerned with applied questions it is much more restricted in its purview. ABA must study behaviors that are socially important. It must produce intervention effects that are large and improve the person's

---

Classical conditioning
Unconditioned stimulus (US) $\longrightarrow$ Unconditioned response (UR)
US paired repeatedly with conditioned stimulus (CS)
Conditioned stimulus $\longrightarrow$ Conditioned response (CR)
Acid in mouth (US) $\longrightarrow$ salivation (UR)
Sight of lemon (CS) repeatedly paired with acid in mouth (US)
Sight of lemon (CS) $\longrightarrow$ salivation (CR)

Operant conditioning
Organism emits various forms of behavior (B1 and B2)
B1 $\longrightarrow$ reinforcement
B2 $\longrightarrow$ no consequences
B1 is strengthened and B2 is weakened
Screaming (B1) $\longrightarrow$ staff come and talk to person
Sitting quietly (B2) $\longrightarrow$ staff ignore sitting quietly
Screaming is strengthened and sitting quietly is weakened

Fig. 9.1 Classical and operant conditioning.

functioning to an extent that the person and others around that person would recognize as meaningful.

Operant and classical conditions could probably only account for a limited amount of human behavior (Skinner, 1953). ABA has extended its reach to account for thinking, feeling and perception through other learning processes, such as stimulus equivalence formation (Reeve & Fields, 2001) and rule-governed behavior. Interest in thinking, stimulated by Skinner's account of verbal behavior (Skinner, 1957), has now led to novel analyses of language in children with pervasive developmental disabilities, and a range of new behavioral verbal therapies such as acceptance and commitment therapy (Hayes *et al.*, 1999). Skinner (1953) also distinguished between three forms of behavioral selection. Operant conditioning is one form of selection. During operant learning more adaptive forms of behavior are selected and refined by their con-sequences. This process occurs during the lifetime of the organism. A second form of selection that determines behavior is natural selection, which takes place over the long span of evolution. Here genes that cause suboptimal forms of behavior are extinguished and genes that cause adaptive forms of behavior are selected. The third form of selection is cultural selection. Cultural practices are patterns of behavior that are specific to a particular culture, such as putting up Christmas trees, burying palm leaves to make it rain or not working on national holidays. In cultural selection cultural practices that contribute to the survival and success of a culture are selected and those that are not are extinguished. Individuals learn these cultural practices, primarily through their verbal interactions with other members of these communities. Thus, behavior-ism includes many forms of learning, not only operant and classical conditioning, and three forms of behavioral selection.

General features and history of applied behavior analysis

Baer *et al.*, (1968) identified six dimensions of ABA that continue to characterize the field today:

(1) ABA must focus on behaviors that are socially important.
(2) ABA involves studies of what people do behaviorally. Self-reports or reports by others are seen as inadequate measures of behavior, since these measures are greatly influenced by factors other than the behavior itself. Publicly observable, reliably observed behavior is essential data for ABA.
(3) ABA is not only interested in changing behavior but in under-standing the functions of behavior and the mechanism of behavior

change. Baer *et al.* define a functional analysis as 'an ability (of) the experimenter to turn the behavior on and off at will'. ABA, like EAB, uses single-subject experimental designs. Traditional group experimental designs are eschewed. This is because they hide individual data within the mean scores of non-existent average subjects and because they emphasize statistical significance over social and educational significance.

(4)   ABA is technological. Its procedures are defined operationally. Saying that the intervention was 'video modeling' is insufficient. The procedure 'video modeling' must be broken down into definable steps and operationally described. In this way the treatment can be replicated in future studies.

(5)   ABA must maintain conceptual integrity by describing its procedures in terms of the learning processes that underlie its interventions. If we say 'planned ignoring' led to a decrease in behavior this is insufficient; if we say 'attention maintained behavior reduced in frequency following attention extinction', the putative learning mechanism behind the intervention is now clear.

(6)   Since ABA is interested in socially significant topics, it must produce changes that are large and important to the participants and clients, rather than merely being statistically significant.

Early work in ABA focused on defining the field and demonstrating the power of positive reinforcement in changing socially important human behaviors. Subsequently, assessing generalization of behavior change and developing a technology of generalized behavior change was addressed. In the late 1970s behavioral technologies were developed and refined to assess the functions of maladaptive behaviors, and demonstrated the importance of basing behavioral interventions on knowledge of the individual function of each person's behavior (see Table 9.1). Subsequently this technology has been refined and taken out of the lab and into the real world, and has been used to focus interventions on positive methods of behavior change in natural settings that are socially acceptable.

Another important recent strand in ABA has been an appreciation of the communicative function of many undesirable behaviors. This perspective has been useful in developing positive behavioral interventions such as *functional communication training* to teach communication skills to replace maladaptive behaviors. Another recent development has been greater use of ABA to teach parents and other carers proactive strategies to prevent problems developing. The area of early intensive behavioral interventions (Lovaas, 1987) is a notable example of this trend. Finally, *positive behavioral support* has developed as an outgrowth of more

Table 9.1 Two examples of functional analysis and implications for treatment.

Function interventions	Indicated interventions	Contra-indicated
Avoiding noise	Remove person before he/she is upset Teach person to request less noise	Turn down noise when upset Time out
Obtain snacks	Increase snacks throughout day Teach person to request snacks Give snack for no disruption	Give snacks to calm down Give snacks when begin to be upset

traditional ABA. Important features of positive behavioral support include a focus on accelerative, educational skills teaching interventions based on functional assessment and analysis of behavior using multi-component interventions. Decelerative methods that focus only on the target behavior are de-emphasized. Emphasis is also placed on broad, quality of life criteria and long-term supports, manipulation of antecedents rather than consequences, use of proactive strategies, and minimizing the use of punishment and emergency procedures (Scott *et al.*, 2000, pp. 167–172).

Applications

Intellectual disability and autism have been traditional areas of application (Matson & Coe, 1992; Matson *et al.*, 1996). ABA has also been widely applied in the area of mental health problems in people with intellectual disabilities (Sturmey *et al.*, in press). There is also a healthy area of behavioral gerontology using ABA (e.g. Schnelle *et al.*, 1983; Burgio & Burgio, 1986). Indeed in later life Skinner became interested in applications of behaviorism to the problems of later life (Skinner, 1983).

The American Association on Mental Retardation's consensus panel, the New York State Education Department and the US Surgeon General have all endorsed ABA as an effective method of intervention (New York State Education Department, 1999; US Department of Health and Human Services, 1999; Rush & Frances, 2000). Meta-analyses have consistently identified ABA as an effective intervention in the area of intellectual disability (Carr *et al.*, 1994; Didden *et al.*, 1997). Advocates of evidence-based intervention have consistently identified ABA as an effective form of treatment. Many other widely practiced forms of interventions have not been evaluated, or have been evaluated and found to be only weakly effective or sometimes harmful to the client (Scott *et al.*, 2000). Thus, ethical standards mandating professionals to select interventions in the best interest of their client, to minimize harm to the public, and to avoid and terminate ineffective treatments (APA 1992), appear to strongly imply the adoption of ABA as a treatment of choice.

ABA intervention with older adults

Social interactive behaviors

There is a long tradition of ABA with seniors. Early work demonstrated that training staff to provide materials, to prompt and praise participation (Jenkins et al, 1977; Felce & Jenkins, 1979; Powell *et al.*, 1979) and to identify individually chosen materials (Cash & Khan, 1985) could increase participation in activities among elders in nursing homes, including those with severe dementia (Cash *et al.*, 1995). More recent work has addressed engagement in daily living activities (Engelman *et al.*, 1999). These studies parallel similar work on increasing activity level and disengagement in people with intellectual disabilities (Sturmey & Crisp, 1990; Jones *et al.*, 2001). Importantly these studies also demonstrate that disengagement is a function of variables in the social and nonsocial environment, that can be manipulated to lead to beneficial behavioral change in seniors.

ABA has been employed to improve conversational and social skills in older adults. For example, Praderas and MacDonald (1986) taught four socially isolated elderly residents of nursing homes to express common courtesies, self-disclosure positively, ask questions and interject with others during telephone conversations. Training was conducted using instructions, modeling, rehearsal, feedback and reinforcement. This intervention was effective in increasing social skills in all these areas to a socially significant degree.

Improving social skills is often regarded as a good preventative strategy for a wide range of mental health problems such as mood disorders. Teaching appropriate social skills may also be important for the adaptation of people with schizophrenia. Teaching socially appropriate ways of interacting may also be a key component for intervening in socially mediated maladaptive behaviors, such as aggression (Griffiths *et al.*, 1998). Social skills have been widely taught to children and adults with intellectual disabilities and autism. Interventions such as modeling, reinforcement, shaping, role-play, prompting and fading, and feedback are especially likely to be effective at teaching social skills. Indeed, a meta-analysis of 73 outcome studies by Corrigan (1991) indicated that people with intellectual disabilities are especially likely to do well with social skills training compared to other populations.

Day *et al.* (1982) taught two women with intellectual disabilities aged 62 and 63 years to interact with two peers aged 59 and 69 who were withdrawn. The intervention took place in an institutional setting. Three intervention techniques were evaluated. The first was minimal instruction in which the participants were verbally instructed to interact with their peers. The second intervention was role-playing in which participants rehearsed appropriate methods of prompting and reinforcing their peers to interact. The third method of intervention was prompting from an experimenter.

Day and colleagues' results showed that elders with intellectual disabilities were effective at intervening with their socially isolated peers. However, verbal instruction was insufficient to produce any meaningful behavior change and both role-play and direct prompting were effective in teaching elders with intellectual disabilities to increase interaction in their socially isolated peers. The study also showed that both role-play and direct instruction could be faded. There was no evidence of generalization outside the teaching setting.

This study is interesting because it demonstrated that elders with intellectual disabilities could be taught to be change agents in the lives of their peers with intellectual disabilities. The study is limited in two respects. First, the lack of generalization may be due to inadequate analysis of the stimuli controlling social behavior in the participants. If the intervention had carefully addressed generalization, through recognized methods such as multiple exemplar training, loose training or training in multiple settings with multiple peers, then generalization may have occurred. Despite these limitations, this is a unique and valuable model for future studies in this domain.

Kleitsh *et al.* (1983) reported a study of social skills training in four socially isolated men with moderate intellectual disabilities. The intervention included verbal prompts, rehearsal of social skills, and contingent social praise. Like the Day *et al.* (1982) study, Kleitsh and colleagues evaluated generalization to a similar training environment and to a regular part of the participant's daily environment.

In baseline no social interaction was observed among the participants. This study demonstrated that the intervention led to an increase in verbal interaction among all four subjects. Further, generalization was observed, across both generalization environments and to peers who did not participate in the intervention. Most impressively, this increase in verbal interaction was maintained four months after training had been withdrawn.

This study was especially impressive in that it demonstrated broad generalization of verbal interaction across settings and to peers who did not participate in the study, as well as maintenance over four months.

These two studies demonstrate that social skills can be readily taught to older adults with intellectual disabilities. Further, with careful attention to design of the intervention, generalization to other settings and non-trained peers can be achieved.

Health-related behaviors

ABA has also addressed a variety of health-related behaviors in older adults. Burgio *et al.* (1986) evaluated prompting and praise to increase independent ambulation and distance traveled in eight elderly nursing home residents. All eight participants increased the distance they walked and six of them began to ambulate more independently.

Other health-related interventions have included improving the diet of seniors. For example, Bunck and Iwata (1978) compared a series of community behavioral interventions to increase participation in a nutritious meal program in three groups of 60 older adults. Two traditional forms of encouraging participation – radio announcements and a telephone follow-up call – were ineffective. However, a personal home visit that prompted participation and an incentive menu for participation were both effective interventions to increase attendance at the program. Analysis of the costs of the intervention indicated that the incentives menu was the most cost effective form of intervention. In a second study these authors addressed increasing attendance in participants who had been to the program once only. They compared activities at the center with a simple incentive program and found that although the former intervention had a modest impact on attendance, the latter had a much greater impact on attendance.

Stock and Milan (1993) found similar beneficial effects on improving the diet of three older adults with health-related dietary restrictions, who usually made poor choices of food. They found that prompting feedback and social reinforcement was effective in changing the choices of food made by all three participants. Other interventions, such as a lottery and adding confederates, did not enhance the outcomes associated with this relatively simple intervention.

Reducing maladaptive behaviors

ABA has also been used to successfully decrease undesirable behaviors in older adults. Heard and Watson (1999) successfully treated wandering in four seniors with dementia who lived in a nursing home. Noting that wandering is often managed by sedation, restraints and other highly restrictive procedures, Heard and Watson (1999) evaluated the use of differential reinforcement of other behavior (DRO) – not wandering. Antecedent-Behavior-Consequence (ABC) charts were used prior to intervention to identify the reinforcer most likely to maintain wandering. For two participants the consequence that was maintaining wandering was hypothesized to be attention, for the third participant access to sweet food maintained wandering, and for the last participant sensory stimulation appeared to be maintaining wandering. In this study the consequence hypothesized to maintain wandering was delivered contingent upon wandering in the baseline. In the intervention the same consequence was delivered, but contingent upon not wandering. Suing an ABAB design the authors demonstrated that wandering dramatically decreased when treated with this DRO procedure. Decreases of 50–75% were achieved using DRO. This study demonstrated that wandering was under the control of environmental stimuli and that manipulation of access to these stimuli could effectively treat wandering.

Behavioral interventions have also effectively addressed incontinence. For example, Burgio *et al.* (1990) developed and evaluated a staff training and management package on continence in four elderly persons. Initially staff members were taught to prompt voiding and monitor their own performance. In addition there was a system of supervisory feedback and external feedback on performance in the program. This program was highly effective in prompting voiding and keeping residents dry. However, over a four to five month period the system gradually deteriorated. Feedback on individual staff members' performance effectively restored the program.

Buchanan and Fisher (2002) reduced disruptive vocalizations in two elderly residents by using non-contingent reinforcement. Prior to intervention functional analyses were conducted to identify reinforcers that may have maintained disruptive vocalization. Intervention in the clients' natural environment consisted of delivering reinforcers independent of the client's disruptive vocalization. Significant reduction in disruptive vocalizations was observed for both participants.

Summary

ABA is a natural science approach to analyzing the environment and its relationship to socially significant behavior. Through this analysis, environmental variables that control behavior are identified and manipulated. This approach has been successful in changing social, conversational and health-related behaviors in older adults with intellectual disabilities and in reducing maladaptive behaviors such as incontinence, wandering and disruptive vocalizations.

References

APA (1992) *Ethical Principles for Psychologists and Code of Conduct*. American Psychological Association, Washington, DC.

Baer, D.B., Wolf, M.M. & Risley, T.R. (1968) Some current dimensions of applied behavior analysis. *Journal of Applied Behavior Analysis*, **1**, 91–97.

Buchanan, J.A. & Fisher, J.E. (2002) Functional assessment and noncontingent reinforcement in the treatment of disruptive vocalization in elderly dementia patients. *Journal of Applied Behavior Analysis*, **35**, 99–103.

Bunck, T.J. & Iwata, B.A. (1978) Increasing senior citizen participation in a community-based nutritious meal program. *Journal of Applied Behavior Analysis*, **11**, 75–86.

Burgio, L.D. & Burgio, K.L. (1986) Behavioral gerontology: application of behavioral methods to the problems of older adults. *Journal of Applied Behavior Analysis*, **19**, 321–328.

Burgio, L.D., Burgio, K.L., Engel, B.T. & Tice, L.M. (1986) Increasing distance and independence of ambulation in elderly nursing home residents. *Journal of Applied Behavior Analysis*, **19**, 357–366.

Burgio, L.D., Engel, B.T., Hawkins, A., McCormick, K., Scheve, A. & Jones, L.T. (1990) A staff management system for maintaining improvements in continence with elderly nursing home residents. *Journal of Applied Behavioral Analysis*, **23**, 111–118.

Carr, E.G., Levin, L., McConnachie, G., Carlson, J.I., Kemp, D.C., & Smith, C.E. (1994) *Communication-Based Interventions for Problem Behavior. A User's Guide for Producing Positive Change*. Paul H. Brookes, Baltimore, MD.

Cash, E.M. & Khan, M.A. (1985) An assessment of factors affecting consumption of entrée items by hospital patients. *Journal of the American Dietetics Associations*, **85**, 350–352.

Cash, J., Bush, D. & Sturmey, P. (1995) The effects of room management and small group procedures on the behavior of older adults with Alzheimer's disease. *Behavioral Interventions: Theory and Practice in Residential and Community-based Clinical Programs*, **10**, 181–195.

Corrigan, P.W. (1991) Social skills training in adult psychiatric populations: a meta-analysis. *Journal of Behavior Therapy and Experimental Psychiatry*, **22**, 203–210.

Day, E.B., Strain, P.S., Fullerton, A. & Stowitschek, J. (1982) Training institutionalized elderly mentally retarded persons as intervention agents for socially isolated peers. *Analysis and Intervention in Developmental Disabilities*, **1**, 199–215.

Didden, R., Duker, P.C. & Korzilius, H. (1997) Meta-analytic study on treatment effectiveness for problem behaviors with individuals who have mental retardation. *American Journal of Mental Retardation*, **30**, 387–399.

Engelman, K.K., Altus, D.E. & Mathews, R.M. (1999) Increasing engagement in daily activities in older adults with dementia. *Journal of Applied Behavior Analysis,* **32**, 107–110.

Felce, D. & Jenkins, J. (1979) Engagement in activities by old people in residential care. *Health and Social Services Journal,* **2**, E23–E28.

Griffiths, D.M., Gardner, W.I. & Nugent, J.A. (1998) *Behavior Supports: Individual Centered Behavioral Interventions. A Multimodal Functional Approach. A Clinical Manual For Practitioners in Dual Diagnosis.* NADD Press, Kingston, NY.

Hayes, S.C., Wilson, K.G. & Strosahl, K.D. (1999) *Acceptance and Commitment Therapy: An Experiential Approach to Behavior Change.* Guilford Press, New York.

Heard, K. & Watson, T.S. (1999) Reducing wandering by persons with dementia using differential reinforcement. *Journal of Applied Behavior Analysis,* **32**, 381–384.

Jenkins, J., Felce, D. Lunt, B. & Powell, L. (1977) Increasing engagement in activity of residents in old people's homes by providing recreational materials. *Behaviour Research and Therapy,* **15**, 429–434.

Jones, E., Felce, D., Lowe, K., Bowley, C., Pagler, J., Galleger, B. & Roper, A. (2001) Evaluation of the dissemination of active support training in staffed community residences. *American Journal on Mental Retardation,* **106**, 344–358.

Kleitsh, E.C., Whitman, T.L. & Santos, J. (1983) Increasing verbal interaction among elderly socially isolated mentally retarded adults: A group language training procedure. *Journal of Applied Behavior Analysis,* **16**, 217–233.

Lovaas, I. O. (1987) Behavioral treatment and normal educational and intellectual functioning in young autistic children. *Journal of Consulting and Clinical Psychology,* **55**, 3–9.

Matson, J.L. & Coe, D.A. (1992) Applied behavior analysis: its impact on the treatment of mentally retarded emotionally disturbed people. *Research in Developmental Disabilities,* **13**, 171–189.

Matson, J.L., Benavidez, D.A., Compton, L.S., Paclawskyj, T. & Baglio, C. (1996) Behavioral treatment of autistic persons: a review of research from 1980 to the present. *Research in Developmental Disabilities,* **17**, 433–465.

New York State Education Department (1999) *Clinical Practice Guideline: Report of the Recommendations. Autism/Pervasive Developmental Disorders, Assessment and Intervention for Young Children (Age 0–3 Years).* Publication No. 4215, New York State Education Department, Albany, New York.

Powell, L., Felce, D., Jenkins, J. & Lunt, B. (1979) Increasing engagement in a home for the elderly by providing an indoor gardening activity. *Behaviour Research and Therapy,* **17**, 127–135.

Praderas, K. & MacDonald, M.L. (1986) Telephone conversational skills training with socially isolated, impaired nursing home residents. *Journal of Applied Behavior Analysis,* **19**, 337–348.

Reeve, K.F. & Fields, L. (2001) Perceptual classes established with forced-choice primary generalization tests and transfer of function. *Journal of the Experimental Analysis of Behavior,* **76**, 95–114.

Rush, J. & Frances, A. (eds) (2000) Treatment of psychiatric and behavioural problems in mental retardation. *American Journal on Mental Retardation,* **104**, 159–228.

Schnelle, J.F., Traughber, B., Morgan, D.B., Embrey, J.E., Binion, J.F. & Coleman, A. (1983) Management of geriatric incontinence in nursing homes. *Journal of Applied Behavior Analysis*, **16**, 235–241.

Scott, J., Clark, C. & Brady, M. (2000) *Students with Autism. Characteristics and Instructional Programming for Special Educators*. Singular Publishing Group, San Diego, USA.

Skinner, B.F. (1953) *Science and Human Behavior*. The Macmillan Company, New York.

Skinner, B.F. (1957) *Verbal Behavior*. Copley Publishing Group, Acton, MA.

Skinner, B.F. (1983) *Enjoying Old Age: A Program of Self-management*. W.W. Norton, New York.

Stock, L.Z. & Milan, M.A. (1993) Improving dietary practices of elderly individuals: the power of prompting, feedback and social reinforcement. *Journal of Applied Behavior Analysis*, **26**, 379–387.

Sturmey, P. & Crisp, A.G. (1990) Organizing staff to provide individual teaching in a group: a critical review of room management and related procedures. *Australia and New Zealand Journal of Developmental Disabilities*, **15**, 127–142.

Sturmey, P., Lee, R., Reyer, H. & Robek, A. (in press) Applied Behavior Analysis and Dual Diagnosis. Behavioral approaches to dual diagnosis. *Training Handbook for Mental Health in Mental Retardation* (eds N.N. Cain, G. Holt, N. Bouras & P.W. Davidson). Paul Brookes, Baltimore, MD.

US Department of Health and Human Services (1999) *Mental Health: A Report of the Surgeon General*. National Institute of Mental Health. Rockville, MD.

Further reading

Beekman, A.T., Kriesgman, D.M. Deeg, D.J. & van Tilburg, W. (1995) The association of physical health and depressive symptoms in the older population: age and sex differences. *Social Psychiatric Epidemiology*, **30**, 32–38.

Burkart, J.E., Fox, R.A. & Rotatori, A.F. (1985) Obesity of mentally retarded individuals: prevalence, characteristics, and intervention. *American Journal of Mental Deficiency*, **90**, 303–312.

Cooper, S.A. (1999) The relationship between psychiatric and physical health in elderly people with intellectual disability. *Journal of Intellectual Disability Research*, **43**, 54–60.

Davidson, P.W., Houser, K.D., Cain, N.N., Sloane-Reeves, J., Quijano, L., Matons, L., Giesow, V. & Ladrigan, P.M. (1999) Characteristics of older adults with intellectual disabilities referred for crisis intervention. *Journal of Intellectual Disabilities Research*, **43**, 38–46.

Fletcher, R.J. & Greene, E. (2002) *Dual Diagnosis: Mental Health/Mental Retardation. A Reference Guide for Training*. New York State Developmental Disabilities Planning Council, Albany, NY.

Fox, R.A., Haniotes, H. & Rotatori, A. (1984) A streamlined weight loss program for moderately retarded adults in a sheltered workshop setting. *Applied Research in Mental Retardation*, **5**, 69–79.

Fox, R.A., Rosenberg, R. & Rotatori, A.F. (1985) Parent involvement in a treatment program for obese retarded adults. *Journal of Behavior Therapy and Experimental Psychiatry*, **16**, 45–48.

Haynes, S.C., McCurry, S.M., Afari, N. & Wilson, K.G. (1993) *Acceptance and Commitment Therapy: A Manual for the Treatment of Emotional Avoidance*. Context Press, Reno, NV.

Jacobson, J.W. (1982) Problem behavior and psychiatric impairment within a developmentally disabled population I: Behavior frequency. *Applied Research in Mental Retardation*, **3**, 121–139.

Mooney, R.P., Mooney, D.R. & Cohernour, K.L. (1995) Applied humanism: a model for managing inappropriate behavior among mentally retarded elders. *Journal of Gerontological Nursing*, **21**, 45–50.

Moss, S. & Patel, P. (1997) Dementia in older people with intellectual disability: symptoms of physical and mental illness, and levels of adaptive behavior. *Journal of Intellectual Disability Research*, **41**, 60–69.

Neef, N.A., Bill-Harvey, D., Shade, M. & Delorenzo, T. (1995) Exercise participation with videotaped modeling: effect on balance and gait in elderly residents of care facilities. *Behavior Therapy*, **26**, 135–151.

Pack, R.P., Wallander, J.L. & Browne (1998) Health risk behaviors of African American adolescents with mild mental retardation: prevalence depends on measurement method. *American Journal of Mental Retardation*, **102**, 409–420.

Pinquart, M. (2001) Correlates of subjective health in older adults: a meta-analysis. *Psychology and Aging*, **16**, 414–426.

Robertson, J., Emerson, E., Gregory, N., Hatton, C., Turner, S., Kessissiglou, S. & Hallam, A. (2000) Lifestyle related risk factors for poor health in residential settings for people with intellectual disabilities. *Research in Developmental Disabilities*, **21**, 469–486.

Rotatori, A.F., Fox, R. & Parish, P. (1980) A weight reduction model for mildly retarded adults living in semi-independent care facilities. *Journal of Advanced Nursing*, **5**, 179–186.

Walkup, J., Sambamoorthi, U. & Crystal, S. (1999) Characteristics of persons with mental retardation and HIV/AIDS infection in a statewide Medicaid population. *American Journal of Mental Retardation*, **104**, 356–363.

Whitman, T.L. (1987) Self-instruction, individual differences and mental retardation. *American Journal of Mental Deficiency*, **92**, 213–223.

10 Psychotropic Medications

Nancy N. Cain and James Mead

Medication plays an important role in the treatment of mental illness. Although psychotropic medications generally work in the same way for those with intellectual disabilities (ID) as for those without, there are a number of unique concerns which must be considered. Some researchers (Rogers *et al.*, 1991; Gingell & Nadarajah, 1994) have suggested that people with ID may be at greater risk of significant side effects and complications from treatment with psychotropic medications due to their already compromised neurological status. This is compounded by the fact that older adults in general are more prone to complications and often more sensitive to the medications. This becomes even more complex in an elderly person with ID because they may demonstrate the presence of complications in unique ways, be less able to articulate what is wrong with them or be less able to express how they feel.

Prior to the mid-1950s, there were minimal medications available to treat mental illness. Many of the medications first available had significant sedating side effects and were often chosen for this effect to control aggressive, destructive or self injurious behaviors, not to treat a mental illness (Clarke *et al.*, 1990; Wressell *et al.*, 1990). Since that time, a tremendous amount of knowledge has been gained regarding the specific mechanisms of different mental illnesses leading to the development of many very precise and effective medications for their treatment. As our knowledge of the mechanisms of these diseases increases, it becomes more important that a correct diagnosis be made for treatment to be effective.

Use of psychotropic medications in aging persons with dual diagnosis

Issues related to the aging process

Age related changes in the various organ systems, including to the liver, kidneys and gastrointestinal system, can lead to changes in blood levels of medications. Progressive changes in the stomach and intestines result in changes in the absorption of nutrients and medications ingested. Degradation of renal function with age leads to decreased filtration and clearance of medications eliminated by the kidneys. Changes to the liver affect drug metabolism. The net result is that psychotropic drug doses may need to be adjusted up or down to compensate for this. Without careful monitoring of direct effects and side effects of the medication, the elderly patient may experience unpredicted debilitating results from otherwise normal dosages. Because these and other changes often make the elderly more sensitive to medications, the adage start low and go slow is wise to keep in mind.

Side effects may be more problematic with aging. The heart slows somewhat and ectopic or irregular beats are more common. Many medications can affect the electrical impulses of the heart, and aging, with slower heart rates and irregular beats, makes older adults more sensitive to these effects. With decreased agility and eyesight elderly individuals are prone to falling. Many medications can make them even more prone to falls by causing postural hypotension (a drop in blood pressure with standing), confusion or unsteadiness. Because of the increased fragility of the bones and length of recovery required for aging adults, they are at greater risk of serious morbidity or mortality as a result of injuries from falls. Older adults are more sensitive to the anticholinergic effects of medications on the urinary tract, which can result in the inability to urinate. This may lead to extreme pain or even injury to the kidneys. Some medications may increase urinary incontinence, leading to decreased independence or skin breakdown, discomfort and infection.

Issues related to people with ID

Persons with ID are often unable to clearly express the nature of their problem or concern, or to understand the treatment being proposed (see Chapters 4 and 11). For this reason, it is especially important to have an individualized data system in place to assess the effects of the medications, to measure the increase or decrease in the symptoms or behaviors targeted and to monitor for side effects. This involves clearly operationalizing the behaviors, picking those that will respond to the medication and adequately training carers to identify the behaviors. To avoid getting distorted descriptions of behaviors they should be assessed across multiple settings. Equally important, this information must then be shared with the psychiatrist when medication reviews occur. Subjective input is also important as those closest to the patient often recognize subtle changes that may not be reflected in the data. This needs to be balanced with the data and changes made to the data collection if needed.

Examples of data collected to assess change might include number of hours asleep each night, length of time out of seat in the work setting, number of episodes of self-hitting or time spent crying, rather than simply getting a subjective evaluation from others of whether or not the patient is manic or depressed. Examples of assessing side effects include data on drooling, incontinence, falls, or general signs of distress such as yelling, belly holding or kicking. Should significant negative change in behavior be seen, the psychiatrist should be made aware of this promptly.

To know if change has really occurred, it is important to establish a behavioral baseline or rate without treatment. Recognizing behavior change early and collecting specific data on rates of behavior without treatment can more easily assess the effect of treatment. In fact, careful recording of the problem behavior, its direct antecedent or preceding event, and how the individual responded to whatever correction or intervention was utilized, may suggest alternative treatments that can be utilized instead of or prior to trials of medication.

Careful data collection is also important for the adjustment of medication dosage. When a person is unable to express when they are experiencing change, it becomes easy to overmedicate. Dosages are often increased rapidly in an attempt to treat an acute illness. The dosage needed to treat the disease initially may not be needed once the illness is under control. With careful documentation of target symptoms, including side effects, the dosage can be titrated to the minimal effective dosage necessary with the least possible side effects.

Specific classes of psychotropic medications

All of the standard psychotropic medications have been utilized with individuals with ID. In the following section we will discuss some of those most commonly used in persons with ID, their indications, possible side effects and potential interactions, especially as related to the aging individual. This section is not meant to be all-inclusive, nor is it meant to replace a psychopharmacology textbook or the *Physicians Desk Reference* for details necessary for the administration of these medications. Individuals seeking this information are referred to the appropriate text.

Antipsychotic medications

Two general types of antipsychotic medications are in use for the treatment of psychotic disorder: the typical and the atypical antipsychotics. Both work through blockade of dopamine receptors in the brain. The atypical antipsychotics were developed more recently and are generally more specific in their dopamine blockade, making them less likely to cause extrapyramidal side effects or tardive dyskinesia (discussed below).

Typical antipsychotics

The typical antipsychotics include thioridazine, chlorpromazine and haloperidal. Numerous studies (Foot, 1958; Campbell *et al.*, 1978, 1982; Cohen *et al.*, 1980; Aman *et al.*, 1984, 1989) have shown that chlorpromazine and haloperidol are effective in reducing stereotyped behavior. While research into the use of neuroleptics for self-injurious behavior, aggression and hyperactivity has generally been positive, showing good effect, the research has been far less sound as noted in the *International Consensus Handbook* (Reiss & Aman, 1998).

Side effects of the typical antipsychotics include extrapyramidal side effects (i.e. akathesia, dystonia, akinesia, tremor and rigidity), weight gain, drowsiness, dizziness, decreased blood pressure, dry mouth, jaundice, leukopenia, pigmentary retinopathy, pigment deposition in the skin and lens, blurry vision and constipation. In older adults, falls can occur from hypotension or sedation and drowsiness can lead to confusion. As discussed previously, older adults can be more sensitive to any of the side effects.

Tardive dyskinesia is an often-irreversible extrapyramidal side effect resulting in spontaneous movements of the face, mouth and possibly of the trunk and limbs. This can occur in any age group. Although caused by the antipsychotic being used, the medication actually serves to mask the symptoms. Therefore they often become apparent following dosage reductions. An increased Q-T interval is an electrocardiogram (EKG) finding showing slowed electrical conduction through the muscles of the heart. This can be seen with the use of many medications, including over the counter medications, but much current attention has been focused on the typical antipsychotics. The concern stems from the fact that, although rare, a prolonged Q-T interval can be potentially lethal. This is especially significant when multiple medications, each of which can have similar but often less significant effects on the heart, are combined, increasing the potential for a lethal dysrythmia. Thioridazine seems to cause the greatest potential increase in Q-T interval and many people are being taken off of it. Caution needs to be exercised, however, in choosing to change from thioridazine to another medication, as some individuals may not tolerate the change. In these individuals, unless the Q-T interval is already dangerously long (i.e. greater than about 460–500 milliseconds), it makes more sense to leave them on the thioridazine and alert all healthcare providers to avoid using other medications which similarly prolong the Q-T interval. Regular monitoring of electrocardiographs should be performed with at least annual monitoring of the stable patient and more often for individuals with frequent medication changes.

Neuroleptic malignant syndrome (NMS) is a rare but potentially life-threatening complication that can be caused by treatment with antipsychotics. It presents as fever, muscle rigidity, autonomic instability and clouding of consciousness. Laboratory testing will often reveal an elevated creatine kinase level and increased leukocyte count. It is more likely in the setting of high dose neuroleptics with rapidly escalating dosages. In the elderly, the potential for developing this complication increases in individuals with dementia or Parkinson's disease who are administered typical antipsychotics (Addonizio, 1992).

Rapid and early treatment of NMS is crucial to recovery. Other medical conditions such as infection need to be ruled out. The neuroleptic needs to be stopped immediately and the patient given supportive measures. A dopamine agonist such as bromocriptine as well as muscle relaxants such as dantrolene can be helpful to the patient. Up to 30% of patients who experience NMS have a recurrence at some point. This potential can be minimized by a delay of two weeks in restarting the neuroleptic and by utilizing a neuroleptic of a different class.

Atypical antipsychotics

The atypical antipsychotics include risperidone, olanzapine and clozapine. They have entered the US market since the late 1980s; some were previously available in the European markets. Like the typical antipsychotics, they work through dopamine blockade. But unlike the typicals, they are more specific in the targets of their blockade and this may be the reason for their improved side-effect profile. Additionally, the atypical antipsychotics show good treatment effect on negative as well as positive symptoms, which may be related to some serotonergic effect as well. The typical antipsychotics usually show minimal effect on negative symptoms.

Research with the atypical antipsychotics in treatment of persons with ID has been limited. Duggan and Brylewski (1999) in a thorough, albeit very restrictive review of the literature, found no real support for the use of atypical antipsychotic medications in the treatment of persons with ID; however, only one trial met their stringent inclusion criteria. Matson *et al.* (2000), in a 10-year review of psychopharmacology and ID, noted evidence suggesting improvement in the treatment of the positive symptoms of psychosis, such as delusions and hallucinations, without causing the blunting of personality often seen with the typical antipsychotics. While research is limited, studies are available showing a positive effect in reducing aggressive behavior (Buitelaar *et al.*, 2001) and behavioral disturbances (Van Bellinghen & De Troch, 2001) in persons with ID without a diagnosed mental illness.

Although less likely than the typical antipsychotics to lead to extrapyramidal side effects, the atypical antipsychotics do manifest a number of potentially significant side effects. Weight gain, which can amount to as much as 0.8 lb per month, is not necessarily reduced by calorie restriction (Cohen *et al.*, 2001). Seizures, sedation, hypotension, development of diabetes mellitus and sexual dysfunction can all be seen with atypical antipsychotic medications. As older adults may be more sensitive to some of these side effects, cautiously escalating the dosage and making attempts to limit falls from hypotension or confusion from sedation are important. Clozapine, the first atypical antipsychotic carries the potential for a life-threatening bone marrow toxicity and thus requires frequent and regular white blood cell count monitoring.

Antidepressants

Four general categories of antidepressants will be discussed. The first two, the monoamine oxidase inhibitors (MAOIs) and the tricyclic antidepressants (TCAs) are used much less today than in the past but for some individuals may still be the most effective. The third category is the selective serotonin reuptake inhibitors (SSRIs) that are the most commonly used antidepressants today. The final category includes other diverse antidepressants such as the serotonin and norepinephrine antagonists. In cases where the depression presents with psychotic features, Hyman and Arana (1995) showed that combining a neuroleptic with an antidepressant leads to improved benefit when compared to either one alone.

Monoamine oxidase inhibitors

The monoamine neurotransmitters include norepinephrine and serotonin, both of which have been linked to depression. By disabling the enzymes that destroy them, the MAOIs cause a relative increase in the levels available, leading to decreased depression. These were among the first antidepressants utilized and have a long history of effectiveness.

The major drawback to the MAOIs has been their potential to cause life-threatening elevations in blood pressure if tyramine-containing foods, such as cheese and aged meats, or certain medications are ingested. For this reason, a tyramine-free diet and close monitoring of co-administered over-the-counter and prescription medications is required. Some MAOIs that do not cause these potentially life-threatening side effects are appearing on the market and may hold future promise.

Tricyclic antidepressants

The TCAs also increase norepinephrine and serotonin but through a very different mechanism, leading to different side effects. The TCAs also have a long history of effective treatment for depression.

Side effects of the TCAs can be significant and include dizziness and orthostatic lowering of blood pressure, dry mouth, blurred vision, urinary retention, constipation, sedation and weight gain. All of these symptoms can be especially debilitating in older adults and their use requires caution and careful monitoring. Monitoring of blood levels is recommended, especially at higher dosages as they can cause cardiac arrythmias. If taken in excess, overdose can be fatal from cardiac arrhythmias. In people who display suicidal behavior and who are capable of self-administering medications, TCAs must be used with extreme care. The SSRIs, as well as medications such as H2 blockers (used for control of dyspepsia) and quinidine (used for cardiac arrythmias), can interfere with the metabolism of the TCAs, resulting in significantly elevated levels.

Selective seretonin re-uptake inhibitors

Introduction of the SSRIs has dramatically changed the treatment of depression. Safe and generally well tolerated, the SSRIs work by decreasing the reuptake of serotonin into the cell, making more serotonin available at the neuronal synapse, where it can be utilized. Previously, many depressed individuals went untreated due to the restrictive diet of the MAOIs or the side-effect profile of the TCAs.

Hellings *et al.* (1996) administered Sertraline to nine persons with mild to moderate ID who demonstrated self-injury or aggression. While it is not clear that a specific diagnosis of depression was made, improvement in the severity of behaviors was seen in eight of the nine patients treated. One patient terminated treatment due to agitation and worsening of the previously seen self-picking behavior. In an open label, uncontrolled preliminary study of adolescents with mild developmental disabilities and depression, paroxetine showed promising results in depressive symptoms with no more than mild side effects.

The major side effects of the SSRIs include minor motor restlessness, occasional GI discomfort, and difficulty with sleep for some people if dosed close to bedtime, and for others significant sedation. These side effects are usually gone after the first several weeks of treatment. However sexual dysfunction, specifically anorgasmia in women and delayed ejaculation in men, does not go away. This can be quite disturbing to those most affected by it. Differences in the metabolism of the SSRIs by the P450 enzyme system can be helpful when treating older adults. Sertraline has minimal interactions with other medications and is generally the best tolerated in older adults.

Other antidepressants

Other recently developed antidepressants work at the neuronal synapse in a manner similar to the SSRIs, but vary in their specificity for serotonin or norepinephrine. These medications, such as mirtazapine, trazodone, venlafaxine and bupropion, are more heterogeneous in both their mechanisms of action and their side-effect profile. For example, venlafaxine is often used in cases of severe or drug resistant depression. In a minority of patients, this medication can lead to substantial hypertension, and blood pressure should be closely monitored, with initiation and dosage change of the medication. Mirtazapine can be quite sedating and useful in an agitated depression. Similarly, bupropion can also be used in agitated depression and is less likely to lead to mania in the treatment of bipolar depression. It is marketed under an alternate brand name as an aide to smoking cessation. This medication is contraindicated in the presence of a seizure disorder. Trazodone has significant sedating properties and can be used quite effectively to promote sleep.

Anxiolytics

Spreat and colleagues (1997) found that almost 10% of individuals with ID were prescribed anxiolytics.

Benzodiazepines

Introduced in the early 1960s, these were the first antianxiety agents that did not function merely by covering anxiety with sedation. They attach to specific anxiolytic receptors in brain cells, called benzodiazepine receptors, and can have an effect within minutes. Because of this mechanism of action, however, they can lead to dependency, symptoms of withdrawal and decreased efficacy over time. Still, they offer a high degree of safety. Because of differences in half-life, their duration of effect ranges from a few hours to days. Most frequently in people with ID they are used to assist in the control of disruptive or aggressive behavior.

Many studies have shown positive effects with benzodiazepines in persons without ID (e.g. Roy-Byrne & Wingerson, 1992; McNally, 1994). Among people with ID, research has primarily focused on children. The *International Consensus Handbook* (Reiss & Aman, 1998) recommends the following guidelines regardless of age:

- The anxiety should be a recent development, disabling and apparent to others. The indication or diagnosis should conform to established indications in adults with discontinuation safely accomplished in a short period of time, such as two months.
- There is a favorable risk/benefit analysis compared to other treatment approaches.
- The effects of treatment can be monitored in terms of therapeutic benefit and adverse effects.

Sedation is the most common side effect of the benzodiazepines. All of the medications are cleared from the body by the liver. Those with a longer half-life can lead to more sedation. This can be a significant problem in the elderly, who are typically slower at metabolizing medications and can become confused and ataxic leading to more falls. In some, the confusion can lead to agitation or aggression.

Tolerance to the benzodiazepines, requiring an increased dose to maintain effect, is common. Cross-tolerance can occur with alcohol use; therefore alcohol use is especially concerning. Physical dependence can follow chronic administration, manifested as anxiety, insomnia and possibly convulsions following the abrupt withdrawal of the medication. Dependence can be avoided by administering the benzodiazepine for no more than a few days at a time, or carefully tapering the dose, often over weeks or months, if long-term use has occurred.

Buspirone

Introduced more recently, buspirone is an anxiolytic more closely resembling many of the antidepressants in its mechanism of action. Specifically, it increases the amount of serotonin available at the neuronal synapse. This leads to its primary advantage; it does not cause dependence or withdrawal and can be used safely in individuals with a history of chemical dependency. Unfortunately, with this advantage comes a greatly decreased rate of response, typically requiring weeks (similar to the antidepressants) for effect. Verhoeven and Tuinies (1996) found that buspirone was not only effective in reducing impulsive and aggressive behaviors in six out of eight people with ID, but also resulted in improved sociability.

Like the benzodiazepines, the liver clears buspirone. As such, liver dysfunction can lead to increased levels. Tachycardia, palpitations, nervousness, gastro-intestinal distress and parathesias are more commonly seen than with the benzodiazepines.

Mood stabilizers

Individuals with bipolar disorder show changes in mood from depression to mania, and in the untreated state they can frequently live at the extremes of these two moods. Simply treating the depressive episodes with antidepressants is ineffective because this can provoke a debilitating manic response.

Lithium

This mood stabilizer has traditionally been the treatment of choice for bipolar disorder. It is a naturally occurring salt that exerts its effects on a number of complex levels, especially through second messengers. Its effect on mood has been known for over 50 years, so it has a long track record. Because of its narrow window of therapeutic effect, its use is not without difficulty,

Research into the usefulness of lithium in individuals with developmental disabilities has been limited. Bowden and colleagues (1994) found both lithium and divalproex to be more effective than placebo in the treatment of acute mania in the non-ID psychiatric population. Manning and Connor (1994) found lithium to be helpful in augmentation of therapy with antidepressants in people with resistant major depression. In aggressive individuals, Peet & Pratt (1993) showed that lithium could reduce episodes of aggression at typical therapeutic doses. Corrigan *et al.* (1993), based on a literature review, suggest that lithium can significantly reduce aggressive acts in persons with ID. However, as noted by the authors, the research contains flaws and limitations.

Side effects of lithium, including nausea, vomiting, diarrhea, acne, sedation, tremor, polyurea, polydipsia, weight gain, weakness and incoordination, can occur when blood levels rise, which can happen for many reasons even in the otherwise stable individual. It has a very narrow therapeutic window of 0.8–1.2 mEq/L and toxicity can occur at serum levels as low as 1.5 mEq/L. Signs and symptoms of toxicity include tremor, blurred vision, nausea, diarrhea, ataxia, hyperreflexia and dysarthria. Thyroid and renal function can be affected by long-term use of lithium. Therefore, in addition to the standard labs, kidney and thyroid function need to be monitored approximately every 6 months, and more often during initiation of treatment and if the patient becomes symptomatic. Less commonly, hypoparathyroidism is seen with chronic treatment so calcium levels should be monitored annually.

Drug interactions are common with lithium. Antibiotics such as tetracycline, non-steroidal antiinflammatory drugs such as ibuprofen, antidepressants such as fluoxitine, beta blockers such as propranolol, as well as many antipsychotic agents, can all increase the lithium level of previously stable patients. For this reason, patients should be advised not to take any over-the-counter medications without talking to their doctor first, and lithium blood levels should be followed closely, with medication changes. Dehydration and physical illness can lead to increased lithium levels and drinking large amounts of fluids is important in hot weather or if exercising strenuously. Sodium loss through excessive perspiration or vomiting can increase lithium levels by causing the kidneys to retain lithium. As lithium is associated with fetal cardiac abnormalities, adequate birth control is important. The use of lithium in those with renal, cardiovascular or thyroid disease must be done with caution and close monitoring of blood levels.

Anticonvulsants

The anticonvulsants such as carbamazepine and valproic acid have been similarly shown to be effective in the treatment of bipolar disorder but with a much improved side-effect profile and less need for close monitoring of blood levels. While the exact mechanism of action is not clear, it is likely that it is different than the mechanism of action for seizure disorder. This is supported by the longer response time in mania.

Studies in people without ID have repeatedly demonstrated the effectiveness of carbamazepine in the treatment of bipolar disorder. Post (1988) found good antimanic effect without many of the side effects that plague lithium use. Combined use with lithium is tolerated well by most patients. In an open treatment trial of lithium or lithium and carbamezapine with ten mild to severely developmentally disabled individuals with rapid cycling bipolar disorder, Glue (1989) found improvement in 50% and total resolution in 20%.

While valproate has been demonstrated effective in the normal population, studies of people with ID are lacking. Older adults with dementia (Lott *et al.*, 1995) showed good response to behavioral agitation with valproic acid.

Carbamezapine causes increased metabolic activity of hepatic enzymes. This leads to increased metabolism of many other drugs metabolized through the liver, requiring careful monitoring of dosages and signs of toxicity of other medications. The most common dose related side effects include diplopia, ataxia, gastro-intestinal complaints and, rarely, water intoxication. Skin rash is occasionally seen. Of primary concern to older adults are rare but often-fatal cases of aplastic anemia and agranulocytosis. Most of these have occurred within the first four months of treatment, and for unexplained reasons have been in patients being treated for trigeminal neuralgia.

The most common side effects of valproic acid are gastro-intestinal complaints such as nausea and heartburn. At higher dosage levels, a fine tremor may be seen. Weight gain is occasionally seen. Two extremely rare but serious side effects are hepatotoxicity (which is more likely to occur in young children) and thrombocytopenia without specific bleeding abnormality documented. Side effects specific to the elderly are lacking.

Psychotropic medications used in the treatment of dementia

Janicki and colleagues (1996) reviewed the practice guidelines for clinical assessment and care management of dementia of Alzheimer type and other dementias among adults with ID. Recommendations included monitoring of the patient for unexpected changes in behavior or function including a baseline screening beginning at age 40 for individuals with Down syndrome and age 50 for everyone else. Medical management called for systematic treatment of all treatable medical conditions such as cataracts, hearing deficiencies and seizure disorders. Importance of case-management services as well as adequate education and training of carers was emphasized. Van Buggenhout and colleagues (1999) support the importance of adequate assessment, identifying increased rates of hearing and vision loss, hypothyroidism and dementia in persons with Down syndrome, increasing with age.

In a meta-analysis of data regarding the psychopharmacologic treatment of pathologic aggression, Fava (1997) looked at evidence suggesting that carbamazepine and valproic acid (both antiepileptics) show evidence of efficacy in the treatment of individuals with dementia, as do the atypical antipsychotics and the beta blockers. The SSRIs and trazodone (both newer antidepressants) have also demonstrated an effect. While benzodiazepines can reduce agitation and irritability, caution must be used as they can also effect behavioral disinhibition and can further cloud the individual's sensorium.

Naltrexone

One theory explaining the cause of self-injurious behavior (SIB) postulates that the injurious behavior becomes linked to the person's own endogenous endorphin release through operant conditioning when the self-injury occurs repeatedly. Naltrexone, an opioid antagonist, would theoretically reduce the occurrence of SIB by disconnecting the link to the endorphin release, thereby leading to a classical extinction paradigm. However, the typical classic extinction burst normally seen when addictive behaviors are interrupted does not occur.

Studies of naltrexone in the treatment of self-injurious behavior in individuals with developmental disabilities have tended to be short-term trials with small populations or even single case designs. In a retrospective study drawing from the entire population of the state institutions of Texas, Casner and colleagues (1996) found that in 56 individuals exhibiting self-injurious behavior treated with naltrexone, over one half showed clinical benefit. Unexpectedly, a trend toward continued improvement was seen over the course of three years.

While it is generally safe without significant side effects, some individuals treated with naltrexone experience transient insomnia and anxiety, loss of energy, headache, muscle cramps and nausea. These are generally mild and tend to resolve.

The psychostimulants

The psychostimulants include pemoline, dextroamphetamine and methylphenidate. Psychostimulants have been noted to have what could be described as a paradoxical effect; that is, they lead to calming rather than stimulation in the hyperactive. It is for this reason that they are utilized in the treatment of attention deficit hyperactivity disorder (ADHD). Just as other disorders can co-occur in people with ID, so can ADHD. However, these medications are not commonly used in older adults for this purpose. When used, it is more often for the stimulant effect in those with debilitating loss of energy or to improve mood in patients with dementia.

Upon initiation of these medications, insomnia and loss of appetite are often seen; giving the medication in the morning and eating before it takes effect can counter these side effects. Headache, nausea, irritability and increased talkativeness are sometimes seen but can typically be avoided by a dosage reduction, with slower upward titration of the medication. Individuals treated with psychostimulants sometimes show a reduction in their spontaneity. Paradoxical sleepiness is occasionally present. Rarely, involuntary muscle movements, such as facial grimacing or jerking of the arms or legs, are seen. Of special concern in older persons is their potential for elevation of the blood pressure and heart rate; while not usually clinically significant, this needs to be monitored more closely in those with pre-existing heart disease. Use of the psychostimulants can lead to elevated serum levels of the tricyclic antidepressants and some anticonvulsants when used in combination. Their use with the MAOIs is contraindicated due to the potential for a life-threatening hypertensive episode.

Sleep medications

Insomnia is a common complaint in older adults. Many medications are utilized for this indication; some are marketed as sleep aides and others utilize the side effect of sedation. A common effect of the benzodiazepines is sedation and those with short half-lives are often utilized for sleeplessness. Triazolam, alprazolam and oxazepam fall into this group. The advantage of utilizing benzodiazepines with a short half-life is in the reduced carry-over effect the next day. Those with a longer half-life tend to lead to more daytime drowsiness and cognitive impairment. All benzodiazepines can lead to tolerance and to rebound insomnia upon termination. To minimize these effects, they should not be used for more than 10 days in a row. Closely related to the benzodiazepines are zaleplon and zolpidem, two recently marketed sleep aides that work at benzodiazepine receptors but are not themselves benzodiazepines. They share a short half-life and therefore less potential for carry-over effect, tolerance and dependence. Chloral hydrate is an older agent that continues to be popular due to its effectiveness as a short-term sleep aide and its low cost. However, it must be used in older adults with extreme caution. It should generally be avoided in those with severe renal, hepatic or cardiac disease and in those taking multiple other medications due to its effect on liver metabolism. Diphenhydramine, an antihistamine, can be a good sedative-hypnotic, but in the elderly the anticholinergic side effects – especially confusion, blurred vision, dry mouth, urinary retention and constipation – can be quite debilitating. Some antidepressants, such as the tricyclic antidepressants, can be used to induce sleep. Amitriptyline is commonly utilized in this manner. However, all of the cautions and side effects noted previously for the TCAs are also applicable here. As mentioned previously, trazodone is an antidepressant that can also be used to induce sleep but without many of the side effects seen with the previously discussed medications. However, when used for older adults, all sleep medications can lead to some degree of confusion and have the potential to increase the likelihood of falls. They therefore must be used with caution.

Medications for side effects

Extrapyramidal side effects are common with the use of psychotropic medications, especially with the neuroleptics. These side effects are acute, dose-related symptoms consisting of muscle spasm, typically of the head or neck, tremor and rigidity, and akathisia or the inability to sit still. They are typically treated with anticholinergic antiparkinson medications such as benztropine. They can also be treated with antihistamines such as diphenhydramine, which also has anticholinergic properties. These medications are typically prescribed on an as needed basis but should be given regularly if these symptoms are persistent. Side-effect medications can have side effects of their own. In older adults, tachycardia, prostatic hypertrophy, urinary retention, glaucoma and confusion are all significant potential problems. In addition, benztropine can lead to the development of irreversible tardive dyskinesia, and in some instances can precipitate an acutely worsened psychosis.

Summary

In this chapter, we have reviewed several issues that are important to providing safe, appropriate and timely psychopharmacological interventions for older persons with ID:

■ Psychoactive medications remain an important component of the treatment plan for older persons with ID as they age. Aging alone should not preclude consideration of either continuing medications started in earlier life, or introduction of new medications not used in earlier life. The underlying mechanisms of psychiatric illness, while somewhat age-dependent, do not wax and wane with the onset of older age.
■ Psychoactive medication for older persons with dual diagnosis, as for younger adults, should not be viewed as a sole response to psychiatric illness. Medications should always be used in conjunction with behavioral or other psychotherapeutic interventions.

- Care must be taken in administering psychoactive medications to older persons with ID, since age-related changes in metabolism or physical status may affect the effectiveness and prevalence of side effects of many psychoactive medications.
- Most medications in the *pharmacopoeia* for persons without ID are applicable for use with persons with ID even through older age.
- Good practice for older persons for ID will follow the principles of *least dosage possible*, and the use of the *least number of psychoactive medications as possible*.

References

Addonizio, G. (1992) Neuroleptic malignant syndrome in the elderly. *Psychopharmacological Treatment Complications in the Elderly* (ed. C.A. Shamoian) pp. 63–70. American Psychiatric Press, Washington DC.

Aman, M.G., Teehan, C.J., White, A.J., Turbott, S.H. & Vaithianathan, C. (1989) Haloperidal treatment with chronically medicated residents: dose effects on clinical behavior and reinforcement contingencies. *American Journal on Mental Retardation*, **93**, 452–460.

Aman, M.G., White, A.J. & Field, C. (1984) Chlorpromazine effects on stereotypic and conditioned behaviour of severely retarded patients – a pilot study. *Journal of Mental Deficiency Research*, **28**, 253–260.

Bowden, C.L., Brugger, A.M., Swann, A.C., Calabrese, J.R., Janicak, P.G., Petty, F., Dilsaver, S.C., Davis, J.M., Rush, A.J. & Small, J.G. (1994) Efficacy of divalproex vs. lithium and placebo in the treatment of mania. The Depakote Mania Study Group. *Journal of the American Medical Association*, **271**, 918–924.

Buitelaar, J.K., van der Gaag, R.J., Cohen-Kettenis, P. & Melman, C.T. (2001) A randomized controlled trial of risperidone in the treatment of aggression in hospitalized adolescents with subaverage cognitive abilities. *Journal of Clinical Psychiatry*, **62**, 239–248.

Campbell, M., Anderson, L.T., Meier, M., Cohen, I.L., Small, A.M., Samit, C. & Sachar, D.J. (1978) A comparison of haloperidol and behavior therapy and their interaction in autistic children. *Journal of the American Academy of Child & Adolescent Psychiatry*, **17**, 640–655.

Campbell, M., Anderson, L.T., Small, A.M., Perry, R., Green, W.H. & Caplan, R. (1982) The effects of haloperidol on learning and behavior in autistic children. *Journal of Autism & Developmental Disorders*, **12**, 167–175.

Casner, J.A., Weinheimer, B. & Gualtieri, C.T. (1996) Naltrexone and self-injurious behavior: a retrospective population study. *Journal of Clinical Psychopharmacology*, **16**, 389–394.

Clarke, D.J., Kelley, S., Thinn, K. & Corbett, J.A. (1990) Psychotropic drugs and mental retardation: 1. Disabilities and the prescription of drugs for behavior and for epilepsy in three residential settings. *Journal of Mental Deficiency Research*, **34**, 385–395.

Cohen, I.L., Campbell, M., Posner, D., Small, A.M., Triebel, D. & Anderson, L.T. (1980) Behavioral effects of haloperidol in young autistic children. An objective analysis using a within-subjects reversal design. *Journal of the American Academy of Child Psychiatry*, **19**, 665–677.

Cohen, S., Glazewski, R., Khan, S. & Khan, A. (2001) Weight gain with risperidone among patients with mental retardation: effect of calorie restriction. *Journal of Clinical Psychiatry*, **62**, 114–116.

Corrigan, P.W., Yudofsky, S.C. & Silver, J.M. (1993) Pharmacological and behavioral treatments for aggressive psychiatric inpatients. *Hospital & Community Psychiatry*, **44**, 125–133.

Duggan, L. & Brylewski, J. (1999) Effectiveness of antipsychotic medication in people with intellectual disability and schizophrenia: a systematic review. *Journal of Intellectual Disability Research*, **43**, 94–104.

Fava, M. (1997) Psychopharmacologic treatment of pathologic aggression. *Psychiatric Clinics of North America*, **20**, 427–451.

Foot, E.S. (1958) Combined chlorpromazine and reserpine in the treatment of chronic psychotics. *Journal of Mental Science*, **104**, 201–205.

Gingell, K. & Nadarajah, J. (1994) A controlled community study of movement disorder in people with learning difficulties on anti-psychotic medication. *Journal of Intellectual Disability Research*, **37**, 53–59.

Glue, P. (1989) Rapid cycling affective disorders in the mentally retarded. *Biological Psychiatry*, **26**, 250–256.

Hellings, J.A., Kelley, L.A., Gabrielli, W.F., Kilgore, E. & Shah, P. (1996) Sertraline response in adults with mental retardation and autistic disorder. *Journal of Clinical Psychiatry*, **57**, 333–336.

Hyman, S.E. & Arana, G.W. (1995) Antidepressant drugs. *Handbook of Psychiatric Drug Therapy*, 3rd edn (eds S.E. Hyman, G.W. Arana & J. Rosenbaum), pp 43–92. Little, Brown and Co, Boston.

Janicki, M.P., Heller, T., Seltzer, G.B. & Hogg, J. (1996) Practice guidelines for the clinical assessment and care management of Alzheimer's disease and other dementias among adults with intellectual disability. AAMR-IASSID Workgroup on Practice Guidelines for Care Management of Alzheimer's Disease among Adults with Intellectual Disability. *Journal of Intellectual Disability Research*, **40**, 374–382.

Lott, A.D., McElroy, S.L. & Keys, M.A. (1995) Valproate in the treatment of behavioral agitation in elderly patients with dementia. *Journal of Neuropsychiatry and Clinical Neurosciences*, **7**, 314–319.

Manning, J.S. & Connor, P.D. (1994) Antidepressant augmentation with lithium. *Journal of Family Practice*, **39**, 379–383.

Matson, J.L., Bamburg, J.W., Mayville, E.A., Pinkston, J., Bielecki, J., Kuhn, D., Smalls, Y. & Logan, J.R. (2000) Psychopharmacology and mental retardation: a 10 year review (1990–1999). *Research in Developmental Disabilities*, **21**, 263–296.

McNally, R.J. (1994) *Panic Disorder: A Critical Analysis*. Guilford Press, New York.

Peet, M. & Pratt, J.P. (1993) Lithium. Current status in psychiatric disorders. *Drugs*, **46**, 7–17.

Post, R.M. (1988) Effectiveness of carbamexepine in the treatment of bipolar affective disorder. *Use of Anticonvulsants in Psychiatry* (eds S. McElroy & H.G. Pope, Jr.) pp. 1–23. Oxford Health Care, Clifton, NJ.

Reiss, S. & Aman, M.G. (1998) *International Consensus Handbook*. The Ohio State University Nisonger Center, Columbus, Ohio.

Rogers, D., Karki, C., Bartlett, C. & Popcock, P. (1991) The motor disorders of mental handicap. An overlap with the motor disorders of severe psychiatric illness. *British Journal of Psychiatry*, **158**, 97–102.

Roy-Byrne, P.P. & Wingerson, D. (1992) Pharmacotherapy of anxiety disorders. *Review of Psychiatry* (eds A. Tasman & M.B. Riba) pp. 360–384. American Psychiatric Press, Washington DC.

Spreat, S., Conroy, J.W. & Jones, J.C. (1997) Use of psychotropic medication in Oklahoma: a statewide survey. *American Journal of Mental Retardation*, **102**, 80–85.

Van Bellinghen, M. & De Troch, C. (2001) Risperidone in the treatment of behavioral disturbances in children and adolescents with borderline intellectual functioning: a double blind, placebo-controlled pilot trial. *Journal of Child and Adolescent Psychopharmacology*, **11**, 5–13.

Van Buggenhout, G.J., Trommelen, J.C., Schoenmaker, A., De Bal, C., Verbeek, J.J., Smeets, D.F., Ropers, H.H., Devriendt, K., Hamel, B.C. & Fryns, J.P. (1999) Down syndrome in a population of elderly mentally retarded patients: genetic-diagnostic survey and implications for medical care. *American Journal of Medical Genetics*, **85**, 376–384.

Verhoeven, W.M. & Tuinies, S. (1996) The effect of buspirone on challenging behavior in mentally retarded patients: an open prospective multiple-case study. *Journal of Intellectual Disability Research*, **40**, 502–508.

Wressell, S.E., Tyrer, S.P. & Berney, T.P. (1990) Reduction in antipsychotic drug dosage in mentally handicapped patients. A hospital study. *British Journal of Psychiatry*, **157**, 101–106.

11 Legal, Ethical and Due Process Issues

Celia B. Fisher, Christine D. Cea, Philip W. Davidson and Nancy N. Cain

Psychoactive medicines have been used for centuries to address challenging behaviors and psychiatric symptoms in persons with intellectual disabilities (ID). Until recently, much of this practice occurred in the context of symptom relief or control with little regard for addressing underlying psychiatric disease. Frequently, the description of these symptoms emanated from other than traditional diagnostic sources including poorly documented reports from carers. More often, the symptoms for which relief was sought may have been an adaptive response by a consumer to inappropriate environmental demands or contingencies that might have been prevented by adjustments in caring practices.

These historical and contemporary practices set the stage for misuse of psychoactive medicines, ineffective treatment for psychiatric disease, unnecessary and potentially permanent and even lethal side effects, polypharmacy, and a reduction in the consumer's functional capabilities. Misapplications of pharmacological treatments may often lead to violations of ethical practice standards issued by professional, governmental and other regulatory organizations, such as the Medicaid program in the US, the American Psychiatric Association and the American Psychological Association. Such violations include compromising the rights of consumers to appropriate treatment and to pre-treatment informed consent.

There are many reasons for the misuse of psychopharmacologic interventions for persons with ID. These include well-intentioned attempts to treat psychiatric illnesses that have been difficult to diagnose or poorly understood in persons with disabilities. But the list also includes the deliberate use of medicine as a substitute for alternate habilitative settings or practices that might be more expensive or more complex to provide or for which family members or other carers may have insufficient skills, understanding or training. These conditions have frequently been associated with institutional settings. However, there is a very high risk that they will emerge in community settings as institutions close, and as personnel shortages, unsatisfactory reimbursement mechanisms and lack of professional experience with ID in the mental health system increase. Aging persons with ID are among the most vulnerable to misuse of psychotropic medications because they manifest psychiatric disorders that began earlier in their lives. With advancing age, there is an increasing likelihood of changes in metabolic responses to pharmacotherapy, carrying with it a higher risk of adverse medication effects. Additionally, there is a high likelihood of age-related functional decline that is often mistaken for new psychiatric morbidity, carrying the possibility of the use of new medications.

For some time, there has been a growing concern among both scientists and practitioners regarding the ethics of psychopharmacological treatment. Much of the focus has been on research and practice with children and adults with mental disorders (Fisher *et al.*, 1996; Gutheil, 1991; Leonard *et al.*, 1996). Special issues emerge when considering psychopharmacological treatment of persons with ID. These ethical crossroads can be classified into categories that may not be mutually exclusive. This chapter is designed to raise several ethical, legal and due process issues in clinical practices involving adults with ID. We begin with a conceptual discussion of each of these issues and follow with illustrative case studies. Throughout the chapter, discussions of legal implications and imperatives are based on US regulations and laws; the principles, however, are applicable internationally.

Informed consent, proxy consent and right to refuse treatment

Psychopharmacological treatment for adults with ID raises ethical questions regarding patient capacity to give informed, rational and voluntary consent to standard and experimental treatments. The serious and often permanent side effects of many of these medications raises complex ethical challenges for practitioners, scientists and family members attempting to balance the obligation to respect the right of adults with intellectual impairments to make autonomous decisions, with the need to protect them from poorly informed or incompetent decisions that place their welfare in jeopardy (Ellis, 1992; Fisher, 1999). Increasing age carries with it the diminishing likelihood that relatives will be available to assist in these decisions.

The moral foundation of informed consent rests on three principles: respect for personhood, beneficence, and justice. Respect for personhood acknowledges the right to self-governance and the obligation to protect from harm persons with diminished autonomy. Beneficence reflects a moral and ethical responsibility to maximize potential treatment and research benefits and minimize potential harm and suffering. Justice requires that all members of society share equally in the allocation of services and treatments, their risks and benefits, and that one particular group does not bear the burden of risks for other groups.

Professional guidelines and governmental regulations around the world draw on these principles in the construction of ethical standards for medical treatment and biomedical research. These guidelines address several issues related to informed consent and the right to refuse treatment (Gutheil, 1991). The Doctrine of Informed Consent (the ethico-clinical principles that protect patient autonomy) has its roots in tort law addressing battery, the act of touching another person without permission (Shouten & Duckworth, 1993). This doctrine requires the provider of care (physician, allied health professional, mental health professional) not only to ascertain the patient's voluntary consent to be treated, but also to assure that the decision is made following the provision of adequate information by a person competent (in a legal sense) to make the decision. United States case law exists that spells out the definition of these requirements (cf. Harnish v. Children's Hospital Medical Center, 1982) and informed consent is viewed by law as a contract (O'Hare, 1983). The law permits a provider to administer treatment without consent only in an emergency, when the consumer has waived the right to informed consent, when a legal caretaker cannot be located, or when seeking consent might worsen the condition to be treated (O'Hare, 1983; Shouten & Duckworth, 1993).

Under the Doctrine of Informed Consent, providers of treatments in the US are legally required to present sufficient information to enable patients to make informed decisions about whether to accept or refuse treatment recommendations or research participation. This information must include:

(1) A description of the expected benefits of the treatment
(2) The reasonable risk or adverse reactions
(3) Steps to ameliorate discomfort
(4) Alternative treatments
(5) The consequences of no treatment at all.

To ensure that valid and informed decisions are made, this information must be presented in a way that is understandable to the person. When consent is sought for a patient or prospective research participant with ID, practitioners and scientists must tailor disclosure information to the differing levels of comprehension and language ability of the individual (Hurley & O'Sullivan, 1999). The manner in which the information is presented must take into consideration other disabling or age-related conditions such as visual or hearing impairments. For persons with visual impairments, for example, the consent form should be written in large print.

The Doctrine of Informed Consent also requires that consent for treatment be given voluntarily, free from coercion, persuasion, manipulation and undue influence. Consent decisions not voluntarily given violate individual rights of autonomy. The cognitive deficits of persons with ID, compounded by emotional or personality disorders, restrictions of their physical and social environments, lack of experience and opportunity in making autonomous decisions, and reluctance to refuse others, make persons with intellectual disabilities especially vulnerable to pressure or coercion to accept treatment (Ellis, 1992; Hurley & O'Sullivan, 1999).

The capacity requirement of the Doctrine of Informed Consent rests on the ability of the decision-maker to receive, understand and use disclosure information to make an informed and voluntary choice. While adults are legally presumed to have the ability to make competent decisions unless it is determined otherwise, persons with diminished capacity may not always have the ability to do so (Dinerstein *et al.*, 1999). Yet under US rules, presumptions of incapacity based on intellectual status alone cannot be used as a reason for denying persons the right to consent to or refuse treatment (Ellis, 1992; President's Commission for the Study of Ethical Problems in Medicine and Biomedical and Behavioral Research, 1982).

Irrespective of varying levels of functioning, impaired decisional capacity of persons with ID may be further influenced by the presence of psychiatric disorders that can be permanent, cyclical, or fluctuate over time. Consequently, the issue of informed consent for treatment or research participation becomes even more complex when it involves persons with dual diagnosis (Cea & Fisher, in press). Due to the large number of individuals with ID and co-morbid psychiatric disorders, assessment of the emotional state of the person prior to seeking consent is essential to understanding his or her capacity for competent decision-making (Freedman, 1998). For older adults with ID, consideration must also be given to any age-related factors such as dementia or sensory impairments that can negatively impact their decision-making ability, as well as the influence of these disorders on the emotional well-being of the individual.

Many factors associated with ID may disrupt contractual obligations under the Doctrine of Informed Consent. For example, competence to consent is often not present in young children or in consumers with severe mental retardation. Thus, depending on the unique characteristics of each patient or prospective research participant, insuring a fair consent outcome may require the use of surrogate (proxy) or guardian consent (O'Hare, 1983; Fisher, in press).

By US law, surrogate decision-makers or guardians appointed by the courts may give consent to treatment or research participation for a person with impaired decision-making ability. Surrogate decision-makers are obligated to make decisions using substitute judgment based on their understanding of what the person with the intellectual disability would have decided if he or she were capable of doing so. If preferences are not known, the surrogate makes decisions in the best interest of the individual. Surrogate decision-makers may give proxy consent to routine medical treatments without involving the courts if the person with intellectual disability agrees to be treated (Freedman, 1998; Hurley & O'Sullivan, 1999). In most US jurisdictions, however, if the person with ID refuses to be treated or if proposed treatments involve 'forcible medication with antipsychotic drugs, electroconvulsive therapy, sterilization, and abortion' (Hurley & O'Sullivan, 1999, p. 49) surrogates cannot give proxy consent. A guardian has the legal authority to make best interest decisions either of the person (all daily decisions) or of property (assets and income) for the individual with ID. Sprague (1994) cautions, however, that individuals acting on behalf of consumers may not always have the consumer's best interest in mind. Care taking responsibilities, economic pressure and other factors may create conflict between consumer and guardian interests. In addition, proxy consent procedures are not considered ethically justifiable unless the person with ID agrees that proxy oversight or assistance is a desirable means of protecting his or her interests, his or her assent to participate is sought, and his or her dissent over-rides proxy opinion (Fisher, 1999; Fisher, 2002, and in press).

Decisions regarding the ability of persons with ID to provide valid consent must take into consideration the individual's vulnerabilities in relation to the context in which his or her consent is being sought. By utilizing a relational framework (Fisher, 1999; Fisher, 2002), care providers and clinical investigators can create a goodness-of-fit between the person and the consent context and thus maximize opportunities for patients or prospective research participants to provide informed, rational and voluntary consent. When such efforts are insufficient to insure consent competence of persons with ID, a relational framework maximizes opportunities for surrogate decision-making that reflect the wishes and concerns of the patient or prospective research participant.

Viewing consent capacity as a product of both person and context shifts ethical inquiry away from focusing exclusively on the intellectual disability of the individual to assessment of aspects of the consent setting that may be creating or exacerbating consent vulnerability, and to consideration of how the setting can be modified to produce a consent process that best reflects and protects the patient's or participant's hopes, values, concerns and welfare (Fisher, in press). The following hypothetical case study utilizes the relational approach to address some of the complex questions and ethical challenges faced by care providers and research investigators in balancing the rights to autonomy of persons with ID while protecting them from harm.

Case study: TJ

TJ, a 40-year-old man with mild ID, has been starting fights in the community residence in which he lives. Standard medications and behavioral treatments for aggressive disorders have not helped him and he may have to move to the local developmental center if his behaviors cannot be controlled. TJ is eligible for participation in a research study at a nearby hospital testing a new drug for aggressive behavior. Fearful about being treated by doctors he does not know, he refuses to participate. His supervisor and the treatment team at the residence think that despite TJ's concern, he should be enrolled in the study because it may be his last chance to stay in the residence where he feels happy and safe.

(Adapted from Fisher, in press)

TJ's case raises some important questions. Prior to a determination of whether TJ's decision not to participate in the study is valid, an exploration into the possible causes of his behavior needs to be made. TJ should be examined by a doctor for the presence of physical problems that may be causing him to act out. A psychiatric evaluation needs to be conducted to rule out any underlying causes for his behavioral symptoms. If such causes were found, treatment with medication specifically designed to alleviate TJ's psychiatric symptoms, rather than merely mollifying his behavior, would avoid subjecting him to experimental treatments that may not target his psychiatric symptoms or alleviate his aggression.

Having eliminated these influences on TJ's behavior, an examination is necessary of the context in which the behavior is occurring. The supervisor and treatment team need to assess the residential environment for antecedents to TJ's behavior, and to explore whether any modifications can be made at the residence, before attempting to enroll him in a study to test an experimental drug with an unknown potential.

Taking into consideration TJ's cognitive limitations, were efforts made to explain all of the issues to him in a manner that he would understand? Did the residential staff discuss their concerns with TJ about the fact that he might have to leave the residence, and did they help him think about the positive and negative aspects of his decision so that his choice can be made based on facts instead of fears. Were efforts made to lessen TJ's fear of new doctors by arranging to have a doctor from the research team visit him at the residence or to have TJ visit the hospital?

In attempting to determine whether or not TJ has the capacity to make this particular decision, his right to autonomous decision-making must be weighed in relation to protection of his welfare. If TJ is presumed competent, the residential supervisor and treatment team would have to respect TJ's right not to participate in the research study since the ultimate decision of weighing of risks and benefits is his to make. To over-ride his decision-making authority could have harmful practical or personal consequences. TJ's legal capacity to consent in other situations may be investigated or his hard won confidence in his own ability to make decisions might be jeopardized, causing repercussions that may be just as dangerous to his welfare as the possibility of his leaving the residence (Fisher, in press).

If TJ is found not competent to make this decision, the residential team might seek proxy consent from a family member or petition the courts to appoint a guardian to make decisions on TJ's behalf. Neither the supervisor of the residence nor the treatment team is authorized to make this decision for TJ. For them to do so would be a violation of his due process rights. Even if a surrogate decision-maker is appointed and TJ is ultimately enrolled in the study, his assent must be sought. Forcing an individual to participate in treatment or experimental research of unknown risk when he or she is unwilling to do so is ethically unjust and technically illegal (Rosenfeld, 2002). Thus, regardless of TJ's capacity for decision-making in this instance, his right to refuse to be enrolled in the study must be respected.

This case study illustrates the importance of viewing consent capacity in the context in which it is sought and engaging adults with questionable capacity as partners in creating respectful and compassionate consent procedures (Fisher, in press). All persons with ID are unique. Consent procedures should be based upon an understanding of each prospective patient's or research participant's special characteristics, their consent strengths and weaknesses, life experiences, and practical concerns. Such understanding can be achieved through ongoing dialogue with patients, family members, legal advocates, and practitioners to insure that consent procedures reflect an ethic of respect and care (Fisher, 2002, and in press).

Drugs used for non-approved applications with adults with ID

Mental health professionals face special ethical challenges in working with children, adolescents and adults with ID. The cognitive and emotional characteristics of these individuals, and their limited social power and relative lack of legal status, make them particularly vulnerable to treatment risks (Fisher *et al.*, 1999). When prescribing psychoactive drugs to treat mental health disorders, care providers and clinical investigators have a professional obligation to ensure the welfare and safety of vulnerable individuals and to minimize potential harm and suffering by carefully weighing and continuously monitoring risks against benefits for treatments they provide.

The pharmacopoeia of psychoactive drugs has grown dramatically over the past 25 years. Drugs are now available for selectively influencing specific neurotransmitter systems and for treating syndromes for which only psychotherapeutic or behavioral treatments were previously available. Unfortunately, many of these medications have been tested for use only with adults and even fewer for use with people with dual diagnosis. Very few of these trials have included efficacy or risk assessments specific to older individuals with ID who are either reaching older age or are already elderly. Some medications, such as Tegretol, Valporate and Impirimine, may have been approved in the US for treatment of one condition (e.g. seizures or depression) but shown in clinical reports to be serendipitously effective in affecting other symptoms (e.g. elevated mood or behavioral dyscontrol). Yet there are only limited controlled randomized clinical trials of these so-called non-standard uses and these applications lack United States Food and Drug Administration (FDA) approval.

Recent rule changes in the US broaden the number of alternative uses of these medications to generate evidence that drugs approved only for adults may be beneficial for applications in pediatric populations (DHHS, 1994). These provisions do not address the concern that pharmaceutical manufacturers may simply extrapolate information on pharmacokinetics on adults without ID for application to adults with dual diagnosis, and may fail to recognize significant age-related and intellectual-status differences in many biological parameters that might affect performance of a drug. There is a lack of consensus guidelines on related issues such as study design, subject enrollment and recruitment, and long-term outcome and risk assessments across these different populations (Leonard *et al.*, 1996).

The non-standard use of a medication, either in terms of target symptom or dosage, has been a very important addition to the intervention spectrum for individuals with disabilities. At the same time, conducting randomized clinical trials or other outcome studies involving drugs and behavior is complicated by difficulties in arguing that the drug's efficacy may justify its non-standard use (Sprague, 1994) or that neurological and biological differences between disabled and non-disabled persons, or between one disabled person and another, are so complex that isolating the effects of specific drugs may be impossible. The following two case studies illustrate ethical issues that can arise from the use of non-approved applications of psychopharmacological interventions for persons with ID in research and treatment situations.

Case study: Efficacy of lithium

The purpose of this study was to test the efficacy of lithium as a treatment for aggressive and self-injurious behaviors in adolescents with ID (see also Fisher *et al.*, 1996 for an in-depth description and discussion of this case). A four-month, parallel group (lithium vs. placebo control), double-blind investigation of adolescents with ID living in a residential treatment center was planned. While the effect of lithium on aggression had been documented in populations with typical mental development, there was little empirical support for its efficacy when prescribed for adolescents with intellectual disabilities.

This case study raises a number of important issues, as follows.

Ethical justification for using randomized placebo controlled trials

The first ethical dilemma faced by the investigators was whether to use randomized placebo trials to evaluate the efficacy of a treatment that was clinically established but not scientifically tested (Fisher *et al.*, 1996). It is not ethically responsible to deprive research participants of a medication whose benefits have been well documented (Levine, 1986; OPRR, 1993). However, when no effective treatments exist, the use of placebo controls is considered to pose few risks and to hold out the potential of direct benefit to both treatment and control groups, with the potential of the latter group being prescribed the medication once its effect was demonstrated.

Despite the absence of rigorous scientific validation, as is common in many treatment settings, center staff were utilizing lithium to treat the aggressive and self-injurious behaviors of some of their residents. As a consequence, staff were reluctant to allow consumers to stop taking the lithium. The investigators believed that the logical extension of research demonstrating a pharmacological agent's efficacy in populations without ID, to minors with ID, could not substitute for direct validation research, so they decided to use a placebo control group in the study. The Institutional Review Board concurred with this decision.

Withholding collateral treatments

Standards for internal validity required that the effects of lithium be studied in the absence of all other psychotropic medications. This presented a second ethical challenge since patients in the lithium or control condition might be expected to exhibit behavioral difficulties when collateral treatments (such as mellaril) were withheld. The investigators were concerned that this could expose patients, their peers and hospital staff to increased risk of self-injurious or assaultive behaviors. Additionally, the investigators questioned the external validity of a study that withheld collateral pharmacological treatment, since it is common in clinical practice to use lithium in concert with other medications (i.e. a tranquilizer). The investigators decided that a clinically and ethically justified approach would be a two-phase design with a lithium alone first phase followed by a lithium plus collateral medication second phase. The clinical staff supported this decision (see Fisher *et al.*, 1996).

Monitoring and protecting participant welfare

Meetings were held with residential staff to discuss potential risks of the study that would determine inclusionary and exclusionary criteria of participants and of monitoring procedures. Since the investigators were using a double-blind methodology, procedures had to be developed that would allow the blind to be broken when a participant had a negative reaction to his or her experimental condition (OPRR, 1993). The investigators wanted to develop a procedure that would both protect participants from potential experimentally induced harm and avoid breaking a blind precipitously and thus endanger the scientific integrity of the study. One way to accomplish this when a negative reaction was suspected was to compare a patient's current behavior to his or her baseline behavior measured prior to the initiation of the clinical trials. If the patient's current behavior was commensurate with baseline behaviors, in consultation with staff and parents the blind need not be broken (see Fisher *et al.*, 1996). It was decided therefore that baseline data be collected for each participant and his or her behavior continually monitored to ensure that it did not fall below baseline levels. A second mechanism developed for protecting participant welfare and the scientific integrity of the study was to avoid potential investigator and staff bias by appointing an independent clinician with no final decision regarding a patient's continued participation (see Imber *et al.*, 1986).

Dissemination of research findings

Data on participant reactions to treatment or control conditions has the potential of uncovering information that can directly benefit research participants (Fisher, 1993). With regard to the study under discussion, an adolescent's response to lithium or placebo trials and his or her reaction to the withdrawal of collateral medicines can provide valuable information for future treatment decisions. Often when a psychopharmacological study is completed, there is little communication between investigators and hospital staff of information that could directly benefit the treatment of individual research participants. In order to avoid this, at the end of the first and second phases of the study, the investigators prepared a summary letter to the parents and (with parental permission) to the hospital staff (Aman & Wolford, 1995). The letter documented the duration and nature of the medication or non-medication condition in which the child had participated and described the patient's observed behaviors at baseline, during and at the end of the experimental period. Where appropriate, treatment based on a child's reactions to the experimental conditions was recommended (see Fisher *et al.*, 1996).

Case study: MA

MA, a 61-year-old woman with severe ID living in a supervised community residence, had a life-long history of concomitant overactivity and screaming. Her behavioral problems had been resistant to treatment with numerous psychotropic drug trials and behavioral interventions. Unrelated to her behavioral disorders, MA developed bilateral corneal abrasions. The ophthalmologic intervention involved bilateral placement of antibiotic ointment followed by covering each eye for 72 hours. Staff were instructed to prevent removal of the patches or any rubbing of her eyes to avoid corneal infections that could result in permanent visual impairment.

The family and the treatment team agreed that MA could not be prevented from removing the patches without some type of restrictive intervention. Three choices were posed:

(1) Maintain MA's least restrictive living conditions with no intervention and subject her to the risk of permanent ophthalmic damage
(2) Introduce a behavioral intervention to restrict her eye-touching behavior, risking failure of the intervention and escalation of her baseline behaviors
(3) Administer medication to sedate her.

The family and the team decided that the risk of MA incurring self-induced blindness was too great to not intervene or use a behavioral intervention with an uncertain outcome. Instead, they chose to sedate her for the 72-hour period during which the ophthalmic treatment was in progress. Following approval of the treatment plan by her agency's

Committee on Humane Treatment, MA was given a benzodiazepine sedative-hypnotic four times per day in a dosage sufficient to sedate her. Staff awakened her every six to eight hours for toileting and to assure that she maintained hydration and food intake. No behavioral outbursts or eye-touching behavior occurred during the 72-hour treatment period. After 72 hours, the benzodiazepine was discontinued with no residual side effects. MA regained full visual function within several hours following removal of the patches.

This case illustrates one of a very few examples of conditions under which chemical restraint may be considered ethical. The decision-making process utilized in MA's case follows Sprague's (1994) model, which considers ethical treatment to be the treatment that is most humane, most effective and least risky to the consumer's health and well-being. In MA's case, all three of these conditions were met. The temporary application of a psychopharmacological agent prescribed in a dosage to sedate MA was beneficial in allowing her corneal abrasions to heal and in avoiding the potential of further damage that may have resulted in blindness. Thus the benefits of the treatment far outweighed the risks. Sprague (1994) also recommends that the deliberative process regarding the use of psycho-tropic medications should involve the family, the consumer (if feasible) and the treatment team staff to assure that all options are fully considered. In addition, a tertiary review process of the treatment decision by an impartial body should be conducted. This review body may from time to time serve in a mediation role when all parties to the treatment decision cannot agree on an option.

Diagnostic-based pharmacological treatment

In the field of ID, most decisions involving consideration of the use of psychoactive pharmacological treatment revolve around behavioral symptomatology. Within that framework, behaviors that threaten phy-sical damage typically receive the greatest attention. Some have argued that this approach may overlook a bona fide psychiatric diagnosis more often than not, and perhaps lead to selection of the incorrect medication to treat behavioral symptoms or to trial-and-error pharmacological man-agement – a strategy that has led to ineffective and inappropriate poly-pharmacy in the past.

The alternative to treating symptomatology is to treat based on diag-nosis. Sturmey (1995) argues that diagnosis-based treatment assumes that either maladaptive behaviors stem from psychiatric disorders, or that maladaptive behaviors are an expression of some underlying disorder. Different psychiatric disorders respond differently to different classes of

medication, while often giving rise to similar behaviors. Specific medications should be used to treat specific disorders as often as possible,
rather than mollify generalized behaviors.

Sturmey (1995) described a three-stage clinical decision-making model
to evaluate the diagnostic basis of behavior disorder. Stage 1 involves
differentiating a true behavior disorder from developmentally normal
behaviors perceived by the carer as abnormal. Stage 2 differentiates
transient behavioral changes from true disorders. Stage 3 follows a
traditional differential diagnostic process to characterize the underlying
cause of the behavioral symptoms.

Not every adult with a behavioral disorder will be diagnosable, and
some consumers may require many visits, extensive observations and
series of laboratory examinations to proceed through the differential
diagnosis. Such adults and their advocates and treatment team will
invariably present compelling cases for pharmacotherapy based on a best
guess diagnosis after only a few visits. Such treatments may even be
desirable on a temporary basis if they can stabilize the adult or his or her
environment by creating the opportunity to apply behavioral interventions. They should not, however, substitute for pursuit of a differential
diagnosis.

Treatment involving application of a psychoactive medication based on
a best-guess cause of behavioral symptoms is often the only option for
some consumers. It is complicated by the frequent lack of correspondence
between the expected effects of a psychoactive medication based on data
from typical consumers, with the effects of that drug on consumers with
ID. Hence, the best guess about a diagnosis may lead to the choice of a
medication to which the consumer has an idiosyncratic and unfruitful
response. The inevitable trial-and-error medicating of behavioral symptoms may actually be the best approach in certain cases. But the process
must be carefully controlled and monitored.

Summary

Mental health practitioners and clinical investigators face special ethical
challenges when working with older adults with ID. This chapter discussed these challenges in relation to treatment recommendations for
psychopharmacological interventions. The limited cognitive and
emotional characteristics of aging persons with ID and their relative lack
of legal status and social power make them particularly vulnerable to
misuse of these drugs and to their risks.

When prescribing psychoactive medications to persons with ID,
practitioners and clinical investigators are obligated to ensure the welfare

and safety of the persons concerned and to minimize harm by continually weighing and monitoring risks against benefits for medications prescribed. As far as possible, these medications should be used in the treatment of diagnostically-based psychiatric disorders and not merely to relieve behavioral and other symptoms for which no clear cause is evident.

The use of psychopharmacological medications in treating older adults with ID also raises complex ethical questions regarding the capacity of these persons to give informed, rational and voluntary consent to standard and experimental treatments. Regardless of level of functioning, the decisional capacity of these individuals may be further impaired by the same psychiatric disorder that the medication is intended to treat, and by age-related factors such as dementia or sensory impairments. All persons with ID are unique. Individual capabilities as well as situational circumstances must be weighted and their implications to informed consent clearly understood.

Finally, if it is determined that an individual with ID is unable to make treatment decisions for him or herself, consent should be sought from a surrogate decision-maker or guardian who makes the decision in accordance with the preferences of the individual or in his or her best interest. It is important to note that with increasing age there is a likelihood that relatives may not be available to assist in these decisions and alternative means of obtaining preferred or best interest decisions for the aging person with ID need to be explored.

References

Aman, M. & Wolford, P. (1995) Consumer satisfaction with involvement in drug research: A social validity study. *Journal of the American Academy of Child and Adolescent Psychiatry*, **34**, 940–945.

Cea, C.D. & Fisher, C.B. (in press). Ethical and legal issues in treating persons with dual diagnosis. *Training Handbook on Mental Health in Mental Retardation* (eds N.N. Cain, G. Holt, N. Bouras & P.W. Davidson) Paul H. Brooks Publishing, Baltimore, MD.

DHHS (1994) Department of Health and Human Services, FDA. *The Federal Register* (21 CFR, Part 201), 59:238, 64240–64250.

Dinerstein, R.D., Herr, S.S., & O'Sullivan, J.L. (eds) (1999) *A Guide to Consent.* American Association on Mental Retardation, Washington, DC.

Ellis, J.W. (1992) Decisions by and for people with mental retardation: Balancing considerations of autonomy and protection. *Villanova Law Review*, **37**, 1799–1809.

Fisher, C.B. (1993) Integrating science and ethics in research with high-risk children and youth. *Social Policy Report: Society for Research in Child Development*, **7**(4), 1–27.

Fisher, C.B. (1999) Relational ethics and research with vulnerable populations. Reports on research involving persons with mental disorders that may affect decision-making capacity Vol. II, (pp. 29–49). *Commissioned papers by the National Bioethics Advisory Commission*, Rockville, MD.

Fisher, C.B. (2002) Respecting and protecting mentally impaired persons in medical research. *Ethics and Behavior*, **12**, 279–284

Fisher, C.B. (in press) A goodness-of-fit ethic for informed consent. *Urban Law Journal*.

Fisher, C.B., Hoagwood, K. & Jensen, P.S. (1996) Casebook on ethical issues in research with children and adolescents with mental disorders. *Ethical Issues in Research with Children and Adolescents with Mental Disorders* (eds K. Hoagwood, P.S. Jensen & C.B. Fisher). Lawrence Erlbaum Associates, Mahwah, NJ.

Fisher, C.B., Hatashita-Wong, M. & Greene, L. (1999) Ethical and legal issues. *Developmental Issues in the Clinical Treatment of Children* (eds W.K. Silverman & T.H. Ollendick) pp. 470–486. Allyn & Bacon, Boston.

Freedman, R.I. (1998) Use of advance directives: Facilitating health care decisions by adults with mental retardation and their families. *Mental Retardation*, **36**, 444–456.

Gutheil, T. (1991) Medicolegal psychopharmacology. *The Practitioner's Guide to Psychoactive Drugs*, 3rd edn (eds A.J. Gelenberg, E.L. Bassuk & S.C. Schooner) pp. 473–485. Plenum Medical Book Company, New York.

Hurley, A.D. & O'Sullivan, J.L. (1999) Informed consent for health care. *A Guide to Consent* (eds R.D. Dinerstein, S.S. Herr & J.L. O'Sullivan). American Association on Mental Retardation, Washington, DC.

Imber, S.D., Glanz, L.M., Elkin, I., Sotsky, S.M., Boyer, J.I. & Leber, W.R. (1986) Ethical issues in psychotherapy research: Problems in a collaborative clinical trials study. *American Psychologist*, **41**, 137–146.

Leonard, H., Jensen, P., Vitiello, B., Ryan, N., March, J., Riddle, M. & Biederman, J. (1996) Ethical issues in psychopharmacological treatment research with children and adolescents. *Ethical Issues in Research with Children and Adolescents with Mental Disorders* (eds K. Hoagwood, P.S. Jensen & C.B. Fisher) pp. 73–88. Lawrence Erlbaum Associates, Mahah, NJ.

Levine, R. (1986) *Ethics and Regulation of Clinical Research*, 2nd edn. Urban & Schwarzenberg, Baltimore-Munich.

O'Hare, T.F. (1983) Legal issues in prescribing psychoactive medications. *The Practitioner's Guide to Psychoactive Drugs*, 3rd edn (eds A.J. Gelenberg, E.L. Bassuk & S.C. Schooner) pp. 399–409. Plenum Medical Book Company, New York.

OPRR (1993) Office for Protection of Research Risks, Department of Health and Human Service, National Institute of Health. *Protecting Human Research Subjects: Institutional Review Board Guidebook*. Government Printing Office, Washington, DC.

President's Commission for the Study of Ethical Problems in Medicine and Biomedical and Behavioral Research (1982) *Making Health Care Decisions: The Ethical and Legal Implications of Informed Consent in the Patient-Practitioner Relationship*. US Government Printing Office, Washington, DC.

Rosenfeld, B. (2002) Competence to consent to research: Where psychology, ethics and the law intersect. *Ethics and Behavior,* **12**, 284–287.

Shouten, R. & Duckworth, K.S. (1993) Medicolegal and ethical issues in the phamacologic treatment of children. *Practitioner's Guide to Psychoactive Drugs for Children and Adolescents* (eds J.S. Werry & M.G. Aman) pp. 161–178. Plenum Medical Book Company, New York.

Sprague, R. (1994) Ethics of treatment evaluation: Balancing efficacy against other considerations. *Destructive Behavior in Developmental Disabilities* (eds T. Thompson & D. Gray) pp. 293–311. Sage, Thousand Oaks, CA.

Sturmey, P. (1995) Diagnostic-based pharmacological treatment of behavior disorders in persons with developmental disabilities: A review and a decision-making typology. *Research in Developmental Disabilities,* **16**, 235–252.

12 Coping with Bereavement: the Dynamics of Intervention

Sandra Dowling and Sheila Hollins

It is at best surprising and at worst shocking to revisit some of the accepted thinking regarding bereavement in the lives of people with intellectual disabilities (ID) up to the mid 1970s. While it is now widely known that these people experience, in essentially the same way as anyone else, the raw and unpredictable emotional upset associated with the death of a relative, friend or colleague (Kloeppel & Hollins, 1989; Oswin, 1991; Hollins & Sireling, 1999), it was previously thought that they did not have adequate intellectual capacity or sufficient emotional maturity to recognise their loss and to grieve for it. In spite of more recent changes in thinking, substantial problems remain. People with ID are known to have significantly higher levels of complicated grief, with many experiencing prolonged grief with increased anxiety, depression and other symptoms of distress (Hollins & Esterhuyzen, 1997).

This chapter is primarily concerned with bereavement in the lives of the growing population of older people with ID, and issues that are specific to them. Firstly, it will consider the historical and social context within which a discussion of bereavement in the lives of people with ID is located, and which informs current thinking, and then will focus on current approaches to bereavement interventions.

The historical and social context framing current discussion

Up to the mid 1970s bereavement in the lives of people with ID was a marginal concern. While a few interested academics and practitioners (e.g. Hollins & Sireling, 1985, 1999; Oswin, 1985, 1991) were drawing attention to the importance of recognizing people's grief and of including them in the loop of family sorrow, established thinking continued to influence culture and practice within services. Naturally this extended beyond attitudes to bereavement, influencing myriad aspects of these people's lives, many of whom had long been excluded from or denied experience of common life events. Educational expectations were low and these individuals were regarded as unlikely to gain employment or to have their own homes. The idea that they may form relationships, marry or have children was, and to some extent still is, anathema to many, and the majority of such people continued to live with their parents until one or both had died. Others inhabited congregate residential services that evolved as contingent expressions of the prevailing philosophy (Towell & Beardshaw, 1991; Atkinson *et al.*, 1997), and which did not embrace the notion of an ordinary life.

Thinking that influenced service development also informed ideas about people's emotional capacity and needs. Marginalization from social norms and activities became merged with disregard for people's emotions and neglect of their need to express or share their feelings. People with ID were thought neither to experience grief nor to recognize or comprehend loss, as though always living in the present. Paradoxically it was also often said that their sorrow would be so great that they should be protected from the harsh reality of death (Dowling, 2000).

How did this thinking impact on practice?

People with ID were, and on occasion still are, not told that someone has died. Sometimes an alternative reality is invented in an attempt to hide the truth of the death. One example of this is the mother who told her daughter that her father had gone away on business. Furthermore, people were often sent to respite care units when a family death was imminent, only returning home after the funeral, thus precluding involvement in any grieving rituals, or the opportunity to witness or share the sorrow of others. In the course of current research (a bereavement intervention study at St. George's Hospital Medical School, London, England) bereaved people are recalling their experiences and many are talking about missed grieving opportunities. Frank's story is illustrative of this. (Personal stories in this chapter are taken from interviews conducted during the bereavement intervention study and all names have been changed and distinguishing details altered.)

Case study: Frank

Frank was 22 when his mother died. He came home from the long-stay hospital, where he had lived since he was 14 years old, on the day of her funeral. He watched from his grandmother's doorway as the rest of the family left for church. He recalls crying and shouting after them to take him along. They did not come back for him and it was not spoken about again.

In this man's culture at that time in the twentieth century, men and women (less commonly children) typically attended the funeral rituals of close relatives and friends. Frank's exclusion suggests that he was being treated in a similar way to a child. Recent research suggests that everyday practice is still limited by such outdated thinking, although it is unclear what part culture, religion and society play in this (Raji & Hollins, 2000). For example, a study of 50 parentally bereaved people, (Hollins & Esterhuyzen, 1997), all of whom had been bereaved in the previous two years, found that 23 of the 50 had not attended their parent's funeral, 42 were unprepared for the death, with no prior discussion having taken place, only eight people had visited their parent while they were ill in hospital, and of the 32 who had lived with their parent prior to death, 18 no longer lived in the family home by the time of the death.

Harper and Wadsworth (1993) studied 43 people who had been bereaved in the previous three years, and proposed a link between life experiences and coping ability and strategies. They suggested that inclusion brings opportunities to accumulate knowledge, and that this can offer a route to providing assistance at times of loss. Not telling people what has happened, leaving them out of the activities that provide a cradle for grief, and not including people or being attentive to how they may feel, does not help, nor is it protective. Instead, such exclusion hinders the resolution of grief and may contribute to the development of complicated grief.

Case study: Frank (*continued*)

Forty years after the death of Frank's mother, he found it incredibly difficult to talk about his memories of her, and breathlessly blurted out what had happened on the day of her funeral. He became extremely anxious when asked how he felt about it and said he didn't want to talk any more. He seemed overwhelmed by what were clearly very painful memories.

All human beings love, and as Parkes (1986) reminds us, 'Grief is the price we pay for love', so without the opportunity to mourn or to be part of the grief of others, people with ID may not have the chance to face the reality of life and death or to learn a language with which to express their feelings. Hollins and Esterhuyzen (1997) noted that grief may be expressed through behavior, and that 'professionals were more likely to attribute behavioral symptoms to a presumed intellectual disability than to other pathology' (Hollins & Esterhuyzen, 1997, p.500). In failing to connect changes in behavior to a loss through death, carers are more likely to address the symptoms (behavior) rather than the cause (bereavement). The following story demonstrates this.

Case study: John

John lived in residential care, he was non-verbal and became more difficult to support when he started to leave his home and wander in nearby woods. He was referred for specialist help, his behavior being described as 'absconding', and staff were concerned about his safety and well-being. His parents had not told him that his grandfather had died; but John missed his regular visits and the walks they used to have together. Understanding his 'absconding' as searching behavior helped John's family understand his grief and his need for explanations and comfort.

While changes in thinking about bereavement in the lives of people with ID are evident, attitudinal shifts have not been fully embraced in practice. The situation is in a state of flux. Because change takes time and is often adopted by new generations, older people with ID are more likely to have experienced the kinds of situations discussed above. In addition to this, older people are more likely to encounter some particular circumstances surrounding bereavement, as discussed below.

Issues of bereavement for older people with ID

In the United Kingdom most people with ID live in the family home with parents, or in later years a sole surviving parent, commonly the mother (Hubert & Hollins, 2000). At its best the familiarity built up over a lifetime provides security and a sense of belonging; likewise the frequently strong relationship between the parent and their adult child gives mutual love, care, continuity and understanding. In many instances people will have already experienced the death of one parent and are extremely fearful that their surviving parent will also die. Fear provokes resistance to discussion or planning for the future. Moira's experiences, described below, demonstrate the difficulty of this situation.

Case study: Moira

Moira is 61 years old; her mother is in her mid-eighties. Spending all of the time she is not at the day centre with her mother, Moira describes a contented home life. She is sure of her mother, she knows she will be there when she gets home and that they will spend the evening together. When her mother visits her friends, Moira goes too. They go to the shops together, they watch television together and may play cards together on a Sunday afternoon. Moira's mother knows what Moira likes to eat, that she likes to have a cup of tea before bed at night, that she doesn't like to be rushed in the mornings and that she enjoys phoning her sister every Saturday evening. No one else knows these details; they are based on a lifetime of understanding. Moira's mother is not just a carer; she is Moira's confidant, her companion and the vessel of her memories. Moira cannot imagine life without her mother. She is aware that her mother is getting older and that her health is declining. Every time her mother has to visit the hospital Moira is terrified that it is serious. She finds it almost impossible to discuss the future and cannot bring herself to think about her mother not being there.

Moira's mother is aware of this and has tried to help her to prepare for the future, but has faced huge resistance from her daughter and little support from professionals, who repeatedly say it is Moira's choice not to discuss her future and there is nothing they can do about it. However, without any plans for the future or any record of the details that make Moira's day-to-day routine her own, the implications and consequences for her response to her mother's inevitable death are grim.

Fearing the future not only diminishes opportunities for planning and preparation, it also impinges on the present, provoking anxiety through sensing a threat to personal well-being. A recent project (Giles, 2001) addressed issues of planning for the future in the lives of 20 people with ID, who still lived in their family home. It was found that notions of planning for the future were either avoided or had a low priority, with the demands of day-to-day life, both for the people with ID and their parents, taking precedence; however, when given the opportunity, through the project, to think about the future and their role in shaping it, both parents and their adult sons and daughters were keen to identify their hopes and dreams and to think about how to make them a reality.

Without such planning older people may be looking to the future through frightened eyes. It is vital that this is recognized and that people's understandable reluctance to talk about it is not simply dismissed as their own choice, but as something that requires time and sensitivity. In some families the surviving parent may be the one who is unable to think about the future and to support their son or daughter in making reassuring plans for a life of their own. The need for a place to live, new relationships and financial security are all easier to establish while parents are in good health.

Many older people with ID who have lost contact with their family following years of institutionalization have recently been resettled in the community. Harry describes his experience of trying to find his family.

Case study: Harry

Harry is 72 years old. He lived in a long-stay hospital from the age of 14 until he was 51 years old. He tried to find his natural mother after his release. He asked for help from social workers and spent several years trying to locate his family, who had moved away from the area where he had lived as a boy. Finally, he discovered that his mother was living in a residential nursing home. He went to visit her. Harry's mother did not look at him or talk to him, she did not respond when he held her hand nor drink the tea a nurse brought for her. She had advanced senile dementia. However, Harry says he thinks his mother knew he had come to see her and that she was pleased to see him. Three weeks later he went to his mother's funeral. He frequently visits her grave and says that he is glad to have seen her before she died.

Older people and their aging parents

People with ID are now far more likely to outlive their parents than ever before, due to increased longevity brought about by advances in medical and social care. People who continue to live in the family home will, as they grow older, find themselves living with aging parents or a sole surviving parent. Families such as these are sometimes unknown to services and may be unwilling to begin to access local services or to ask for help. They may have resolved to live without outside assistance for their adult son or daughter, a decision which may be based on inadequate or out of date knowledge about what services are available, or a fear of being thought unable to cope. Horne (1989) described such households as members of a hidden population.

Many such families, often with simultaneously conflicting and shared needs, may be isolated from both formal and informal support networks (McGrath & Grant, 1993), and may be vulnerable to any alteration in the precarious equilibrium of everyday life. Services may only be alerted to the existence of these vulnerable households at times of crisis. The death of one member of the family can be a critical turning point (Hubert & Hollins, 2000).

Individual and family needs alter with the passage of time. As people grow older they may find themselves in declining health, their social network may have narrowed or their economic situation may have deteriorated. Relationships within a family will necessarily respond to the influence of changes within individual's lives. The parent of a son or daughter with ID may have seen themselves as mother/father, carer and advocate, but as the years go by the parent may come to rely on their adult child for companionship and as someone with whom to share everyday tasks and events. The relationship may have become symbiotic, or in some cases a role reversal will have happened, with the disabled family member becoming their aging parent's carer. This is Sarah's experience.

Case study: Sarah

Sarah's mother died three years ago at the age of 83; Sarah was 62 at the time. Her mother had been in failing health for several years prior to her death and had become increasingly dependent on her daughter. Sarah is a very able woman. She took on many household tasks and responsibility for much of her mother's care. As her mother grew more frail Sarah found it increasingly difficult to cope.

The situation altered dramatically when Sarah's mother was taken into hospital early in the new year. Sarah contacted her sister who lives abroad, to tell her that mother was very ill.

Sarah's mother died about two weeks after being admitted to hospital. Sarah visited her every day. She had been her mother's companion for many years, and while her mother cared for her as a child and young woman, Sarah had adopted this role in later years. Yet it was her sister to whom the doctor spoke in muted tones when they arrived at the hospital to visit, and her sister to whom the doctor expressed his condolences at her mother's death.

Having drawn attention to some of the additional difficulties experienced by older people with ID at times of bereavement, this chapter will now consider how to intervene to encourage more helpful dynamics and patterns of behaviour.

Intervening before a death

Although it is not possible for anyone to be fully prepared for the emotional distress following a death, it is vital to have an appreciation of the idea of loss and, therefore, a sense that the intense feelings of grief are both an expected and normal reaction to it.

What does preparation entail?

Preparation is about information, inclusion and detail. Information is acquired in a variety of ways: it can be communicated directly, attained metaphorically through stories or images, or it can be acquired experientially, through inclusion in rituals associated with death and dying. Understanding cannot be achieved without information. Direct communication about death, dying and bereavement can be difficult. It is a sensitive subject and needs to be discussed with due regard for its emotive potential. No one likes talking about death; however, ignoring or avoiding the subject may lead to complications at a later date. Using visual materials can assist discussions, and some have been produced specifically for people with ID (Hollins *et al.*, 1994; Luchterhand & Murphy, 1998; Cooley & McGauran, 2000; Hollins *et al.*, 2002). These accessible products can be used in preparatory work, helping people to comprehend the ubiquity and naturalness of death as part of the life cycle, to understand that the deceased will be absent and missed, and to help people think about their feelings in the face of such a loss. It should be noted that metaphoric and euphemistic allusion and language without explanation are rarely effective communication tools for people with ID, often creating confusion rather than dispelling it. A good example of this is portrayed in the novel *Walter*, (Cook 1982), where confusion about death results from an unexplained euphemism.

Most families experience the death of a family member or friend. However, 'death does not signify the ending of the relationship between an individual and society' (Harrell-Bond, 1990); rather it brings about a critical time when emotional responses are contained in socially and culturally prescribed rituals of mourning, burial or cremation and the later reallocation of roles and responsibilities. Some theorists, Harrell-Bond (1990) and Eisenbruch (1991), suggest that when people are deprived of adequate opportunities for mourning, grief is likely to remain unresolved, possibly predicating complex grief or psychological dysfunction.

Furthermore, Klass *et al.*'s (1996) notion of 'continuing bonds' with the deceased is also important, but they require an acknowledgement of individuals' internal emotional worlds. People with ID may be denied the opportunity to share their feelings of loss with other family members, to witness the sadness of others and to in some way find a template to express their own grief, or a way of declaring their feelings that can be interpreted and therefore effectively understood. Sorrow at the death of a loved one is expressed variously within different families and more diversely within different social and cultural settings. Individuals who have not had the opportunity to equip themselves with a culturally appropriate language of grief, by for example being included in customary rituals and events and witnessing the way in which people commonly express their feelings, may find alternative ways to show how they feel. In some instances this is through changes in behavior or attitude, which neither they nor their carers are likely to connect to their emotional state. A comprehensive record of people's bereavement history and details of any other significant losses could usefully inform carers about the possible reasons why someone's behaviour, outlook or attitude may have changed. Appropriate connections may then be made, and suitable support can be offered.

Oswin (1991) wrote about the common pattern of people with ID being moved from one residential setting to another several times in the year following the death of a sole surviving parent. The consequential upheaval of this virtually nomadic existence, after what is likely to have been a fairly routine lifestyle, is likely to exacerbate difficulties for the bereaved individual. Such disruption though is not merely geographical. In these circumstances the bereaved person is likely to have lost access to the familiar community where they may have lived for many years, often in a close and sometimes exclusive relationship with a parent who may have been their companion, confidant, advocate and perhaps the vessel of their memories (Hollins & Sireling, 1999).

While the relationship that has been lost through the death of the parent is irreplaceable, some of the concomitant losses mentioned above could be mitigated through careful planning and recording of important details. Such 'important details' will include the kinds of things that add colour to life, that please rather than irritate and encourage opportunity instead of stasis. A comprehensive record of the past through a life-story book, memory box or family tree provides people with a record of their personal history, that may otherwise be lost or forgotten. People's preferences and established routines, if known and prioritized by carers, can provide important continuity to everyday life and can help people to reassert their identity with familiar signifiers, in the face of other major changes. It is also significant to identify, with people, their hopes and plans, and to consider ways that these can be achieved. The future is as important as the past, and with adequate systems to record the important details of people's lives, a bridge can often be built between before and after a major transitory event such as death. Although this will not take away the pain and sorrow of grief, it may hinder additional unnecessary losses.

Whose job is it?

Findings from current research suggest that the social and professional input into the lives of people with ID primarily focuses on practical rather than emotional aspects of people's lives. Neither day center nor residential staff, whose opinions have informed a current bereavement intervention study (see later in this chapter), regard it as within their remit to address issues that may affect people on an emotional plane, both regarding it as the other's responsibility. Some parents stated that as a result they had been given little help in addressing issues related to a bereavement, with their adult sons or daughters, and that they frequently found the subject too painful to confront without support.

It is vital that information is available to people with ID about the fact of death and its likely emotional impact, and that details of their life stories are effectively collected and recorded so as to help smooth the transition following a bereavement of someone close to them. Service managers need to address these issues (and other emotional aspects of people's lives), and plan appropriate service responses, as a priority within their everyday provision.

Identifying people at risk

For some individuals the prospect of loss through death is overwhelming. Given the anxiety that contemplation of the future arouses for some people, it is reasonable to assume that the reaction to an bereavement may be overwhelming. Preparation and planning for the future in the security of the present, however difficult, are a better option than waiting until circumstances have become critical.

Inclusion at bereavement

The preceding discussion has shown that people with ID are keenly aware of loss and that they do indeed grieve. It is therefore of the utmost importance that people with ID are included in every possible part of the customary, collective expression of grief. This may be (if culturally appropriate) by participating in planning and perhaps taking a role in the funeral, welcoming other mourners, having time to cry or shout in sadness, anger or upset, being comforted and later choosing mementoes and talking with others to help remember the person who has died. The notion that people will be shielded from their own feelings by failing to include them is a delusion.

A current bereavement intervention study

A current bereavement intervention study by the Department of Psychiatry of Disability, St. George's Hospital Medical School, University of London, is using quantitative and qualitative methodologies to test the usefulness, effectiveness and practicability of two different interventions for people with ID following bereavement. One intervention is based on a traditional counseling model and is delivered by trained bereavement counselors following additional bespoke training. The other is a practical adaptation of Stroebe and Schut (1999) *Dual Process Model*, developed within the Department of Psychiatry of Disability at St. George's Hospital Medical School in London and delivered by people who see the bereaved persons on a day-to-day basis.

Many of the people participating in this study fall into an older age group. They have faced many of the issues and experienced many of the difficulties outlined above and may have lived with the emotional consequences for many years. Yet they have been willing to share their experiences and are eager to address some longstanding difficulties, by becoming involved in the therapeutic opportunities available in this study.

Specialist bereavement services for people with ID are limited. However, there are many generic services that offer counseling and other types of therapy to the population as a whole, but they are often unwilling to work with people with ID, thinking that they lack appropriate skills to do so. In the course of ongoing research by the authors, it has become apparent to many of the counselors involved in the study that with a few adaptations, mainly in terms of communication techniques and time-scale, their existing counseling skills are fully appropriate for working with people with ID. This has highlighted issues for development and training in existing bereavement counseling services so as to foster and facilitate the inclusion of people with ID. It is, however, important to note that not everyone requires a specialist intervention following a bereavement, but with thought, time and care from those who regularly support the bereaved person, and consideration of some of the issues discussed above, grief may take a common course and the individual may find resolution and the passing of pain with time.

Summary

Much has changed in the lives of people with ID in the past 25 years. People can now expect to live longer and in some cases to live fuller lives. Lifestyle has altered. Many more people live in the 'community' rather than in more segregated, restrictive environments. For some, opportunities have broadened in the fields of employment and education, while barriers to the development of personal relationships are gradually lifting.

The degree to which these positive changes can be found in people's lives varies; change is influenced by a multitude of factors, though prominent among these are the attitudes and perspectives of those who are in direct contact with people with ID on a day-to-day basis. Many people continue to have limited autonomy or scope for personal development in a society fraught with inequity and prejudice.

The circumstances of an individual's day-to-day life influence the way in which they are able cope with major life events such as bereavement. As this chapter has stated, thinking about loss and grief in the lives of people with ID has altered in the past 25 years. There is now a considerable body of work, which acknowledges the presence of grief in the emotional lives of people with ID, but also highlights the potentially increased complexity of their loss. However, our ongoing research and practice indicate that there is a still a gulf between thinking and practice in many arenas in which people with ID live and work. It is still common for people to be said not to have responded to the death of a parent or other significant person, or for them to have had no chance to say 'goodbye' to a dying person, or to be excluded from attending a funeral. Older people are more likely than their younger peers to experience these kinds of disabling attitudes and practices. Wider social change has contributed to the dissipation of the taboo surrounding death and dying. It is now time that this social endorsement of the importance of mourning and of the rituals surrounding death is extended to all people with ID.

References

Atkinson, D., Johnston, M. & Walmsley, J. (1997) *Forgotten Lives; Exploring the History of Learning Disability*. BILD Publications, Kidderminster.

Cook, D. (1982) *Walter*. Penguin, Harmondsworth.

Cooley, J. & McGauran, F. (2000) *Talking Together about Death: A bereavement pack for people with learning disabilities, their families and carers*. Winslow Press Ltd, Oxon.

Dowling, S. (2000) Exiled grief: The social context of bereavement in the lives of people with intellectual disability. *Grief Matters*, **3**, 32–35.

Eisenbruch, M. (1991) From post-traumatic stress disorder to cultural bereavement diagnosis of Southeast Asian refugees. *Social Science and Medicine*, **33**, 673–680.

Giles, J. (2001) *Looking forward project*. Unpublished Wandsworth Rathbone Report.

Harper, D.C. & Wadsworth, J.S. (1993) Grief in adults with mental retardation: preliminary findings. *Research in Developmental Disabilities*, **14**, 313–330.

Harrell-Bond, B.E. (1990) Dealing with dying: some anthropological reflections on the need for assistance by refugee relief programmes for bereavement and burial. *Journal of Refugee Studies*, **3**, 228–243.

Hollins, S. & Esterhuyzen, A. (1997) Bereavement and grief in adults with intellectual disabilities. *British Journal of Psychiatry* **170**, 497–501.

Hollins. S. & Sireling, L. (1985) *The Last Taboo*. St. George's Hospital Medical School, London.

Hollins, S. & Sireling, L. (1999) *Understanding Grief: Working with People who have Learning Disabilities*. Pavilion Publishing, Brighton.

Hollins, S., Sireling, L. & Webb, B. (1994) *When Mother Died. Books Beyond Words*. Gaskell, Royal College of Psychiatrists, London.

Hollins, S., Dowling, S. & Blackman, N. (2002) *When Somebody Dies. Books Beyond Words*. Gaskell, Royal College of Psychiatrists, London.

Horne, M. (1989) Identifying hidden populations of older adults with mental handicap: outreach in the UK. *New Zealand Journal of Developmental Disabilities*, **15**, 207–218.

Hubert, J. & Hollins, S. (2000) Working with elderly carers of people with intellectual disabilities and planning for the future. *Advances in Psychiatric Treatment*, **6**, 41–48.

Klass, D. P., Silverman, R. & Nickman, S.L. (1996) *Continuing Bonds: New Understandings of Grief*. Taylor Francis, Philadelphia and London.

Kloeppel, D.A. & Hollins, S. (1989) Double handicap, mental retardation and death in the family. *Death Studies* **13**, 31–38.

Luchterhand, C. & Murphy, N. (1998) *Helping Adults with Mental Retardation Grieve a Death Loss*. Taylor and Francis, Philadelphia.

McGrath, M. & Grant, G. (1993) The life-cycle and support networks of families with a person with a learning difficulty. *Disability, Handicap and Society*, **8**, 25–42.

Oswin, M. (1985) Bereavement. *A Multi-Disciplinary Approach to Mental Handicap* (eds M. Craft, J. Bicknell & S. Hollins). Balliere Tindall, London.

Oswin, M. (1991) *Am I Allowed to Cry? A Study of Bereavement Amongst People who have Intellectual Disabilities*. Human Horizons, London.

Parkes, M. (1986) *Bereavement: Studies of Grief in Adult Life*. Penguin, Harmondsworth.

Raji, O. & Hollins, S. (2000) Exclusion from funerary rituals and mourning: implications for social and individual identity. *Madness, Disability and Social Exclusion: The Archaeology and Anthropology of Difference* (ed J. Hubert). Routledge, London.

Stroebe, M. & Schut, H. (1999) The dual-process model of coping with bereavement: rationale and description. *Death Studies*, **23**, 197–224.

Towell, D. & Beardshaw, V. (1991) *Enabling Community Integration and the Role of Public Authorities in Promoting an Ordinary Life for People with Learning Disabilities in the 1990s*. The Kings Fund, London.

13 Psychosocial Concerns Among Aging Family Carers Of Persons with ID

Philip McCallion and Stacey R. Kolomer

In most, if not all countries, family carers provide the majority of support for adults with intellectual disabilities (ID). There is an increasing likelihood that they will continue to be the primary carers of these adults as they enter their aging years. Many of the carers are themselves older adults. This chapter will position the psychosocial issues of family caring for aging adults with ID within the generic literature on old age caring and in the specific literature on caring for an adult with ID. Challenges posed by growing outreach and service provision to families from diverse cultures are discussed. A newer population of family carers, grandparents, will also be described. The potential for psychosocial concerns will be identified, information will be provided on what is known about such concerns, interventions and their effectiveness will be discussed, and recommendations for future research and practice will be presented.

Demography of caring

Until recently, large numbers of persons with ID did not live to old age, and those in later adulthood were further hidden because families, their primary carers, were able to provide lifetime care (Roberto, 1993). In recent decades the likelihood of aging persons with ID living into retirement years and outliving family carers has increased (Fujiura, 1998). It seems likely that this poses additional stresses and concerns for families.

Adults with ID are experiencing an extended old age. There are no accurate and complete counts in the US of people who are aging with ID. Estimates suggest that life expectancy for persons with ID has increased from an average 18.5 years in 1930 to 59.1 years in 1970 and an estimated 66.2 years in 1993 (Braddock, 1999). Janicki and colleagues go further and based on analyses of New York State data, they project continued growth to match life expectancy of the general population (Janicki *et al.*, 1999). Indeed, there are estimates that by 2020 the number of persons with developmental disabilities aged over 65 will have doubled (Janicki & Dalton, 2000). Other estimates suggest that in the US alone there are approximately 4.3 million persons with varying levels of intellectual and other developmental disabilities, of whom only about 10% are in formal out-of-home placements. There are approximately 2.6 million (61%) residing at home and being cared for by family members. Almost 700 000 have carers aged over 60 and an additional 900 000 are estimated to live with babyboom age carers about to cross that threshold (Fujiura, 1998; Braddock, 1999).

Many individuals with ID are, therefore, already in households where the carer is older. There is every expectation that the majority of those today being cared for by older carers will themselves be over 60 by 2020, likely to be cared for by the same but much older carer, and that those currently being cared for by carers in their forties and fifties will by 2020 still be cared for by these individuals, then in their sixties and seventies. There are aging needs for both the person with an ID and their carer, and there is the likelihood that greater demands will be placed on service systems because the person with an intellectual disability has different service needs and the carer has growing aging related limitations on her/ his ability to provide care.

Primary family carers

There is generally one primary carer in a family, usually the mother of the individual with ID. The primary carer makes most decisions regarding care of the care recipient, offers emotional support, and assists with a range of adaptive activities of daily living and critical instrumental tasks. Frequently provided types of assistance include transportation; shopping; doing household chores; coordinating assistance from social service and health care providers; routine health care such as administering and monitoring medications; personal care such as bathing, feeding, toileting, and dressing; supervision; financial management; and financial assistance (Toseland & McCallion, 1997).

The identification of a primary carer has led many service providers to focus attention solely on this family member. However, there is increasing evidence of the importance of the additional support provided by siblings (Connidis, 1997), spouses (Kleban *et al.*, 1989), and even favorite nephews and nieces (Atchley & Miller, 1986). This has also been found in the caring literature related to ID (Seltzer *et al.*, 1991; Bigby, 1997). There is also evidence that other family members are affected by caring and impact the stress experienced by the primary carer (Kleban *et al.*, 1989; Toseland *et al.*, 1995; Beach, 1997). Recognizing and responding to the effects of caring on the physical, mental and emotional health of carers are important elements to consider when studying and providing services to adults with ID.

Family caring and psychosocial distress

Even though it is often demanding and stressful, caring is frequently perceived as a rewarding experience. Rewards include greater intimacy and love, finding meaning through the experience of caring, personal growth, improved relationships, and experiencing satisfaction and appreciation of received social support from others. To the extent that caring is perceived as rewarding, it has been associated with better health among carers and reduced perceptions of burden or stress (Kramer, 1997).

There is also evidence that caring can negatively impact the health and well-being of carers. Physical problems that have been reported by carers include exhaustion and fatigue from constant attendance to the care recipient's needs. This situation is often exacerbated by carers' aging related health problems. Physical exhaustion and deteriorating carer health, in turn, often contribute to psychological problems such as depression or increased anxiety. Frustrations and misunderstandings, the long duration of disabilities combined with the lack of hope for improvement, difficult interactions with service systems and the guilt many carers feel about their own negative feelings, frequently produce additional psychological distress and restriction of beneficial carer contacts with friends and neighbors (McCallion & Toseland, 1993; Toseland *et al.*, 2001).

Service system issues

Often service systems are not well prepared to address aging concerns for persons with ID and their aging carers, adding to potential stressors. At least in the US, historically, state disability systems gave more of their attention to developing educational and vocational services for children and work-age adults with ID, and many aging adults with ID living at home have been unknown to and/or unplanned for by the services system as previous insititutionalization options alienated many families from services (McCallion & Tobin, 1995; Braddock, 1999). More recently, programs to address the growing needs of this population have been stymied by conflict over which is the responsible service system – aging or intellectual disabilities; who the primary client should be – the aging carer, the person with an intellectual disability or the family; and what are appropriate service models – maintaining the family living situation, planning for transitions to out-of-home placement, or promoting the independence of the person with an intellectual disability (McCallion & Janicki, 1997).

The further complication of frequent long-standing conflictual relationships between older carers who provide long-term care and formal
service providers is also well documented (Smith & Tobin, 1993;
McCallion & Tobin, 1995). Therefore, at the moment when older carers'
needs and stresses are such that they become willing to seek formal services, there are the potential added stressors that those services will not be
available, that carers will be referred around between agencies and that
they will be 'assisted' by staff they have never trusted.

Differences between mothers and fathers as carers

In families with a child who has a disability the role assignments of the
parents have been found to be even more traditional than in homes where
a child does not have a disability (Heller *et al.*, 1997). Most often in these
homes fathers work and earn money to support the family while mothers
stay at home to take care of the child. Several studies have also identified
that even after retirement fathers are unlikely to take on additional
responsibilities within the home (Heller *et al.*, 1997; Essex *et al.*, 1999).
Heller and colleagues (1997) found that mothers perceived themselves as
helping the child for more hours than fathers, were involved in more
organizations, worked out of the home for fewer hours than fathers, and
provided the child with more support. Only in the area of providing
financial aid did fathers score higher than mothers (Heller *et al.*, 1997).

There may be a number of psychosocial consequences associated with
these gender-based roles in caring, but research findings are contradictory. Brubaker *et al.* (1989) in a study of 337 carers of adults with ID
found that mothers identified their children's disabilities as more severe
than did the fathers. In contrast Pruchno and Hicks-Patrick (1999) found
in their study of parents caring for children with lifelong disabilities,
including intellectual disabilities and mental illness, that it was the
mothers who reported higher functioning levels than fathers. Fathers who
participated in Pruchno and Hicks-Patrick's study also reported that their
children were more non-compliant and violent in comparison to the
reports from the mothers. Fathers have also been found to experience
more pessimism than their wives about their adult children with ID
(Essex *et al.*, 1999). Conversely, other researchers have suggested that
mothers are at greater risk for dysphoria and strain (Heller *et al.*, 1997).
Finally, consistent with gender-based roles, fathers have been found to be
more likely to be concerned about who will provide financial support to
their child in the future, as well as who would manage that support (Essex
et al., 1999).

In their study of 113 families, Heller and her colleagues (1997) identified women as experiencing more subjective burden than their caring male counterparts. Women in this study scored significantly higher than men on almost every item of a burden scale, excluding financial worrying and caring causing harm to the chances of having a good marriage. Items on which women scored significantly higher than men included worrying about the future, having little time for self, feeling exhausted, limited social life, fewer vacations, and not having enough time left (Heller *et al.*, 1997). Again, in contrast, Essex and colleagues (1999) measured psychological distress among married couples caring for adults with ID and found no significant difference between spouses in depressive symptoms and subjective burden. However, fathers of sons were found to experience increasing symptoms of depression over an 18-month period in comparison to fathers of daughters. Pruchno and Hicks-Patrick (1999) also found no significant differences between mothers and fathers who provide care to an adult child with a chronic disability on either the CES-D (Center for Epidemiology Studies Depression Scale) which measures symptoms of depression or the LSIA (Life Satisfaction Index) which measures life satisfaction.

More research is clearly needed on differences in views of disability caring across the sex of carers. What does appear to be established is that regardless of sex there are many carers who do experience symptoms of depression and other strains.

Stress and coping differences among carers

Coping can be defined as the different ways in which people respond to stressful events (Essex *et al.*, 1999). Mothers have been found to use a variety of coping strategies as they provide care for their adult child with an intellectual disability. Adaptive coping strategies used by mothers of adults with ID include acceptance, positive reinterpretation and growth, turning to religion, and planning (Hayden & Heller, 1997). In a longitudinal study Essex and colleagues (1999) found that mothers were significantly more likely than fathers to use problem-focused coping strategies as a means of addressing stress with their dependent children with intellectual disabilities. Problem-focused coping includes using cognitive and behavioral problem-solving efforts as a technique of reducing stress.

The coping strategies of older carers have also been found to differ from younger carers. For example, Hayden and Heller (1997) found that older carers sought spiritual support more often than younger counterparts and the younger carers experienced more of a sense of personal burden. Seltzer and Krauss (1994) have previously posed the possibility that what we are looking at here is greater adaptation to the caring situation by older carers. Hayden and Heller (1997) suggest that we also need to look at greater expectations of younger carers of assistance from the formal service system and other family members. More research on these differences may offer insight both into the areas where family carers need assistance and the nature of the assistance needed.

Carers from diverse cultures

More developed countries with well-established formal service systems need to be concerned that the effects, perceptions and prevalence of caring may vary according to the racial or ethnic background and immigration history of the family. Recent evidence from generic caring studies in the US, for example, suggests that African American families may be more resilient to negative psychological effects of the stress of caregiving than are European heritage families (Connell & Gibson, 1997). European heritage carers generally report higher levels of adverse emotional responses such as depression and burden. In contrast, Aranda and Knight (1997) concluded that Latino/Hispanic carers experience at least similar and possibly higher levels of burden and depression than European-origin carers. One frequently offered explanation is a greater availability of support for African American and other primary carers of diverse cultures from other family members (Johnson, 1995). However, it is often difficult to separate the effects of ethnicity from socioeconomic, educational, cultural and historical differences (Connell & Gibson, 1997; Pruchno et al., 1997). Looking specifically at family carers of persons with ID, it has been found that stereotyping families by ethnicity may lead practitioners to assume a level of adjustment to caring and availability of extended family support that is not true for a caring family. This may result in practitioners not recognizing a caregiver's need for assistance because of inappropriate assumptions (McCallion & Janicki, 1997).

Some studies suggest that little is known about how carers from diverse cultures respond to specific stressors, or about whether intervention programs designed to alleviate caring stress are effective for these families (Toseland & McCallion, 1997). Therefore, greater attention to the needs of these family carers by practitioners and researchers is urgently needed. Investigations of lower usage of carer intervention programs by members of cultural minorities have found a greater reliance on filial piety, greater availability of extended family supports, distrust of formal structures, and cultural beliefs that one should take care of one's own (for a review see McCallion and Janicki, 1997). However, society's structural barriers to service use may also result in needy caring families from these cultural groups receiving the least amount of services. Barriers include the experience of historical discrimination, legal status concerns for some, and alienation from services which have been developed for rather than by the families to be served (Lockery, 1991; Johnson, 1995). In addition, there are economic, religious, transportation, financial and insurance barriers, and carers from cultural minority groups report not feeling welcomed by other participants, feeling like outsiders in the locations chosen for the intervention, and interventions not meeting their needs (Henderson *et al.*, 1993, McCallion & Janicki, 1997).

Practitioners can respond by first understanding the preliminary norms and attitude of the cultural group and then developing and implementing culturally sensitive interventions. For example, strategies that have been found to be successful include involving locally-based multicultural service agencies in outreach and service delivery, and having participants from the cultural groups choose the intervention leader, the location of the intervention, the timing of the sessions, and the range of issues to be addressed (Henderson & Gutierrez-Maya, 1992; Henderson *et al.*, 1993; McCallion & Janicki, 1997; McCallion & Grant-Griffin, 2000; McCallion *et al.*, 2000).

Grandparent carers

It has been estimated that one in ten grandparents will take on the role of primary carer to a grandchild for at least six months before the child is age 18 (Silverstein & Vehvilainen, 1998) including children with a developmental delay or disability. Almost 6% of all children in the US are living in grandparent headed-households and in one-third of these homes the children's parents are not present (Fuller-Thomson *et al.*, 1997; Silverstein & Vehvilainen, 1998; Emick & Hayslip, 1999; Fuller-Thomson & Minkler, 2000). It is only recently that attention has been drawn to the growing population of grandparent carers. It has been suggested that the number of grandparent headed-households is greatly underestimated and these families genuinely fall in the chasms between service agencies resulting, for example, in denials of services to which the needs of their grandchild with a developmental disability entitle them (Szinovacz, 1998; Kolomer, 2000; McCallion *et al.*, 2000).

Reviewing studies of children known to the foster care system, Kolomer *et al.* (2002) found that compared to their peers, children cared for by their grandparents often have a higher incidence of health problems, more frequent difficulties in school and more serious emotional challenges. These children have also been found to have higher occurrences of visual and hearing problems, asthma, arrested growth, obesity, anemia, developmental disabilities, psychosomatic complaints and dental problems. Also, given that the most frequent reasons for placement of a child with a grandparent are substance abuse and child abuse and neglect, it should not be surprising that children are likely to have emotional difficulties and disabilities. What is of concern is that many conditions or disabilities are not recognized and are not appropriately addressed. Grandparents caring for a child with a disability report receiving less social support, and they experience higher levels of role strain and financial strain, and more life disruption than either custodial grandparents raising children without problems or traditional grandparents (Emick & Hayslip, 1999; McCallion *et al.*, 2000). They are particularly at risk for symptoms of depression and alienation (Minkler *et al.*, 1997; McCallion & Grant-Griffin, 2000).

Interventions

The generic literature provides considerable information on interventions to address the psychosocial concerns of carers and their relative effectiveness (for an extensive review see Toseland *et al.*, 2001). There are also a number of specific interventions related to helping people with ID.

Respite

There are two broad types of respite programs: temporary inpatient placement in residential facilities, nursing homes, or hospitals; and in-home respite using paid aides. Respite is frequently cited as one of the programs most desired by family carers and most likely to reduce stress and promote continued maintenance of the caring situation (Heller, 2002). Time off from the unrelenting demands of caring is believed to be directly therapeutic for the carer, and indirectly therapeutic for the care recipient (Lawton *et al.*, 1989). However, a rigorous review of the generic family caring literature by Flint (1995) concluded that there were only five high quality studies, and these studies indicated little evidence that respite care had a significant effect on carers' functioning, psychiatric status or physical health, or on care recipients' functioning and rate of institutionalization. More research is needed and the importance of respite for family carers of persons with ID needs to be specifically targeted for investigation.

Cash subsidies

Innovative approaches to supporting family carers are voucher or cash subsidy programs (Simon-Rusinowitz *et al.*, 2001). The premise is that families know best what it takes to maintain an adult (or child) with a disability in the family home. These programs also recognize that informal networks of relatives, neighbors and friends are the most available and most cost effective support resource. The programs allow families to pay informal helpers for support services. Families receive cash subsidies to spend for supports as they choose or within certain parameters. In 2000, 19 states in the US had cash subsidy programs for families (Heller, 2002). Heller *et al.* (1997) conducted one of the few studies of a state-wide family support program for adults with ID. Compared with families not receiving these services, participating families reported greater caring satisfaction, feelings of competence and self-efficacy in helping the adult with an intellectual disability. There was also evidence of more community integration and improved interpersonal relations for the adult with an intellectual disability, fewer unmet service needs, more satisfaction with services received, less need for out-of-home placement and more legal and financial planning. However, there are policy concerns about the appropriateness of cash subsidy programs for family carers; their reach even in the 19 states where they are available is not to all families who might benefit (for a review, see Yamada, 2001).

Support groups

Support groups are a primary intervention method for generic family carers. Most support groups mix education, discussion and social activities in a warm, empathic atmosphere that emphasizes mutual sharing and mutual help. Others are more psycho-educationally oriented, focusing on the acquisition of specific problem-solving and coping skills (McCallion et al, 1994a,b; McCallion & Toseland, 1996). Groups may be short-term or long-term and may have closed or open membership policies. Support groups can prevent and alleviate stress in many ways:

(1) Providing carers with a respite
(2) Reducing isolation and loneliness
(3) Encouraging ventilation of pent-up emotions and the sharing of feelings and experiences
(4) Validating, universalizing and normalizing each carer's experiences
(5) Instilling hope and affirming the importance of the carer's role

(6) Educating carers about the aging process, the effects of chronic disabilities, and community resources
(7) Teaching effective problem-solving and coping strategies
(8) Helping carers to identify, develop and implement effective action plans to resolve pressing problems related to caring

(Toseland *et al.*, 2001)

Clinical literature suggests that family carers find participation in support groups highly beneficial and satisfying (Toseland & Rossiter, 1989). Studies utilizing larger sample sizes and more rigorous research designs are more equivocal but they support beliefs that the groups improve carers' mental and physical well-being, increase their knowledge of community resources and the size of their informal support networks, and alleviate pressing problems associated with caring (for reviews see Bourgeois *et al.*, 1996; McCallion & Toseland, 1996; Toseland & McCallion, 1997).

A randomized trial of a psycho-educational support group for grandparents was shown to significantly reduce symptoms of depression among treatment subjects and to increase their senses of caring mastery and empowerment. The combining of the support group intervention with six months of intensive case management appeared to increase efficacy in addressing symptoms of depression (McCallion *et al.*, 2000). More research on the value of support groups for all carers of persons with ID, not just grandparents, may expand the range of effective services to address the psychosocial needs of carers.

Individual interventions

There is less information available about individual and family-oriented counseling interventions to address caring stress, and the little available focuses on the generic family carer population. Gallagher and her colleagues (Gallagher & Czirr, 1984; Gallagher *et al.*, 1989) found that individual therapy reduced depression among carers and helped them cope with anticipatory grief over the impending loss of a frail elderly care recipient. Toseland and Smith (1990) found that short-term individual counseling was effective in decreasing symptoms of psychological distress and in increasing feelings of competence and well-being. Mittelman and colleagues developed an intervention program for carers of persons with Alzheimer's dementia that used a combination of individual, group and family intervention strategies; it was very effective in increasing the psychosocial well-being of carers as well as delaying the institutionalization of care recipients (Mittelman *et al.*, 1993, 1995, 1996). Similar sys-

tematic consideration of such programs for carers of adults with intellectual disabilities is needed.

Family interventions

There is little doubt that caring is associated with increased family conflict
and with heightened concerns and anxieties about neglecting other family
members (see, for example, Horowitz, 1985; McCallion & Toseland, 1993).
Yet there are few reports of interventions. In a review article Zarit & Teri
(1991) suggested that the lack of attention to family interventions may be
because of their cost and the limited availability of third-party reimbursement. Others, however, have suggested that the paucity of these
interventions may reflect practitioners' discomfort with family strife
(Couper & Sheehan, 1987), or primary carer reluctance to ask other family
members to become involved in family counseling because of long-
standing family conflicts, and fears that key family members' feelings will
be hurt (Toseland *et al.*, 1995).

Most of the reports of family counseling for carers are based on accumulated clinical practice experience, case examples, studies without
randomized control groups, or multi-modal intervention programs that
included family counseling along with other types of interventions. When
family members are willing to participate, family therapy can be effective
in improving communication and reducing interpersonal conflict, for
developing care plans, and for resolving specific problems (see, for
example, Herr & Weakland, 1979; Carter & McGoldrick, 1980; Lowy, 1985;
Ferris *et al.*, 1987; Quayhagen & Quayhagen, 1994).

Education

Specialized education and training programs have been developed for
family carers. In the intellectual disabilities field these are a frequently chosen option to address future planning issues. Some programs are one-session community forums sponsored by religious,
civic and governmental agencies where service providers describe the
available community programs and services, and carers are encouraged to ask questions and to find out how to apply for service. These
programs reach out to carers who might not otherwise learn about
the programs and services available to help them in caring. Other educational programs provide weekly or monthly seminars that focus on
different topics such as guardianship, residential options and financial planning.

Permanency/futures planning

Heller (2002) has summarized information on the principal research-based approaches to planning. These efforts are pre-emptive and are designed to relieve stress by engaging family carers in constructive planning for themselves and their adult offspring with ID. Such planning can help provide more control for the family and thus relieve pressures that otherwise could result in psychopathologies, abuse and a family disintegration. One such effort, the Family Futures Planning Project in Rhode Island (Clark & Susa, 2001) offered a 10-session curriculum addressing housing options, estate planning, home and community-based services and carers' emotional, physical and recreational health (Clark & Susa, 2001). A paid facilitator assisted families with developing a plan and building a support network. A unique feature of this approach was that the focus was on family and not just the individual's needs.

The Planned Lifetime Advocacy Network (PLAN) in Vancouver, Canada, is a family operated non-profit organization. The number of families reached is limited to those who can afford the membership fee. A six-step approach guided the development of a personal future plan: clarifying the family's vision, building relationships, controlling the home environment, preparing for decision making, developing wills and estate planning, and securing a plan. The PLAN program provides many levels of support and services including workshops, technical assistance, mentor families and paid facilitators.

The Family-to-Family Project in Massachusetts was a response to the waiting lists for residential services in that state. Eight Family-to-Family Support Centers were developed across the state. The centers offered presentations on special needs trusts and wills, home ownership and consumer-controlled housing, circles of support, and presentations; a resource manual with information concerning funding sources, housing options and legal issues (translated into several different languages); and outreach to unserved families.

The Family Future Planning Project is an ongoing project using paid facilitators and mentor families to provide information on available supports to both the family carers and the person with a disability so that they can make informed choices. Families are encouraged to think about their plans for the future of their relative with a disability and to get involved in advocacy activities that can lead to systems change; also, to develop long-term financial plans for their relative with a disability and facilitate more involvement by the person with an intellectual disability in self-advocacy groups (Heller, 2002).

Like most specific programs, all of these projects are dependent on funding for continuation. They must balance requiring family payments, as does PLAN, which may restrict which families participate, with the absence of ongoing public funding for such activities. This is an area where continued advocacy is needed to ensure available resources, where localities with waiting lists for services may be targeted to fund this interim step (as happened in Massachusetts), and where cases need to be made that funding of planning assistance is an appropriate use of family subsidy monies provided by governments.

Summary

Families have been the backbone of care for persons with ID and yet have rarely received the respect of being recognized for this by society. Not acknowledging their role also permits a lack of awareness of the stresses involved, the psychosocial consequences of these stresses and the need for supportive services. The increased longevity of persons with intellectual disabilities and their growing numbers are putting additional pressures on these family carers, and it is at least unclear if siblings and other family members are willing or able to assume this responsibility when parents are no longer able. This is all occurring at a time when resources for out-of-home living situations and other support services are stagnant, if not declining. In the short term this will mean increasing stresses and psychosocial concerns for family carers. In the longer term, these stresses and psychosocial concerns will become an individual, family, service system and societal crisis for more developed countries, and will magnify the inadequacy of care present in many less developed countries. Now is the time to target these families for support in ways that are respectful of their histories and cultures of care.

References

Aranda, M.P. & Knight, B.L. (1997) The influence of ethnicity and culture on the caregiving stress and coping process. *The Gerontologist*, **37**, 342–354.

Atchley, R. & Miller, S. (1986) Older people and their families. *Annual Review of Gerontology and Geriatrics* (ed. C. Eisdorfer) pp. 337–369. Springer, New York.

Beach, D. (1997) Family caregiving: The positive impact on adolescent relationships. *The Gerontologist*, **37**, 233–238.

Bigby, C. (1997) Parental substitutes? The role of siblings in the lives of older people with intellectual disability. *Journal of Gerontological Social Work*, **29**, 3–21.

Bourgeois, M., Schulz, R. & Burgio, L. (1996) Interventions for caregivers of patients with Alzheimer's disease: A review and analysis of content, process, and outcomes. *International Journal of Aging-Human Behavior*, **43**, 35–92.

Braddock, D. (1999) Aging and developmental disabilities: demographic and policy issues affecting American families. *Mental Retardation*, **37**, 155–161.

Brubaker, T.H., Engelhardt, J.L., Brubaker, E. & Lutzer, V.D. (1989) Gender differences of older caregivers of adults with mental retardation. *The Journal of Applied Gerontology*, **8**, 183–191.

Carter, E. & McGoldrick, H. (1980) *The Family Life Cycle*. Gardner, New York.

Clark, P.G. & Susa, C.B. (2001) Promoting personal, familial, and organizational change through futures planning. *Community Supports for Aging Adults with Lifelong Disabilities* (eds M.P. Janicki & A.F. Ansello) pp. 229–242. Paul H. Brookes, Baltimore, MD.

Connell, C.M. & Gibson, G.D. (1997) Racial, ethnic and cultural differences in dementia caregiving: Review and analysis. *The Gerontologist*, **37**, 355–364.

Connidis, I. (1997) Sibling support in older age. *Journals of Gerontology*, **49**, S309–317.

Couper, D. & Sheehan, N. (1987) Family dynamics for caregivers: An educational model. *Family Relations*, **36**, 181–186.

Emick, M.A. & Hayslip, B. (1999) Custodial grandparenting: stresses, coping skills, and relationships with grandchildren. *International Journal of Aging and Human Development*, **48**, 35–61.

Essex, E.L., Seltzer, M.M. & Krauss, M.W. (1999) Differences in coping effectiveness and well-being among aging mothers and fathers of adults with mental retardation. *American Journal on Mental Retardation*, **104**, 545–563.

Ferris, S., Steinberg, G., Shulman, E., Kahn, R. & Reiserg, B. (1987) Institutionalization of Alzheimer's disease patients: Reducing precipitating factors through family counseling. *Home Health Care Services Quarterly*, **8**, 23–51.

Flint, A. (1995) Effects of respite care on patients with dementia and their caregivers. *International Psychogeriatrics*, **7**, 505–517.

Fujiura, G.T. (1998) Demography of family households. *American Journal of Mental Retardation*, **103**, 225–235.

Fuller-Thomson, E., Minkler, M. & Driver, D. (1997) A profile of grandparents raising grandchildren in the US. *Gerontologist*, **37**, 406–411.

Fuller-Thomson, E. & Minkler, M. (2000) America's grandparents: Who are they? *Grandparents Raising Grandchildren: Theoretical, Empirical, and Clinical Perspectives* (eds B. Hayslip & R. Goldberg-Glen) pp. 3–22. Springer Publishing, New York.

Gallagher, D. & Czirr, R. (1984) *Clinical observations on the effectiveness of different psychotherapeutic approaches in the treatment of depressed caregivers*. Paper presented at the Annual Meeting of the Gerontological Society of America, San Antonio, Texas.

Gallagher, D., Lovitt, S. & Zeiss, A. (1989) Interventions with caregivers of frail elderly persons. *Aging and Health Care: Social Science and Policy Perspections* (eds M. Ory & K. Bond) pp. 167–190. Routledge, London.

Hayden, M.F. & Heller, T. (1997) Support, problem-solving/coping ability, and personal burden of younger and older caregivers of adults with mental retardation. *Mental Retardation*, **35**, 364–372.

Heller, T. (March 2002) *Assisting older family caregivers of adults with an intellectual disability*. Paper presented at the IASSID 12th International Roundtable on Aging and Developmental Disabilities, Koriyama City, Japan.

Heller, T., Hsieh, K. & Rowitz, L. (1997) Maternal and paternal caregiving of persons with mental retardation across the lifespan. *Family Relations*, **46**, 407–415.

Henderson, J. & Gutierrez-Maya, M. (1992) Ethnocultural themes in caregiving to Alzheimer's disease patients in Hispanic families. *Clinical Gerontologist*, **11**, 59–74.

Henderson, J., Gutierrez-Maya, M., Garcia, J. & Boyd, S.(1993) A model for Alzheimer's disease support group development in African-American and Hispanic populations. *Gerontologist*, **33**, 409–414.

Herr, J. & Weakland, J. (1979) *Counseling Elders and their Families*. Springer, New York.

Horowitz, A. (1985) Family caregiving to the frail elderly. *Annual Review of Gerontology and Geriatrics* (eds C. Eisdorfer, M.P. Lawton & G.L. Maddox) Vol. 5, pp. 194–246. Springer, New York.

Janicki, M.P. & Dalton, A.J. (2000) Prevalence of dementia and impact on intellectual disability services. *Mental Retardation*, **38**, 277–289.

Janicki, M.P., Dalton, A.J., Henderson, C.M. & Davidson, P.W. (1999). Mortality and morbidity among older adults with intellectual disability: Health services considerations. *Disability and Rehabilitation*, **21**, 284–294.

Johnson, T. (1995) Utilizing culture in work with aging families. *Strengthening Aging Families: Diversity in Practice and Policy* (eds G. Smith, S. Tobin, E. Robertson-Tchabo & P. Power) pp. 175–201. Sage, Newbury Park, CA.

Kleban, M., Brody, E., Schoonover, C. & Hoffman, C. (1989) Family help to the elderly: Perceptions of sons-in-law regarding patient care. *Journal of Marriage and the Family*, **51**, 303–312.

Kolomer, S.R. (2000) Kinship foster care and its impact on grandmother caregivers. *Journal of Gerontological Social Work*, **33**, 85–102.

Kolomer, S.R., McCallion, P. & Janicki, M.P. (2002) African-American grandmother carers of children with disabilities: Predictors of depressive symptoms. *Journal of Gerontological Social Work*, **37** (3/4), 45–63.

Kramer, B. (1997) Gain in the caregiving experience: Where are we? What next? *Gerontologist*, **37**, 218–232.

Lawton, M., Brody, E. & Saperstein, A. (1989) A controlled study of respite service for caregivers of Alzheimer's patients. *Gerontologist*, **29**, 8–16.

Lockery, S. (1991) Family and social supports: Caregiving among racial and ethnic minority elders. *Generations*, **15**, 58–62.

Lowy, L. (1985) *Social Work with the Aging: The challenge and promise of the later years* 2nd edn. Longman, New York.

McCallion, P. & Grant-Griffin, L. (2000) Redesigning services to meet the needs of multi-cultural families. *Community Supports for Older Adults with Lifelong Disabilities* (eds M.P. Janicki & E. Ansello), pp. 97–108. Paul H. Brookes, Baltimore, MD.

McCallion, P. & Janicki, M.P. (1997) Area agencies on aging: Meeting the needs of persons with developmental disabilities and their aging caregivers. *Journal of Applied Gerontology*, **16**, 270–284.

McCallion, P. & Tobin, S. (1995) Social worker orientations to permanency planning by older parents caring at home for sons and daughters with developmental disabilities. *Mental Retardation*, **33**, 153–162.

McCallion, P. & Toseland, R.W. (1993) An empowered model for social work services to families of adolescents and adults with developmental disabilities. *Families in Society*, **74**, 579–589.

McCallion, P. & Toseland, R.W. (1996) Supportive group interventions with caregivers of frail older adults. *Social Work with Groups*, **18**, 11–25.

McCallion, P., Diehl, M. & Toseland, R. (1994a) Support group intervention for family caregivers of Alzheimers Disease patients. *Seminars in Speech and Language*, **15**, 657–670.

McCallion, P., Toseland, R. & Diehl, M. (1994b) Social work practice with caregivers of frail older adults. *Social Work Practice Research*, **4**, 64–88.

McCallion, P., Janicki, M.P., Grant-Griffin, L. & Kolomer, S.R. (2000) Grandparent caregivers II: Service needs and service provision issues. *Journal of Gerontological Social Work*, **33**, 57–84.

Minkler, M., Fuller-Thomson, E., Miller, D. & Driver, D. (1997) Depression in grandparents raising grandchildren: results of a national longitudinal study. *Archives of Family Medicine*, **6**, 445–452.

Mittelman, M., Ferris, S., Steinberg, G., Shulman, E., Mackell, J., Ambinder, A. & Cohen, J. (1993) An intervention that delays institutionalization of Alzheimer's disease patients: Treatment of spouse caregivers. *Gerontologist*, **33**, 730–740.

Mittelman, M., Ferris, S., Shulman, E., Steinberg, G., Ambinder, A., Mackell, J. & Cohen, J. (1995) A comprehensive support program: Effect on depression in spouse-caregivers of AD patients. *Gerontologist*, **35**, 792–802.

Mittelman, M., Ferris, S., Shulman, E., Steinberg, G. & Levin, B. (1996) A family intervention to delay nursing home placement of patients with Alzheimer's disease. *Journal of the American Medical Association*, **276**, 1725–1731.

Pruchno, R. & Hicks-Patrick, J. (1999) Mothers and fathers of adults with chronic disabilities. *Research on Aging*, **21**, 682–713.

Pruchno, R., Hicks-Patrick, J. & Burant, C. (1997) African-American and white mothers of adults with chronic disabilities: Caregiving burden and satisfaction. *Family Relations*, **46**, 335–346.

Roberto, K.A. (ed.) (1993) *The Elderly Caregiver: Caring for Adults with Developmental Disabilities*. Sage, Newbury Park, CA.

Quayhagen, M. & Quayhagen, M. (1994) Differential effects of family-based strategies on Alzheimer's disease. *Gerontologist*, **29**, 150–155.

Seltzer, M.M. & Krauss, M.W. (1994) Aging parents with coresident adult children: The impact of lifelong caregiving. *Lifecourse Perspectives on Adulthood and Old Age* (eds M.M. Seltzer, M.W. Krauss & M.P. Janicki) pp. 3–18. American Association on Mental Retardation, Washington, DC.

Seltzer, G., Begun, A., Seltzer, M.M. & Krauss, M.W. (1991) The impact of siblings on adults with mental retardation and their aging mothers. *Family Relations*, **40**, 310–317.

Silverstein, N.M. & Vehvilainen, L. (1998) *Raising Awareness about Grandparents*

Raising Grandchildren in Massachusetts. Gerontology Institute, University of Massachusetts-Boston.

Simon-Rusinowitz, L., Mahoney, K.J., Shoop, D.M., Desmond, S.M., Squillace, M.R. & Sowers, J.A. (2001) Cash and counseling as a model to structure and finance community supports. *Community Supports for Aging Adults with Lifelong Disabilities* (eds M.P. Janicki & A.F. Ansello) pp. 229–242. Paul H. Brookes, Baltimore, MD.

Smith, G.C. & Tobin, S.S. (1993) Casemanagers perceptions of practice with older parents of adults with lifelong disabilities. *The Elderly Caregiver: Caring for Adults with Developmental Disabilities* (ed. K.A. Roberto). Sage, Newbury Park, CA.

Szinovacz, M.E. (1998) Grandparents today: a demographic profile. *Gerontologist*, **38**, 37–52.

Toseland, R. & McCallion, P. (1997) Trends in caregiving intervention research. *Social Work Research*, **21**, 154–164.

Toseland, R. & Rossiter, C. (1989) Group intervention to support caregivers: A review and analysis. *Gerontologist*, **29**, 438–448.

Toseland, R. & Smith, G. (1990) The effectiveness of individual counseling for family caregivers of the elderly. *Psychology and Aging*, **5**, 256–263.

Toseland, R., Smith, G. & McCallion, P. (1995) Supporting the family in elder care. *Strengthening Aging Families: Diversity in practice and policy* (eds G. Smith, S. Tobin, B.A. Robertson-Tchabo & P. Power) pp. 3–24. Sage, Newbury Park, CA.

Toseland, R., Smith, G. & McCallion, P. (2001) Family caregivers of the frail elderly. *Handbook of Social Work Practice with Vulnerable and Resilient Populations* (ed. A. Gitterman) pp. 548–582. Columbia University Press, NY.

Yamada, Y. (2001) Consumer direction in community-based long-term care: Implications for different stakeholders. *Journal of Gerontological Social Work*, **35**, 83–98.

Zarit, S. & Teri, L. (1991) Interventions and services for family caregivers. *Annual Review of Gerontology and Geriatrics* (ed. K.W. Schaie) Vol. II, pp. 241–265. Springer, New York.

**Part 3
Service System Issues**

14 Community Mental Health and Support Services

Nick Bouras and Geraldine Holt

The mental health needs of people with intellectual disabilities (ID) have received increasing recognition since the early 1980s. There is now also a consensus view of the need to respond more adequately to them. A number of countries have developed clinical services and specialist training and devoted significant resources to research in this field. As the ID population ages, we already know that we must create options for serving their mental health needs. Data suggest that the mental health needs of older persons with ID may be quite similar to those of younger adults; thus it may be possible to adapt existing models for community-based mental health services initially designed for younger adults with ID. This chapter presents the current position of community-based services for adults of all ages with ID and mental health needs.

Policy and planning

In many countries the main focus of policy since the 1960s has been the drastic reduction of institutional care for people with ID and the rapid development of alternative community services. The speed of implementation of these new service developments has been varied and uneven in different parts of the world, and even within the same country. Jacobson (1998) critically reviewed policy initiatives for people with ID internationally. In some countries de-institutionalization programs have been well advanced (e.g. USA, UK and Scandinavia); in other places they have lacked impetus and services are still behind (Hatton *et al.*, 1995). In the UK the number of adults with ID in long-stay institutions dropped from 55 000 in 1980 to 12 000 in 1999 and is planned to further decrease through the 2000s; in Scotland the plan is for the closure of all institutions by 2005.

Achievements of community care include a wide range of residential settings, and models of respite care, daytime activities, employment opportunities and mainstream education. A variety of positive outcomes for adults from the closure of institutions have been demonstrated (Allen, 1989; Felce, 1994; Haney, 1998), although there are considerable differences in observed results (Emerson & Hatton, 1995). The presence of psychiatric disorders is an important factor affecting adaptation to living in the community, limiting quality of life (Reiss, 1994) and increasing the risk of institutional admission (Emerson, 1995).

Kon and Bouras (1997) followed up 74 people aged 24 to 65 from a long-stay institution, one and five years after their resettlement. They found that the frequency of psychiatric diagnosis and behavioral problems remained fairly consistent over the five-year period, but there was a marked increase in their utilization of local health and mental health services.

However, research of people with ID resettled into community establishments provides evidence that without very careful planning it is possible for the environment to deteriorate, for the residents to become understimulated and withdrawn and for psychiatric and behavioral problems to become more overt. Linaker and Nottestead (1998) reported that 109 individuals in Norway who were resettled in the community showed an increase in their physical and psychiatric/behavioral problems over a 12 year follow-up (1987–1995). As persons with ID and concomitant mental health issues grow older, maintaining the stability of their environments may be complicated by a variety of factors, including their own age-related health and functional decline, loss of family supports, and inadequacy of generic community services to address aging issues.

Holt and associates (2000) reported the current state of mental health services for people with ID in five European countries (Austria, Greece, England, Ireland and Spain). Overall, the needs of this client group had not been specifically addressed at a national level, with the exception of England and Ireland where even so there were gaps in services. In each of the five countries there had been adoption of the principle of normalization, with a move towards de-institutionalization, integration, inclusion and empowerment. Families and self-advocacy groups had grown steadily. The pace of this change varied between and even within countries. The main findings included: unclear policies, trends for legislation changes, increased prevalence of mental health problems, inadequate generic mental health service provision, need for specialist mental health services, need for improved interconnections of services, and need for training developments. Policy and legislation in the five European countries under consideration tended to separate the disability aspects of people with ID from their mental health needs. Consequently, the service needs of this group remained largely invisible. The effect on the lives of people with ID, their families and carers had been detrimental. Several gaps were described, particularly in relation to generic mental health service provision, which was unable to respond to service demands for people with ID and mental health needs. In many cases service provision to this group was *ad hoc* and dependent on the goodwill and the personal commitment of the professionals and volunteers involved. The availability of specialist training varied from country to country and not surprisingly bore a close relationship to the level of specialist service development (Day, 1999). Our experience suggests that these issues may grow into highly significant barriers to successful aging in place.

Where interagency working is required it is essential that there are agreed protocols as to which service is responsible for what. This is often not the case, and for those people whose needs are changing – notably at times of transition such as from child to adult, from living with family to living in a different setting, to becoming less active and frailer – people with ID are particularly liable to fall between services. A new National Service Framework for Older People (DoH, 2001) published in England identifies the needs of older people with ID as being similar to other older people, but also recognizes their specific vulnerabilities (e.g. dementia in people with Down syndrome). While taking an antidiscriminatory stance it emphasizes the need for integrated planning and delivery of services around the particular needs of an individual. If this is to be realized, agreed protocols between local services are vital. Hogg and Lambe (1998) in a review of the literature report that services for people with ID are unprepared for the changing needs of people as they get older, and that they are largely segregated from generic services. Meanwhile it is difficult for people with ID to access generic services for older people. There is generally poor provision for older people with mental health needs (Barron & O'Hara, 2000). The essential element is that the individual is able to access the services that he/she needs, even when this means collaboration between different service elements, as has been described in projects in the US by Janicki *et al.* (1995).

There is a lack of good quality information about aging and mental health status at a clinical and an epidemiological level. At present, adequate standardized diagnostic criteria to identify mental health problems are not established, and information regarding the relative efficacy of various interventions is not available. This hinders service planning and policy formulation.

Service models

The move from long-stay institutions to community-based provision signaled the development of specialized services for adults with ID. Historically, institutions used to provide a base for all services for people with ID, including mental health services.

As institutional beds were closed, people with ID were moved to less restrictive environments, or remained longer with their families. There was an assumption that the mental health problems shown by people with ID were exaggerated as a consequence of institutional lifestyles, and that they would substantially diminish when large-scale community care programs had been put in place. A significant number of people with ID, despite progress in the care delivery systems, have however continued to pose major difficulties in their management. Recent data also suggest that these problems cannot be expected to diminish with age (Davidson *et al.*, in press; Janicki *et al.*, 2002).

The progress in standardized assessment methods revealed that psychiatric disorders were frequently underdiagnosed in this population, and that in some cases aggressive behavior was associated with a mental illness. This has implications for services.

With the progress of resettlement programs, the term 'challenging behavior' replaced 'behavior problems'. It originated as a service concept to identify people with ID and an additional behavioral disorder, and allocate service resources accordingly (Emerson, 1995). It also attempted ideologically to shift the emphasis of the problem away from the individual and on to the service. Unfortunately, it is now often used as a clinical diagnosis, and worse still, it is sometimes used to absolve service providers of responsibility for the management of such an individual.

Davidson *et al.* (1999) outlined the development and delivery of care of several models of community-based services for people with ID and mental health challenges in the English-speaking world (nine in the US, one in Canada, one in Australia and one in the UK). These models offered a variety of services, including crisis intervention, to people with ID and mental health needs or challenging behavior problems. Most of the models described had both conceptual and operational problems between mental health and ID service systems. Interagency communication was not well established and access to services across systems was limited. The need for consensus among providers, consumers and purchasers in establishing a comprehensive service network for those adults with ID with these needs, was emphasized. Bringing everyone together to sanction the need for and the characteristics of the service program can facilitate this before it is established.

The main issues relating to services for people with ID and mental health challenges since the implementation of community care programs can be seen under the following headings:

- Distinguishing between challenging behaviors and mental health problems/psychiatric disorders
- Developing a continuum of generic and specialist mental health services

- Provision of adequate assessment and treatment
- Provision of essential supports and services for people with ID and challenging behaviors or mental illness and their carers.

Distinguishing between challenging behaviors and mental health problems or psychiatric disorders

Challenging behaviors are the most common reason for which people with ID are referred for psychiatric assessment (Day, 1985; Jacobson, 1998). Having a formal diagnosis of a psychiatric disorder, rather than a non-specific description of a behavior disorder, is important because it may lead to a specific treatment modality and funding for care. It may also be of prognostic significance and it is important for planning services and for research purposes.

There has been, however, considerable uncertainty regarding the relationship between challenging behaviors and psychiatric disorders. This uncertainty arises partly because of the lack of clarity surrounding the definition of behaviors and symptoms, and the lack of relevant research. Understanding the possible links between challenging behaviors and psychiatric disorders is important, from a theoretical and a clinical perspective, as greater understanding may lead to the subsequent development of more effective treatment methods (Emerson *et al.*, 1999).

Regarding the nature of possible links between challenging behavior and psychiatric conditions, there is some evidence that psychiatric disorders may in some cases underlie or exacerbate problematic behavior. Thus, for example, evidence suggests that some forms of self-injurious behavior may be associated with obsessive-compulsive disorder (King, 1993; Borthwick-Duffy, 1994) and that fluctuations in mood state associated with affective disorders may provide the motivational basis for some self-injury (Sovner *et al.*, 1993). A number of studies have also suggested that challenging behaviors may sometimes be symptoms of affective disorders (Jawed *et al.*, 1993; Reiss & Rojahn, 1993; Meins, 1995; Emerson *et al.*, 1999; Moss *et al.*, 2000).

Age-related changes in health status occur in persons with ID just as they do in individuals without ID (Evenhuis, 1999). There is evidence that compromised health status may affect behavior and psychiatric status in older persons with ID (Davidson *et al.*, in press). Therefore, vigilance and timely assessment of functional decline in later age will be an essential element of a community network of services. Few such options are now available for older persons with ID.

In the UK, specialist outreach services for people with challenging behaviors have been developed to provide assessment and treatment. It is estimated that in 1995 about £10 million per annum was spent in the UK on community-based assessment and treatment of people with ID and challenging behavior (Emerson *et al.*, 1996). There is, however, little information available on the outcomes associated with such services (Lowe *et al.*, 1996). Bouras and Holt (2001a) have reviewed specialist challenging behavior services in the context of community-based mental health services; the results are reported below.

Developing a continuum of generic and specialist mental health services

In line with the principle of normalization, some planners have proposed that psychiatric problems in people with ID could be adequately catered for within mainstream mental health services. However, services are needed from both the ID network and the mental health system, for when community-based programs to provide comprehensive services are not available, problems become apparent (Bouras & Holt, 1997). Services should be provided according to need rather than being dependent on a primary diagnosis of ID or mental health problems, and should be delivered in the context of two or more coexisting disabilities, allowing for more appropriate treatment and support (Reiss, 1994; Russell, 1997).

Various parts of the UK have developed differing service models depending on their local situation (Gravestock & Bouras, 1997; Bailey & Cooper, 1998). Some services center around residential, usually hospital, provision (perhaps with outreach work) while others are more community-based, sometimes with access to inpatient facilities (Bouras & Holt, 2000).

In the US and other countries, where there is an overall lack of specialist mental health services for people with ID, there are considerable adverse consequences (Jacobson, 1998; Davidson *et al.*, 1999). Additionally, there appears to be a need for specialized geriatric assessment for persons with ID. Such services are designed to sort out causes of functional decline, including dementia (Henderson & Davidson, 2001) and may be an essential element in the process of diagnosing and treating mental illness in this population. There are very few models for this type of diagnostic service. The prevailing view is that people with ID with mental health needs have often been underserved or inappropriately treated because of interorganizational barriers, leading to unnecessary hospitalization and lengthy delays in returning to their community housing.

Provision of adequate assessment and treatment

Admissions for assessment and treatment of psychiatric disorders still remain a serious problem for both ID and generic mental health services. Only 70% of health services in the UK who provide ID services offer specialist admission beds (Bailey & Cooper, 1998). Boundary disputes between general adult and ID services frequently lead to a reduced quality of care for people with complex needs (Chaplin & Flynn, 2000).

Of 424 consecutive new referrals to the Community Specialist Mental Health Service in south-east London, admission was required for 47 persons (11%) to generic psychiatric wards of the local adult mental health services (Bouras & Holt, 2001a). The people who were admitted were older (mean age = 36.8 years, SD = 14.1) than those treated in the community (mean age = 32.6 years, SD = 13.5) and most (86%) had mild ID. Of those admitted, 87.3% fulfilled the criteria for a DSM III-R psychiatric diagnosis compared with 38.7% of those who received a community intervention. The highest number of people admitted (44.7%) suffered from psychotic disorder, 14.9% from depressive disorder and 8.5% from personality disorder. Physical aggression was present in 50% of those admitted, compared with 29.8% of those not admitted ($\chi^2 = 5.9$, p < .01). Physical aggression, whether related to psychiatric diagnosis, as in our service, or not (Davidson et al., 1994) seems to be an important factor for determining admission.

There is still a paucity of evaluative research of psychiatric services for adults with ID. A study by Gustafsson (1997) in Sweden examined the prevalence of people with ID admitted to general hospital psychiatric units and found a lower frequency of utilization as compared to the general population. Those people with ID who had depression or were living on their own tended to have longer inpatient stays than those with other psychiatric diagnoses or living in supported accommodation. Similarly, in the Netherlands, Dreissen et al. (1997) examined the determinants of referrals to psychiatric services and the amount of consumed mental health services by people with ID, using a case register in a defined geographical area. Being older and having milder ID predicted a higher probability of receiving psychiatric treatment, while living alone was associated with higher levels of mental health service consumption. Raitasuo et al. (1999) found in a prospective study of 122 admissions to a special psychiatric unit in Finland that the typical inpatient was a young man with mild ID and a diagnosis of psychosis, who had lived in several residential places.

A growing number of specialist ID inpatient units linked with mental health services have been started in various parts of the world. Their main aim is to support different community programs of people with ID but their evaluation is still awaiting publication. The authors' personal clinical experiences suggest that in countries where community care for people with ID has been fully implemented since the early 1980s (e.g. south-east London in England), new service issues are gradually emerging. For example, community services are required to deal with an increasing number of people with autism or Asperger's syndrome with no or a degree of mild ID and mental illness (MI), of older adults with dementia, of people functioning at the borderline of cognitive impairment, and of people with ID and mental health challenges and a forensic history.

In the UK, with universal health care, large sums of money have been spent by social and health services in buying psychiatric services for people with ID and mental health needs from specialist private units. In recent years there has been an increase in the number of private secure and medium secure units that care for people with mild ID and a forensic history. Unfortunately, these new facilities are often a long way from a person's home, family, supporters and friends, which makes retaining links difficult and planning for a return home a rather remote possibility. The implications for the local services are also detrimental because they are deprived of the funds necessary to develop their required services. In London, 37% of people with ID originating from a borough are living outside it and 49% of those people have some form of mental illness or challenging behavior (Piachaud, 1999). Even if local solutions continue to be developed it will be some years before the current geographical dispersion will be resolved.

Provision of essential supports and services

The emphasis on a community-based, non-institutional service model has meant that deficiencies in the system are much more overt, and clear action has to be taken to address them. Community services cannot rely on the structures and safety of long-stay hospitals to contain their problems or mask poor quality. They also require that staff members who work in them are very clear about their function and competent in their skills (Holt & Joyce, 1999)

Fletcher et al. (1999) pointed out that in addition to empowering individuals with ID, appropriate residential and vocational services are needed to maximize their skills. Smaller settings, organized to respond to a wide range of needs particular to one or a few people, appear to offer the best environment for prevention of behavioral difficulties that have jeopardized community living situations in the past. No one model, however, will necessarily meet the needs of all individuals with ID and mental health challenges. Some people may become isolated and lonely in one or two person settings, or have difficulties that cannot be managed in housing where additional staff or clinical support is not readily available. Some adults may simply prefer to live in a supervised group-living situation rather than supported living and should be given the opportunity to live in a place they prefer. Residential services should include a full range of alternatives to enhance an individual's capacity for community living. The individual receiving residential services should be allowed to have as much comfort, ownership, and autonomy as possible.

Current policy directions also point toward greater individualization in vocational and lifestyle options. For people with ID and mental health challenges, the feasibility of persistent community presence and the longevity of supported or integrated vocational situations are greatly influenced by the individualization and flexibility of the support process and the available clinical and support skills (Bouras & Holt, 2001b). As in the development of appropriate residential supports, the benefits of day, vocational and therapeutic activities, as well as social and community presence, will be greatly influenced by the capability of organizations and clinicians to provide timely, individually responsive and minimally restrictive, but clinically sufficient and appropriate, direct staff support and therapeutic services. Delivery of supports and services in this manner represents one of the most important challenges to organizational and clinical effectiveness in services for people with ID. The development of residential and other community support services such as daytime activities and employment opportunities for people with ID/MI has rather been neglected.

Most existing community facilities do not have the expertise to support older people with ID who have such complex behavioral needs. Staff personnel find working with people with ID and mental health needs stressful. Giving them skills in this area so that, with support, they can manage people with challenging behavior and mental illness enables them to find this work more rewarding. The most basic and vital role of support staff in this context is the awareness that a person with ID may suffer a mental illness, as we all may. They need to be aware of the range of therapeutic options that might be helpful, including environmental changes, behavioral strategies, psychotherapeutic techniques, and medications. A fuller knowledge and consideration of this topic will help to dispel myths and prejudices (e.g. that medication is to be avoided at all costs, or that its use signifies that staff have in some way failed the adult). Specific knowledge about some disorders will provide insights into why and how interventions must be tailored around someone's strengths and needs (e.g. someone with autistic spectrum disorder may hit himself when his routine is changed). The intervention chosen may be to provide a timetable, which the staff and the adult can follow. Several flexible training packages, which can be used by staff groups in their own setting, are now available. One, the Training Package in the Mental Health of Learning Disabilities (Bouras & Szymanski, 1997) developed in the UK, contains materials for a series of workshops and stresses active participation in individual and group activities, some based on information in the workshop materials and some based on the participants' experiences. Accompanying the training package is a handbook (Holt & Bouras, 1997a), which can be used for references and for further reading by the workshop facilitators. A video, *Making Links* (Holt & Bouras, 1997b), is also available and complements the package. Evaluation reports of the use of this training method have shown encouraging results (Holt *et al.*, 2000). Cain *et al.* (in press) have also produced a training manual for use in the US with similar staff groups. Similarly, Janicki and McCallion (2001) have published a training manual and CD rom-video as an aid to staff helping adults with ID affected by Alzheimer's disease and related dementias.

A conceptual framework of services

Moss *et al.* (2000) postulated a matrix model to guide the development and evaluation of mental health services for people with ID. The matrix model has a geographical dimension that refers to three levels (national/regional, local and user/patient) and a temporal dimension referring to three phases (input, process and outcome). Using these two dimensions a matrix is constructed that focuses on critical issues for community mental health services for people with ID. This model can facilitate the understanding of how persons with ID and mental health services operate by explaining clinical events in terms of their location in time and space. That is the 'where and when', which helps our understanding of the 'how and why'. There are two major advantages for the adoption of such a model. Firstly, it provides a logical framework for identifying areas for research and development. Secondly, it offers a way of identifying common service dimensions, offering the possibility of comparing and evaluating services operating in diverse national contexts. These factors are particularly relevant to mental health services for people with ID, which are characterized by the involvement of a variety of agencies and organizations, strong ideologies and conflicting professional views.

The matrix model can also be used to prioritize actions, which will assist clinicians, planners, administrators, managers, commissioners of services, users and their carers to develop local service responses. The actions necessary in each area will be specific to local circumstances. One of the issues likely to require action in many areas is to ensure that quality standards, equivalent to those used for physical health care services, are applied to mental health services, including for those with ID. The matrix model can be used to assist in the assessment of local and users' needs. It can also be used to develop a research agenda for people with ID, to improve the diagnosis and detection of the mental health problems in this population, to identify their causes and to evaluate treatment outcomes.

The mental health needs of people with ID are complex, involving interconnected clinical, organizational and service factors. Achieving sustainable improvements in mental health service provision is going to need coherent policies to guide its development. For instance, the agencies responsible for regulating such services should seek evidence that service providers are taking appropriate steps to meet the mental health needs of this population. Broadly speaking, there needs to be a commitment to an evidence-based approach, with a recognition that all levels of staff have a contribution to make in the assessment process, the provision of treatment, and the longer-term support of the individual and his/her carers. At present, services have reached a crisis point (Jacobson, 1999; Bouras & Holt, 2001a), characterized by unclear policies, interagency disagreements and limited service responses, with unpredictable consequences for the quality of life of users, their families and carers. The conceptual framework of the matrix model may contribute to a clearer formulation of these complex issues.

Summary

Since 1990 there has been a development of more individualized, empowering and inclusive approaches to services for people with ID and mental health challenges. Most of these developments are based on a process of person-centered planning. Self-advocacy supports people with ID to take more control over their lives and involve them in decision-making for service planning. The mental health needs of those with ID continue, however, to be overlooked and remain grossly unmet. Of special concern is an even greater lack of services and supports for older adults with ID as they age. More efforts are required from all concerned to address this major gap constructively and to reflect evidence-based practice.

References

Allen, D. (1989) The effects of de-institutionalisation on people with mental handicaps: A Review. *Mental Handicap Research*, **2**, 18–37.

Bailey, N. & Cooper, S. (1998) NHS beds for people with learning disabilities. *Psychiatric Bulletin*, **22**, 69–72.

Barron, P. & O'Hara, J. (2000) Mental health services for people with learning disabilities. *British Medical Journal*, **321**, 582–583.

Borthwick-Duffy, S.A. (1994) Epidemiology and prevalence of psychopathology in people with mental retardation. *Journal of Consulting and Clinical Psychology*, **62**, 17–27.

Bouras, N. & Holt, G. (eds) (1997) *Mental Health in Learning Disability Training Package*, 2nd edn. Pavilion Publishing, Brighton.

Bouras, N. & Holt, G. (2000) The planning and provision of psychiatric services for people with mental retardation. *The New Oxford Textbook of Psychiatry* (eds M.G. Gelder, J.J Lopez-Ibor Jr. & C. Andreasen). Oxford University Press, Oxford.

Bouras, N. & Holt, G. (2001a) Psychiatric treatment in community care. *Handbook of Treatment of Mental Illness and Behavior Disorders in Children and Adults with Mental Retardation* (eds A. Dosen & K. Day) pp. 493–502. American Psychiatric Press, Washington, DC.

Bouras, N. & Holt, G. (2001b) Community mental health services for adults with learning disabilities. *Textbook of Community Psychiatry* (eds G. Thornicroft & G. Szmukler) pp. 397–407. Oxford University Press, Oxford.

Bouras, N. & Szymanski, L. (1997) Services for people with mental retardation and psychiatric disorders: US-UK comparative overview. *International Journal of Social Psychiatry*, **43**, 64–71.

Cain, N.N., Holt, G., Bouras, N. & Davidson, P.W. (in press) *Training Manual on Mental Health in Mental Retardation*. Paul Brookes Publishing, Baltimore, Maryland.

Chaplin, R. & Flynn, A. (2000) Adults with learning disability admitted to psychiatric wards. *Advances in Psychiatric Treatment*, **6**, 128–134.

Davidson, P.W., Cain, N.N., Sloane-Reeves, J., Van Speybroeck, A., Segel, J., Gutkin, J. & Quijano, L. (1994) Characteristics of community-based individuals with mental retardation and aggressive behavioral disorders. *American Journal on Mental Retardation*, **98**, 704–716.

Davidson, P.W., Morris, D. & Cain, N.N. (1999) Community services for people with dual diagnosis and psychiatric or severe behaviour disorders. *Psychiatric and Behavioural Disorders in Developmental Disabilities and Mental Retardation* (ed. N. Bouras) pp. 359–372. Cambridge University Press, Cambridge.

Davidson, P., Janicki, M., Ladrigan, P., Houser, K., Henderson, C.M. & Cain, N.N. (in press) Associations between behavior problems and health status in older adults with intellectual disability. *Journal of Aging and Mental Health*.

Day, K. (1985) Psychiatric disorder in the middle aged and elderly mentally handicapped. *British Journal of Psychiatry* **147**, 660–667.

Day, K. (1999) Professional training in the psychiatry of mental retardation in the United Kingdom. *Psychiatric and Behavioural Disorders in Developmental*

Disabilities and Mental Retardation (ed. N. Bouras) pp. 439–457. Cambridge University Press, Cambridge.

DoH (2001) *National Service Framework for Older People*. Department of Health, London.

Dreissen, G., DuMoulin, M., Haveman, M.J. & van Os, J. (1997) Persons with intellectual disability receiving psychiatric treatment. *Journal of Intellectual Disability Research*, **41**, 512–518.

Emerson, E. (ed) (1995) *Challenging Behaviour: Analysis and Intervention in People with Learning Difficulties*. Cambridge University Press, Cambridge.

Emerson, E. & Hatton, C. (1995) *Moving Out. Relocation from Hospital to Community*. The Stationery Office, London.

Emerson, E., Forrest, J., Cambridge, P. & Mansell, J. (1996) Community support teams for people with learning disabilities and challenging behaviour. *Journal of Mental Health*, **5**, 395–406.

Emerson, E., Moss, S. & Kiernan, C. (1999) The relationship between challenging behaviour and psychiatric disorders in people with severe intellectual disabilities. *Psychiatric and Behavioural Disorders in Developmental Disabilities and Mental Retardation* (ed. N. Bouras) pp. 38–47. Cambridge University Press, Cambridge.

Evenhuis, H. (1999) Associated medical aspects. *Dementia, Aging, and Intellectual Disabilities: A Handbook* (eds M.P. Janicki & A.J. Dalton) pp. 103–118. Brunner-Mazel, Philadelphia.

Felce, D. (1994) Costs, quality and staffing in services for people with severe learning disabilities. *Journal of Mental Health*, **3**, 495–506.

Fletcher, R., Beasley, J. & Jacobson, J.J. (1999) Support service systems for people with dual diagnosis in the USA. *Psychiatric and Behavioural Disorders in Developmental Disabilities and Mental Retardation* (ed. N. Bouras) pp. 373–390. Cambridge University Press, Cambridge.

Gravestock, S. & Bouras, N. (1997) Survey of services for adults with learning disabilities. *Psychiatric Bulletin*, **21**, 197–199.

Gustafsson, C. (1997) The prevalence of people with intellectual disability admitted to general hospital psychiatric units. *Journal of Intellectual Disability Research*, **41**, 519–526.

Haney, J.I. (1998) Empirical support for deistitutionalisation. *Integration of Developmentally Disabled Individuals into the Community* (eds L.W. Heal, J.I. Haney & A.R. Novak) pp. 123–144. Paul H. Brookes, Baltimore.

Hatton, C., Emerson, E. & Kiernan, C. (1995) People in institutions in Europe. *Mental Retardation*, **33**, 132.

Henderson, C.M. & Davidson, P.W. (2001). Comprehensive adult and geriatric assessment. *Community Supports for Older Adults with Lifelong Disabilities* (eds M.P. Janicki & E.F. Ansello) pp. 373–386. Paul H. Brookes, Baltimore.

Hogg, J. & Lambe, L. (1998) *Older People with Learning Disabilities: A Review of the Literature of Residential Services and Family Caregiving*. White Top Research Unit, University of Dundee, Dundee, Scotland.

Holt, G. & Bouras, N. (eds) (1997a) *Mental Health in Learning Disabilities: Handbook* 2nd edn. Pavilion Publishing, Brighton.

Holt, G. & Bouras, N. (eds.) (1997b) *Making Links*. Pavilion Publishing, Brighton.

Holt, G. & Joyce, T. (1999) Mental health and challenging behaviour services. *Tizard Learning Disabilities Review*, **4**, 36–42.

Holt, G., Costello, H., Bouras, N., Diareme, S., Hillery, J., Moss, S., Rodriguez-Blasquez, C., Salvador, L., Tsiantis, J., Weber, G. & Dimitrakaki, C. (2000) BIOMED-MEROPE Project: Service provision for adults with mental retardation: A European comparison. *Journal Intellectual Disability Research*, **44**, 685–696.

Jacobson, J. (1998) Psychological services utilization: relationship to severity of behavior problems in intellectual disability services. *Journal of Intellectual Disability Research*, **42**, 307–315.

Jacobson, J. (1999) Dual diagnosis services: History, progress and perspectives. *Psychiatric and Behavioural Disorders in Developmental Disabilities and Mental Retardation* (ed. N. Bouras) pp. 327–358. Cambridge University Press, Cambridge.

Janicki, M.P. & McCallion, P. (2001) *Dementia and People with Intellectual Disabilities – What Can We Do?* (CD-Rom) New York State Developmental Disabilities Planning Council, Albany, New York.

Janicki, M.P., Heller, T., Seltzer, G. *et al.* (1995) *Practice guidelines for the clinical assessment and care management of Alzheimer and other dementias among adults with mental retardation.* American Association on Mental Retardation, Washington, DC.

Janicki, M., Davidson, P., Henderson, C.M., McCallion, P., Taets, J., Force, L, Sulkes, S., Frangenberg, E. & Ladrigan, P. (2002) Health characteristics and health services utilization in older adults with intellectual disabilities living in community residences. *Journal of Intellectual Disability Research*, **76**, 287–298.

Jawed, S.H., Krishnan, V.H., Prasher, V.P. & Corbett, J.A. (1993) Worsening of pica as a symptom of depressive illness in a person with severe mental handicap. *British Journal of Psychiatry*, **162**, 835–837.

King, B.H. (1993) Self-injury by people with mental retardation: A compulsive behavior hypothesis. *American Journal on Mental Retardation*, **98**, 93–112.

Kon, Y. & Bouras, N. (1997) Psychiatric follow-up and health services utilisation for people with learning disabilities. *British Journal of Developmental Disabilities*, **84**, 20–26.

Linaker, O.M. & Nottestead, J.A. (1998) Health and health services for the mentally retarded before and after the reform. *Tidsskirft for Den Norske Laegeforening*, **118**, 357–361.

Lowe, K., Felce, D. & Blackman, D. (1996) Challenging behaviour, the effectiveness of specialist support teams. *Journal of Intellectual Disability Research*, **40**, 336–347.

Meins, W. (1995) Symptoms of major depression in mentally retarded adults. *Journal of Intellectual Disability Research*, **39**, 41–45.

Moss, S., Bouras, N. & Holt, G. (2000) Mental health services for people with intellectual disabilities: A conceptual framework. *Journal Intellectual Disability Research*, **44**, 97–107.

Piachaud, J. (1999) Issues for mental health in learning disabilities services. *Tizard Review*, **4**(2), 47–48.

Raitasuo, S., Taiminen, T. & Salokangus, R.K. (1999) Characteristics of persons with intellectual disability admitted to psychiatric inpatient treatment. *Journal of Intellectual Disabilities Research*, **43**, 112–127.

Reiss, S. (1994) *Handbook of Challenging Behavior: Mental Health Aspects of Mental Retardation*. IDS Publishing Co, Worthington, OH.

Reiss, S. & Rojahn, J. (1993) Joint occurrence of depression and aggression in children and adults with mental retardation. *Journal of Intellectual Disability Research*, **37**, 287–294.

Russell, O. (ed.) (1997) Historical overview: concepts and concerns. In *Seminars in the Psychiatry of Learning Disabilities*, pp. 1–15. Gaskell, London.

Sovner, R., Fox, C.J., Lowry, M.J. & Lowry, M.A. (1993) Fluoxetine treatment of depression and associated self-injury in two adults with mental retardation. *Journal of Intellectual Disability Research*, **37**, 301–311.

15 Community Education and Prevention Strategies

Lynda L. Geller and John C. Pomeroy

Since the 1980s there has been a virtual revolution in the demand and expectations of gerontologic services in developed countries. Not only has there been a substantial increase in length of life for healthy individuals, but also in life expectancy coupled with reductions in age specific morbidity. This trend has affected society in general, including older persons with intellectual disabilities (ID). Generally, the same factors of improved health care and health technology that have given the population at large improved quality of life in old age, have also benefited people with ID. However, this population has unique problems associated with aging, and individuals with additional mental health problems present with complexities that create additional burden for the affected individual and need to be addressed in terms of service provision, research and training. As noted in Chapter 14, there are multiple contributing factors to successful delivery of services and supports in a community setting; hence, a multisystemic, biopsychosocial, transdisciplinary approach is required to address the complicated diagnostic and treatment questions. While service design may be the most important aspect of this equation, certainly personnel preparation is a close second in importance. The goals of any training and education necessary to assist the wide range of professionals and carers necessary to achieve this collaborative model should provide the basis for both prevention strategies and best practice service models.

When clinical and service systems overlap, members of the individual systems often lack knowledge, or even appreciation, for the major issues in each other's fields. This is particularly relevant to the intersection of gerontology, mental health and ID. For persons considered to have a 'dual diagnosis' (those with ID and psychiatric or behavioral disorders) who are aging, there is commonly significant fragmentation of services, partly due to the lack of training that each professional discipline has in each other's area of experience.

Cross-discipline training between the ID and mental health (MH) communities has been an issue for more than two decades. The realization of the importance of this type of training has been instrumental in the formation of organizations such as the National Association for the Dually Diagnosed (NADD) and numerous curricula for training. However, few in either the ID or MH fields are as well trained or experienced in aging, despite sociological trends since the 1980s making this lack of expertise a crucial issue.

With deinstitutionalization in both psychiatric and developmental centers, hundreds of thousands of older adults with dual diagnosis are now living in the community. Community resources are undoubtedly overburdened trying to cope with the complex challenges presented in serving and supporting persons with dual diagnosis. In general, MH support systems were designed for chronically mentally ill patients who were in good physical health and for whom there was a reasonable expectation of functional self-help skills. In the MH system, a decline in self-help skills would typically indicate relapsing mental illness and therefore probable rehospitalization. This model does not necessarily account for the physical and cognitive declines of aging. Similarly, community resources for persons with ID were largely designed to provide residential, vocational and day services for adults relatively free of psychiatric disability and ill health. As participation in daily vocational or day treatment activity is often required of adults with intellectual disabilities, there is often no provision for the retirement years, and there is limited understanding of how to help an aging population confront an often inflexible system of care. Workers in both systems may stereotype aging adults with intellectual disabilities as uninteresting, unlikely to respond to therapeutic intervention, and often non-compliant. Furthermore, providers may be underinformed about the special health needs of aging individuals who may also lack the communication skills to inform others of their distress.

In a report of the International Association for the Scientific Study of Intellectual Disabilities (IASSID) and the World Health Organization (WHO), a number of specific issues were identified that directly pertain to the lack of transdisciplinary knowledge and the potential for negative outcomes (Thorpe et al., 2000). In considering aging individuals with dual diagnosis, there are some unique issues that need to be well understood by anyone caring for them. Many of these individuals have syndrome-specific cognitive and health issues, many of which are not well understood, because of the relatively recent increases in life-span in this population and the lack of an adequate contemporary knowledge base. Many have had long-term use of psychotropic medications including recently marketed treatments for which there are limited data on the effects of chronic use. Lifestyles of those with dual diagnoses tend to be passive, sedentary or institutional, which bring their own set of unfortunate outcomes.

Professionals with aging expertise working with older persons with ID tend to be unaware of the potentially atypical expression of various cognitive, health and mental health problems that may be seen in the persons with intellectual disabilities, and the poor communication about these issues they might expect from their patients. The IASSID/WHO report (Thorpe *et al.*, 2000) identified several issues where training is universally needed if general community providers are to be effective with this population. These include training in ID on:

- The unique health issues related to specific syndromes and lifelong cognitive impairment
- A well-informed, multisource medical history
- Specialized examination techniques for those with cognitive deficits and behavioral/psychiatric disorders
- The availability of expert support when problems are particularly complex
- Obtaining informed consent with disabled populations

Of particular importance for everyone dealing with this population is the realization that individuals with both ID and mental illness tend to be devalued or stigmatized and thus often do not receive the quality of treatment that is available to others. Before aggressive advocacy can be developed, community members must have a fuller understanding of the unique problems presented by aging adults with dual diagnoses, and the possible solutions.

The fields of ID and MH have both begun to address their aging populations. However, the subspecialty of dual diagnoses, being relatively new, is still grappling with the basic issues of interdisciplinary training, and has not given as much consideration to the particulars of aging. The many issues highlighted in this book will prove to be crucial for all professionals and carers supporting aging individuals with dual diagnoses. This chapter provides a structural model that could be incorporated into existing or new regional programs for training in dual diagnoses, and addresses the many levels of needed information from parent to clinician and direct care worker to administrator.

Training model

Some of the major issues that need to be addressed in any training about aging and dual diagnoses are not unlike the generic issues related to every aging person, but with the awareness of the additional pressures of lifelong disability. For all aging individuals there may be increased loneliness and social isolation as peers and relatives die, and a defined role in society may decrease as opportunities to integrate into the community diminish with declining health (Lebowitz & Niederehe, 1992.) As adults with ID frequently do not have spouses or children and tend to have limited social networks, those providing care must insure that formal supports are in place. Those with less severe ID often participate in typical senior network programs (Selzer *et al.*, 1989), but with increased ID there is a need for specialized age-related programs. The necessity for geriatric programming illustrates two separate but interlinked training requirements. The staff of geriatric facilities need to understand lifelong cognitive and/or psychiatric disability, and the staff supporting adults with dual diagnoses need to understand how to develop an appropriate age-related support program for their clientele. In developing a comprehensive training model to address the combination of ID, psychiatric and behavioral disorders, and aging, it is necessary to consider the most important core curriculum, the highly varied level of skills of the target trainees, and the varying levels of information that need to be considered.

The optimal model for training in dual diagnoses and aging has as its basis the concept of interdisciplinary interaction as a crucial element in the learning and problem-solving process. A common basis of essential information must be established and a system to appropriately disseminate this knowledge must be devised. Any successful model needs to provide training at a need-to-know level and within a role-based framework.

Training levels

There are essentially three need-to-know levels. These levels are a reflection of the difference in necessary levels of expertise between clinicians with specialization in dual diagnoses or dual diagnoses and aging, those who provide program and residential services to those with dual diagnoses or aging, and others who have only limited clinical roles with these populations:

(1) *Professional staff.* The individual to be trained will be developing a career in dual diagnosis or dual diagnosis and aging and needs to gain the expertise to provide interdisciplinary leadership in assessment and treatment, research, and best practices training. Target groups include health care professionals (physicians, physician assistants and nurses), mental health professionals (psychiatrists, psychologists and social workers) and developmental disabilities professionals and behavioral specialists.

(2) *Direct care staff.* The individual to be trained will be working regularly with adults with dual diagnosis or aging as a career path. Target groups include professional service providers (occupational

therapists, physical therapists, speech and language pathologists and specialists on aging), direct care staff, and families.

(3) *Administrative leadership*. The individual to be trained needs to have adequate knowledge of dual diagnosis and aging to participate in a team addressing salient issues for a client, service system or research topic. Target groups include administrators, service coordinators and advocates.

Ideally, the training model would be enhanced by the development of specific strategic sites as training centers. The centers would be responsible for developing specific core curricula based on salient issues from the separate fields of ID, MH and aging, emphasizing the intersecting points of importance. Centers would be responsible for developing courses that address the following needs.

- A core course in dual diagnoses, with emphasis on aging, gerontological and geriatric issues, for professionals who intend to make a career in the field. A mixture of disciplines would participate and a goal of instruction would be to develop a cadre of potential trainers in dual diagnosis.
- A parallel core course in dual diagnoses, with emphasis on aging issues, for individuals who would be providing everyday care and/or life management services (direct care, group home supervisors, case managers, parents).
- Time limited core mini-courses that serve as an introduction for professionals and administrators who would be receiving ongoing technical assistance.
- Time limited core mini-courses that serve as an introduction for carers, who would be receiving ongoing technical assistance.

Time limited core courses would focus more specifically on certain areas of knowledge depending on the course enrollees. For example, some mini-courses could address dual diagnoses issues for an audience of specialists in aging, or physical and cognitive sequelae of aging for those in the field of ID.

Sequence of training

Every individual receiving training in dual diagnoses or dual diagnoses and aging would receive a core course that is either center-based or web-based and is appropriate to an individual's role and need-to-know. After the core course, a number of alternate training packages, developed by the designated center, would be available based on each trainee's specific needs. Additional training elements should include:

- *Transdisciplinary traineeships*. Clinical/research facilities currently specializing in intellectual disabilities, mental health, gerontology or geriatric psychiatry with specific interests in one of the other fields, could serve as designated sites. The teaching faculty should represent a wide range of professional disciplines with demonstrated knowledge and experience in all three fields. Traineeships should be offered based on each profession's standards of training. The trainees would regularly participate in the ongoing core course and transdisciplinary clinical activities. Involvement in clinical research would also be desirable. Each trainee would receive both discipline-specific and cross-discipline supervision in their work. Length of participation and weekly hours would be discipline specific but have minimum guidelines to insure adequate transdisciplinary experience. Financial support for both the center and the trainees would be essential to success.

- *Community technical assistance*. Members of the teaching faculty with skills in providing technical assistance and training would, as part of their center responsibilities, conduct group community training. Agencies could contract with the center to provide such technical assistance and training. Depending on the general issues to be addressed, a member of the center staff would be assigned to develop an individualized training package specific to the agency's needs. The first part of this process should be all agency staff receiving the appropriate time limited core mini-course. There would always be a community-based follow-up that would vary in time and intensity based on agency need. For example, an agency opening a group home for aging adults with dual diagnosis has very different needs from a day treatment center with one adult who is aging and has a dual diagnosis. However, the critical aspect of team assessment and problem-solving is the continuity and support of the center trainer. Whether trainees of all roles and all need-to-know levels were trained concurrently or consecutively would depend on the philosophy and training package elements agreed on by the trainer and the agency.

- *Workshop*. From a basis of knowledge and experience in the composite fields of intellectual disabilities, mental health and aging, professionals designated as trainers would elicit opportunities to educate systems and provide accessible training at various levels. By spreading knowledge of the intersection of these three fields, information is provided to carers, who may have previously been experienced in only one or two of these areas. This education can help with problem-solving for ongoing cases or can encourage development of a level of knowledge so that individuals providing care or support feel more empowered to act effectively to assist aging adults with dual diagnoses. A long-term benefit is the development of increasing numbers of staff at community support programs who will feel able to cope with the problems such complicated adults can present. The support and education that competent, trained multidisciplinary professionals could provide would theoretically reinforce the training and quality of service, but inevitably some governmental support for this type of endeavor would also be essential to sustain the effort.

Prevention strategies

In addition to the inevitable improvement in knowledge and clinical care that training models can provide, there is the opportunity to develop the quality of preventive care that can be built into a well-informed focused care system that will give attention to the important issues of reducing morbidity by good clinical practice and shared interdisciplinary responsibility.

The IASSID/WHO report on mental health (Thorpe *et al.*, 2000) stresses the importance of well-conceived training as a crucial element in all aspects of prevention. Primary prevention is the anticipation and prevention of problems before they occur. Quality of life issues are of particular importance in that appropriateness of living situation, support systems, and general health care can mitigate the occurrence of many typical problems associated with aging for those with disabilities. Home care versus institutional care, uninformed polypharmacy versus diagnosis-specific prescription, or intergenerational support versus isolation, can all have a profound impact on the development or prevention of an array of problems.

Secondary prevention includes the early detection and aggressive treatment of emerging problems. Again, the type of interdisciplinary training being proposed mitigates problems by training diverse groups of carers to recognize, specify and creatively treat problems that require interdisciplinary intervention.

Tertiary prevention is the minimization of impairment in established problems. Cross-training helps carers recognize and refer problems to appropriate disciplines because of the exposure they have had to issues beyond their own field and to professional disciplines with whom they may previously have had no contact. For family and direct care workers, the realization of the wide range of resources available to address problems may influence more timely referral and a greater understanding of the necessary monitoring needed to minimize further harm that existing problems can create. Thus, interdisciplinary training should also be thought of as an essential element of prevention, as well as a crucial underpinning of the development of knowledge and the delivery of best clinical care.

Summary

To successfully develop a system of center-based and community training, there is a need of sufficient funds for training and a critical mass of committed individuals from all three clinical fields to develop specific training agendas. The development of designated centers could logically proceed from programs currently in existence in dual diagnoses, geriatric psychiatry, or aging in developmental disabilities. Financial resources for cross-training would enhance these programs and provide an incentive to develop courses of study in aging and dual diagnoses.

Geriatric psychiatry provides a useful model for development. In 1978 there was one program in the US for geriatric psychiatry. Ten years later there were 30 such programs and the field continues to expand, with concurrent growth in this specialty within psychology, social work and nursing. The crucial elements in this development were the establishment of Geriatric Research, Education, and Clinical Centers in the Department of Veteran's Affairs, funding initiatives from the National Institute of Health on mental health and aging, the establishment of the National Institute on Aging, and the legitimization of geriatric psychiatry as a field through Board Certification in Psychiatry (Cohen, 1992.) These same elements of ongoing governmental support, financial incentive and credentialing need to be activated for the development and continued existence of effective training in aging and dual diagnoses. The research agenda described throughout this book needs to be coupled with educational initiatives to insure that training is linked to sources of current knowledge, and that research experts and funding organizations set an appropriate investigational agenda.

Thus, in addition to the above-mentioned transdisciplinary training goals, increased communication between basic and clinical researchers and service professionals is an important element in the development and maintenance of the field. The rapid progress that has been made in geriatric psychiatry in areas of applied and basic research in biomedical and psychosocial areas, health promotion, and the differentiation between mechanisms of aging and courses of psychiatric illness, need to be replicated in professions affected by dual diagnoses and aging. By developing similar supports for this field, through governmental, private and community cooperation, vital training initiatives can be developed and maintained that will enhance the field and similarly advance quality of life for aging adults with dual diagnoses.

References

Cohen, G.D. (1992) The future of mental health and aging. *Handbook of Mental Health and Aging* (eds J.E. Birren, R.B. Sloane, & G.D. Cohen) pp. 893–914. Academic Press, Inc, San Diego.

Lebowitz, B.D. & Niederehe, G. (1992) Concepts and issues in mental health and aging. *Handbook of Mental Health and Aging* (eds J.E. Birren, R.B. Sloane & G.D. Cohen) pp. 3–26. Academic Press, Inc, San Diego.

Selzer, M.M., Krauss, M.W., Litchfield, L.C. & Modlish, N.J.K. (1989) Utilization of aging network services by elderly persons with mental retardation. *The Gerontologist*, **29**, 234–238.

Thorpe, L., Davidson, P. & Janicki, M. (2000) *Healthy Ageing – Adults with Intellectual Disabilities: Biobehavioral Issues*. World Health Organization, Geneva.

Further reading

Committee on Personnel for Health Needs of the Elderly Through the Year 2020 (1988) *Personnel for Health Needs of the Elderly Through the Year 2020*. Government Printing Office, Washington, DC.

Evenhuis, H., Henderson, C.M., Beange, H., Lennox, N. & Chicoine, B. (2000) *Healthy Ageing: Adults with Intellectual Disabilities: Physical Health Issues*. World Health Organization, Geneva.

Herr, S.S. & Weber, G. (1999) Prospects for ensuring rights, quality supports, and a good old age. *Aging, Rights, and Quality of Life* (eds S.S. Herr & G. Weber) pp. 343–370. Paul H. Brookes Publishing Co, Baltimore.

Lieberman, M.A. & Peskin, H. (1992) Adult life crisis. *Handbook of Mental Health and Aging* (eds J.E. Birren, R.B. Sloane & G.D. Cohen) pp. 893–914. Academic Press, Inc, San Diego.

Rodin, J. & Langer, E. (1980) Aging labels: The decline of control and the fall of self-esteem. *Journal of Social Issues*, **36**, 12–29.

Seltzer, G.B. (1993) Psychological adjustment in middle life for persons with mental retardation. *Older Adults with Developmental Disabilities* (ed. E. Sutton) pp. 157–184. Paul H. Brookes Publishing Co, Baltimore.

Seltzer, M.M. (1992) Aging in persons with developmental disabilities. *Handbook of Mental Health and Aging* (eds J.E. Birren, R.B. Sloane & G.D. Cohen) pp. 583–599. Academic Press, Inc, San Diego.

Stone, R., Cafferta, G.L. & Sangl, J. (1987) Caregivers of frail elderly: A national profile. *Gerontologist*, **27**, 616–626.

16 Nurse Roles in Supporting Aging Persons with Mental Health Problems

Mary McCarron and Colin Griffiths

Aging persons with intellectual disabilities (ID) often face a multitude of coping challenges, such as dealing with an increasing array of mental and physical health care conditions, coming to terms with the loss of family and friends, and adapting to changing environmental and social support structures. These challenges are further compounded by the communication deficits that many persons with ID experience. For some people with ID, mental and physical illness may manifest early and repeatedly over the life-span. For others such problems may only become apparent in later life. This is of course also true for people in the general population. People with ID also experience major mental disorders, with an estimated overall prevalence of about 10% (Day & Jancar, 1994). Comparable to the generic population, an increase in both physical and mental health problems is evidenced with increasing age (Cooper, 1999). Some disorders such as dementia display an increased prevalence with age and are particularly common in people with Down syndrome (Oliver & Holland, 1986; Prasher & Krishnan, 1993). For detailed discussion on these topics see Thorpe (1999) and Chapter 3 of this book.

Environmental stress may further overwhelm the individual's current coping capacities and lead to a variety of maladaptive behaviours. Mental health disorders in people with ID often have a negative impact on cognition, behavior and general functioning, and impede and distort normal aging. Consequently the quality of life for affected individuals, their family, those with whom they live and their carers can be greatly reduced. For example, the psychological and emotional impact for families in dealing with adults who have severe psychopathology has been reported (e.g. Heller *et al.*, 1997; McIntyre *et al.*, 2002), and a number of authors have also reported a relationship between characteristics of the person with ID and staff stress (e.g. Bersani & Heifetz, 1987; Jenkins *et al.*, 1997).

Detection and intervention to address mental health issues are important. However, many prodromal signs and symptoms of mental health problems in this population may go unidentified because of confused expectations by carers, lack of understanding of the significance of these behaviors, and the tendency to often attribute unusual behaviors to the individual's ID as opposed to the potential underlying mental health problems. Mindful that in this population many conditions are not mutually exclusive and often coexist, behavioral change may represent a symptom of an underlying condition that can be reversed or managed. Since many people with ID are often not able to self-report symptoms, detection of physical and mental health problems and subsequent referral for appropriate diagnostic work-up are highly dependent on professionals such as nurses during the course of assessment or visits.

Nurse training for people with ID differs from country to country. In the UK and Ireland separate branches of the register exist for nurses who have been trained specifically in this unique discipline. In the US, however, nurses are taught through generic programs which mostly contain little theoretical and clinical content relevant to intellectual disability (Nehring, 1994). Thus nurses in the US who work in the field of ID tend to specialize in the field post initial training.

Nehring (1994) suggests that the special roles of the nurse in the community are concerned with coordinating health care and acting as educator, supporter and advocate for adults with ID. Nurses' roles are centered around supporting people with ID to obtain the highest quality of life possible in the community, and the focus for the nurse is the provision of holistic care for both clients and families. Jukes (1994) also regards the nurse as having a vital community-based role, and states that the role of the nurse in the community is to assess their clients and to devise plans of care that meet identified needs, to offer a range of therapeutic interventions to clients, to promote self-advocacy for people with ID and to provide information and links for people with ID to the generic services that they require.

This chapter includes case studies that illustrate the challenges and opportunities for nurses and other carers to improve diagnosis and care of mental health problems in persons with ID. Underpinning the practice approach espoused here is the belief that mental health and quality of life issues are so closely interconnected that an imperative exists to ensure accurate identification of the issues and consequent appropriate intervention as an integral part of health care for all.

Contrasts and challenges in aging persons with ID

The following case studies illustrate similarities and differences in the older years of persons with and without ID.

Case study: Mary and Patricia

Mary, age 55 years, has worked as a health care assistant for most of her working life at the local hospital. She lives in an urban community, is married and has three grown-up children and two grandchildren. Financially she is comfortable and has secured herself a modest pension. She plays an active role in her local community, is involved in her church and swimming club, plays bridge two nights per week and has a large circle of friends both through her work and local community. Over the past 18 months Mary has experienced a number of significant life events marked by the sudden death of her husband, and six months later a close friend. Her own physical health has deteriorated and on advice from her primary care physician, Mary has decided to retire from her job.

Patricia is a 50-year-old woman with Down syndrome, moderate ID and limited verbal communication skills. She lives in a community residence in an urban community with four other women who also have a moderate ID. She works two days per week at a local supermarket and for the remaining three days attends a small community workshop for people with ID. Patricia has two sisters who occasionally visit. Patricia's job at the supermarket is very important to her; she has got to know staff members; however, her contact with them is during work only. She has very little involvement in her local community, other than attending the local church and shops, and while neighbours are friendly and polite, Patricia's engagement in social or leisure activities is limited. Her social network centers mainly on the people in her house and workshop and she has limited financial resources. Over the past 18 months Patricia has experienced a number of significant life events marked by the sudden death of her sister. Her own physical health has deteriorated (a combination of arthritis and recurrent lung infections) and on advice from her primary care physician and care team Patricia retired. Soon afterwards, Patricia was transferred to another community residence that was staffed to cater for people with more severe ID. Since her transfer she has become quiet and withdrawn.

In contrast to the generic population, persons with ID often have little previous experience of successfully negotiating life crises, and consequently they do not bring with them the same array of life experiences and skills to bear on situations and challenges that arise (Moss, 1999). These contrasting case scenarios serve to highlight similarities in life events and transitions that are common to all. The crucial difference however is that in Patricia's case limited social network and lack of outside interest and life experiences increase her risk of suboptimal mental health. This is further compounded by societal expectations and limited services options and support structures to support aging-related challenges. Those quality of life factors that Moss (1999) contends have the greatest impact on promoting and ensuring positive mental health (i.e. physical health and social support networks) are not present in Patricia's case. This apparent isolation of the person with an ID can limit perceived supports for the person when he or she needs them. Absent friends, lack of or no meaningful relationships and few interests or hobbies may mean that the person with an ID is very susceptible to the stressors of modern life. The paucity of life experiences and avenues means that there are few cushions that can soften the impact of stress, exposing the person to mental health concerns rather more quickly than would happen to someone with a richer social life. In Patricia's case lack of service planning to address issues of aging, combined with inadequate vision and preparation for retirement, substantially increase Patricia's risk of reduced quality of life in later years. In common with persons who are not disabled, people with ID need preparation for healthy adjustment to retirement. Developing social and leisure competence is a skill, one that all people regardless of disability should be encouraged to acquire early in life. Thus nurses and carers must give vigilant attention to the need to establish avenues that will help to broaden the person's social network, and provide opportunities which encourage interaction with others at both a local and community level.

General approaches

As people with an ID grow older, having resources and supports to cushion this transition and adapt to change and loss is necessary for successful living. In order to support aging people with ID through this transition, nurses must promote a positive attitude towards aging, emphasizing retained abilities over disabilities, and placing high value on assisted autonomy, independence and/or interdependence to allow persons with ID to maintain some control over their own lives. The question for nurses and other carers is how can people with ID be enabled to enjoy the later years of life in this optimum manner? In the organization of day-to-day programming some reflection and active planning is needed to determine:

- Are service structures and care approaches aimed at minimizing the risk of mental health problems?
- Are steps being taken to empower the person with ID to gain more control over those factors that cause stress?
- Have strategies been identified by carers to help cushion and buffer the impact of stress and adverse life events?
- Are there health education strategies and guidelines for healthy life-styles for persons with ID themselves and for their primary carers?

Mental health is a much broader notion than the absence of mental illness.

A subjective sense of well-being is a distinctive feature of positive mental health, and generally demonstrated by features such as happiness, humor, creativity, self-expression, self-respect, relaxation, assertiveness and affection. This ultimately suggests that mental health must be viewed as a continuum rather than simply the presence or absence of mental illness. Successful aging and mental health care are achieved through a positive interaction of the psychological, biological, sociological and spiritual aspects of the person. A health promotion attitude towards optimizing positive mental health emphasizes the need for healthy living practices, positive social relationships, adequate personal income, varied interests and leisure pursuits, and having a sense of individual self-worth and esteem. The successful interaction between biological, psychological and social aspects of aging remains the most important factor in functional outcomes for the person with ID (Thorpe *et al.*, 2001).

Nursing roles in assessment and intervention

As can be seen in Fig. 16.1, accurate diagnosis of mental health problems in persons with intellectual disabilities is an area fraught with difficulties. Underlying intellectual impairment and communication, combined with poor baseline records against which to measure decline present problems even for the enlightened diagnostician. Diagnosis of mental health problems relies on knowing not just the course but also the context in which the symptoms have developed. Assessment and monitoring should address a number of issues, as follows.

Monitoring health status

Physical health examinations in persons with intellectual disabilities are important because of the difficulties they have in understanding their health care needs, and the inability often to self-report symptoms. Many aging people with ID may have multiple pathology and treatments, which makes assessment complex (Turner & Moss, 1996; Evenhuis *et al.*, 2000). Frequently the result is that an important dysfunction is not apparent until the person presents with acute symptoms. Where nurses have regular contact with persons with ID, they have a fundamental role to play in being alert for and documenting subtle markers such as change in personality and mood – the clues to potential underlying physical or mental health care problems. It is also part of the nurses' role to educate family and primary carers about the relevance of change and the importance of assessment and diagnosis of mental health problems in this

The person with ID
- Cognitively and emotionally functions at an earlier developmental level which affects their understanding of the world and their ability to express themselves
- Increased sensitivity and fear of unfamiliar environments such as clinics and offices
- Communication difficulties and inability to self-report feelings/difficulties
- Difficulty in using standardized assessment procedures
- Physical problems associated with increasing age often become the principle focus for carers, overshadowing other problems such as mental illness
- Atypical presentation of disorders increases complexity of assessment

Service issues
- Lack of experience and education of generic health care professional in dealing effectively with people with intellectual disabilities
- Impoverished care environment
- Lack of specific mental health services with appropriate trained personal to respond appropriately

Carers
- Lack of knowledge and inability to recognize and report changes
- Confused expectations among carers: diminished cognitive abilities may be viewed as an excepted consequence of aging, or attributed to the person's intellectual disability instead of the result of other factors
- Inability to distinguish between signs of ill-being and well-being

Fig. 16.1   Mental health assessment: common sources of difficulties.

population. Nurses and carers need to be familiar with a variety of medical difficulties (which may be expressed atypically in people with ID), that are more common with increasing age such as increased sensory impairment, hypothyroidism, diabetes, heart disease and cancer (see Burt *et al.*, 1998; van Schronjenstein Lantman-deValk, 1998; Evenhuis *et al.*, 2000). Similarly, owing to communication difficulties many people with ID will be unable to describe and articulate feelings or physical problems that they may be encountering, such as pain, discomfort, malaise, the adverse effects of prescribed medications, or psychological problems such as loneliness, sadness, frustration, confusion or depression. These feelings may then generate behaviors in individuals that can be very disruptive and likely to be labeled as 'challenging' The feelings may also generate withdrawn unobtrusive behaviors that go unnoticed.

Nurses must be alert to making subjective judgments that may lead to incomprehensible behaviours being attributed without supporting evidence to underlying mental illness. A lack of knowledge of the symptoms of these conditions may result in inappropriate or inadequate treatment to address factors that are reversible. The lack of knowledge may also result in decreasing the likelihood of proactive and necessary planning to assist those with irreversible decline to cope more effectively with the increased disability that so often accompanies decline.

The Royal College of Nursing (1993) offered useful guidelines on the assessment of mental health needs in old age in the generic population; the issues addressed are also relevant for nurses working with persons with ID. In the current health care climate where frequent staff changes are not uncommon, it is important that nurses are proactive in ensuring that there are objective measures and documentation of the person's personality, level of engagement and participation in daily life activities as well as checking and alerting for changes in memory, communication, mobility and cognition.

Monitoring functional status

Information regarding what level of independence the person previously had in activities of daily living can provide an indicator of change. A clear, precise and unambiguous record of the person's abilities, such as the person's capacity to self-feed, use the toilet or wash independently, are helpful markers with which to measure decline. Indeed there would seem to be some virtue in recording such data on an ongoing, perhaps annual, basis so that the person's cognitive and functional status can be regularly tracked. Best practice suggests that this should be done annually for people with Down syndrome over the age of 40 years and for all people with ID over the age of 50 years (Janicki *et al.*, 1995).

Monitoring behaviour and personality

There should also be periodic assessments to alert for fluctuations and change in behavior and personality. For example, if the person's personality was generally described as happy and sociable, spontaneously interacting with peers, staff and others, and now the individual 'keeps to self', is easily irritated and has lost interest in previously enjoyed activities/events, then this is clearly important. The significance of major life events such as loss, change and bereavement are also clearly important. Possible correlations between symptom presentation and environmental events can help aid the diagnostic process.

Educative role

Nurses have an educative role for other health care professionals as well as for clients and their families. Health and social services personnel need training and support in anticipating and recognizing difficulties and if this is done effectively it will increase the probability of prompt intervention. Nurses also help in differential diagnosis and in ensuring that affected individuals and their families and carers receive appropriate education and the services that are essential to maintain optimum quality of life. Nurses, by the very nature of their role, have the knowledge and ability to communicate information and thus to educate other health care workers.

Advocacy role

Nurses working in this field also have an important advocacy role. Zerwekh (1991, p.32) defines advocacy as 'the process of promoting patients rights of self-determination'. Many persons with ID are not able to speak for themselves and are thus dependent on others, such as nurses, to advocate on their behalf. The nurse, for example, may need to advocate on the person's behalf to ensure equity of access to services along with identifying needed resources necessary to promote optimal quality of care. The nurse also has an important role in supporting the people with ID to attain skills and self-confidence they need to advocate for themselves.

Holistic orientation

Nurses need to caution against overfocusing on diagnostic categories, as used in isolation, because they medicalize the way we interpret the behavior of the person and may lead to care and support interventions that limit rather than empower and result in fragmented care. As can be seen in Fig. 16.2, in a sensitive and respectful manner, nurses must lead efforts to use a variety of sources to build up a picture of the whole person, emphasizing their strengths and needs, likes and dislikes, personality and interests, and their unique life story. In the face of deteriorating mental abilities the person with ID will become increasingly dependent on nurses and carers to uphold their identity; including a biography-based approach in the overall assessment process will help to facilitate this (Wilkinson & Janicki, 2002).

Interventions

As illustrated in Fig. 16.3 nurses are called on to take a comprehensive multifaceted approach to care. Nurses need to be proactive as early

- Alerts nurses and carers to current or potential mental health difficulties, which facilitates timely and appropriate referral
- Provides a baseline from which sources of difficulties and response to treatment/interventions can be evaluated
- Holistic picture which acknowledges the uniqueness of the person
- Helps to identify areas of increasing need and highlights areas requiring additional support
- Identifies strengths and retained abilities to guide establishing care approaches which empower the person to maintain a sense of independence
- Highlights areas of interests from which future care and therapies/interventions can be planned
- Helps to monitor rate of decline

Fig. 16.2   Important outcomes of assessment.

- Promote a culture with the core basic principles of respect, dignity, choice, and privacy to underpin care
- With all care activities be sure to orientate the person, ask their permission if possible, and try and help them understand their environment and what is happening
- Avoid confrontation with the person, as it is generally counterproductive
- Minimize life stressors
- Establish a multi-element intervention plan
- Develop a trusting relationship and a person-centered holistic approach to care
- Empower persons to be involved and to influence their care
- Be innovative and develop outlets for person to express feelings
- Encourage and promote the person with intellectual disability in valued social roles and life enhancing activities
- Develop good observation and communication skills
- Teach therapeutic communication and skills in behavior modification, gentle teaching, validation therapy and positive reinforcement
- Pharmacological treatment where appropriate
- Prevent injury and harm to self, others or property
- Consider the environment to be a form of therapy, consider possible modifications
- Use a non-judgemental approach
- Prevent isolation and ensure approaches are minimally restrictive
- Monitor the efficacy of all interventions, and make appropriate revisions
- Ensure there a structure in place to support staff and a system for ongoing education and training
- In the case of dementia understand that it may demand a continuum of care, and decisions for later care should begin early in the process

Fig. 16.3   Therapeutic approach to care: points for reflection.

interventions and treatments of an emerging problem will be necessary to prevent its escalation. It is fundamental that nurses are tuned in to the function of behavior, enabling preventative strategies to be put in place prior to the onset of the cycle of behavioral episodes. The focus of care must be on understanding a person's sources of difficulties, and the reasons for behaviors or actions. Maladaptive behaviors often become an effective means of communication for people with intellectual disabilities who have difficulties with expressive language. When working with people with ID the channels of communication can be complex, and this is further exacerbated by the onset of mental health problems. Often very little communication takes place through the realms of speech and nurses need to reach past the silence and become creative listeners. There is a need to be sensitive to those non-verbal cues of facial expression, tenseness, gestures, sounds and posture, and respond appropriately (see Goldsmith, 1996; McCallion, 1999). Aggressive and agitated behavior may be the person's means of indicating that something is wrong and cannot be adequately expressed. For example the person with ID who starts to pace the floor, wave hands or engage in rapid repetitive speech, may be providing clues for staff of increased stress and anxiety, enabling early intervention and thus the aversion of a behavioural cycle. Ultimately this approach serves to prevent escalation of emerging problems and also to minimize their impact.

Mindful of Kitwood's work on dementia care (Kitwood & Bredin, 1992; Kitwood, 1997), one of the most fundamental prerequisites is the establishment of a care philosophy and the development of a multi-element intervention plan with short and long-term goals for practice. It is imperative that all staff are clear on the strategies and basic principles for dealing with behaviors that challenge. Uniformity and consistency in approach are necessary for effective management. All members of the multidisciplinary team, the person themselves (if appropriate) and family need to be involved in the following processes

Establishing a care philosophy

Ensure that all members of the care team and family are working towards agreed stated goals. For example, an education program could be instituted for members of the care team and family to help them understand current sources of difficulties and opportunities for improved care for the person with ID who has mental health issues. A care vision reflecting interdependence rather than independence can be encouraged. Happiness and reduced stress should be viewed (accepted) as important outcomes of care.

Supporting peers in the group home

Using a variety of sources and training materials (see for example Kerr & Innes, 2000), an educational program should be instituted for work colleagues and peer members in the group home to help them to understand sources of difficulties and need for support. This will greatly reduce stress and confrontations among all concerned and help to restore tranquillity in the group home.

Offering comfort

In order to reduce sources of stress and anxiety, consider and introduce a variety of supports. For example, assisted and reduced choice with respect to items of clothing; sequencing items of clothing in correct order for dressing; pictorial daily planners for persons with symptoms of dementia or confusion. Sensitive and tactful assistance from the care team and peer group empowering the person to continue to the running of the group home, is important in retaining self-esteem and self-worth.

Redesigning occupation

Job sharing, restructuring hours of work and rethinking chore responsibilities will reduce pressure on the person with ID experiencing difficulties, and also help to address the concerns of peers and staff in the group home. Organize leisure pursuits and relaxation therapies utilizing previously identified areas of interest.

Case study: Peter

Peter is a 40-year-old man with a severe ID. He had a cerbrovascular accident (CVA) when he was 37 years old, resulting in a residual hemiplegia. He has no speech but can make his basic needs known through gestures. Peter has some receptive language. He has lived in a bungalow in the community for the past 20 years. He attends supported employment for two hours weekly. He also attends recreational activities locally. Peter has recently had to deal with the death of the man with whom he shared a room for many years and who was his friend. Peter has started to develop mental health problems that have manifested as daily aggressive behavior.

As a result of both his physical deterioration and his developing mental health problems, Peter has had to retire from his work and spends his daytime in the activity unit where he previously only spent one day a week. He finds he is bored in this situation, a state of affairs that seems to exacerbate his aggressive behaviors. Because of his behavioral changes Peter has been relocated from his community home to a group home on the campus of a large service provider. Here he is lonely, missing his old friends even more, and he finds his freedom to engage with the local community is severely curtailed.

To resolve this situation, nurses and carers, in conjunction with Peter, undertook a number of interventions and actions. The loss of his friend, loneliness, lack of autonomy, dislike of change, combined with the effect of a stroke a couple of years ago which seemed to precipitate Peter's decline, have all played a part in inducing the situation in which he appears to be suffering from a mild but deteriorating depression. The strategy was to address the precipitating factors and to build or rebuild the supports that can cushion Peter from further pressures that might cause a relapse.

The problem regarding Peter's placement is that he can no longer meet his friends and contacts whom he has come to know over the past 20 years. In view of this the nurse will suggest that Peter might share his current placement with his previous one. The plan calls for him to spend three days a week in his former home in the community on an experimental basis.

Work for Peter was an integral part of his life and it facilitated his social connections. When Peter's functional behavior deterioration made it impossible for him to continue working, his aggressive behavior became more prominent as a result of his frustrations. To help overcome this, in tandem with Peter's tentative moves back to community residential placement, it was recommended that he also return to work for one day per week on an experimental basis.

His friend's death, which followed a month of severe illness, upset Peter. He and his friend had roomed together for many years, they had spent much of their social life together, had holidayed together, and although neither could communicate well verbally they had an affinity that had grown over the years into a firm friendship. As his friend's health deteriorated he had been moved to hospital where Peter would visit him most days. After his friend's death Peter became withdrawn and was far less active than he had been. Since he had not formed close attachments to the other people who lived in his house, he became more isolated in his own home. Peter's retirement from work meant that he no longer met the other people with whom he was friendly. As a result of these changes Peter had no cushioning effect from friends to be with him and to help him over his dual bereavement. The question of linking Peter with his old friends needed to be addressed.

Art, music and massage therapies have provided Peter with an opportunity for a cathartic expression of his grief and sorrow. As these continued, Peter became very tearful during these sessions but they coincided with an eventual lessening of the aggression that Peter displayed.

The sequelae of Peter's CVA consist primarily of an impaired ability to get around independently. Steps, stairs, maneuvering in tight corners and lengthy walks are all impossible now. His mobility might be improved if the home could be modified and certain aids introduced; it has been suggested that an occupational therapist be consulted regarding this.

The effects of change appeared to be compounding Peter's grief reactions. The nurse encouraged other team members to consider reversing some of the changes in Peter's residential and occupational life to offer more stability. On reflection, it now seems obvious that where major life changes occur, great care should be taken to ensure that they occur slowly and that their reversibility is also possible.

Peter's remedial plan resulted from a close analysis and assessment of the situation as well as a willingness among Peter's carers to accept that they had made mistakes in changing his life too quickly. This in turn suggested that including Peter in his life planning process might have avoided such problems.

Summary

Nurses and carers are often in contact with adults with ID for longer periods than any other member of the multidisciplinary care team. They are in a unique position to develop close trusting relationships, which have the potential to be a powerful therapeutic resource. These relationships are in fact a key tool through which all the therapeutic approaches that are suggested in this chapter may be enacted.

A crucial aspect in working effectively with people with ID and mental health problems is an individualized approach, an approach that includes the development of preventative strategies, accurate and adequate assessment and effective, monitored interventions. It is the contention of the authors that the mental health needs of the person with ID are best met in a context where the person is at the center of the caring process. This person-centered approach must be linked with care approaches that promote a mentally healthy lifestyle. Such an approach emphasizes physical health and activity along with the adoption of a healthy diet, exercise and appropriate health screening as essential prerequisites in the enhancement of health and well-being for all older people, including persons with ID.

It also includes providing a range of supports for the person on a graduated basis, so that least restrictive environments are offered as ways of maintaining and assisting clients to manage their lives. Finally, empowerment, assisted autonomy and independence/interdependence are also critically important in providing a sense of self and self-worth, and contribute to mentally healthy aging. Such a holistic caring view of aging and mental health must be at the center of nursing responses to the needs of persons with ID.

References

Bersani, H.A. & Heifetz, L.A. (1987) Perceived stress and satisfaction of direct-care staff members in community residences for mentally retarded adults. *American Journal of Mental Deficiency,* **90**, 289–295.

Burt, D.B., Loveland, K.A., Primeaux-Hart, S., Chen, Y-U., Phillips, N.B., Cleveland, L.A., Lewis, K.R., Lesser, J. & Cummings, E. (1998) Dementia in adults with down syndrome: diagnostic challenges. *American Journal on Mental Retardation,* **103**, 130–145.

Cooper, S.A. (1999) Psychiatric disorders in elderly people with developmental disabilities. *Psychiatric Disorders in Developmental Disabilities* (eds N. Bouras) pp. 212–225. Cambridge University Press, Cambridge.

Day, K. & Jancar, J. (1994) Mental and physical health and aging in mental handicap: a review. *Journal of Intellectual Disability Research,* **38**, 241–256.

Evenhuis, H., Henderson, C.M., Beange, H., Lennox, N. & Chicoine, B. (2000) *Healthy ageing – Adults with intellectual disabilities: Physical health issues.* World Health Organization, Geneva.

Goldsmith, M. (1996) *Hearing the Voice of People with Dementia: Opportunities and Obstacles.* Jessica Kingsley, London.

Heller, T., Miller, A.B. & Factor, A. (1997) Adults with mental retardation as supports to their parents: effects of parental caregiving appraisal. *Mental Retardation,* **35**, 338–346.

Janicki, M.P., Heller, T., Seltzer, G. & Hogg, J. (1995) *Practice guidelines for the clinical assessment and care management of alzheimer and other dementia among adults with mental retardation.* American Association on Mental Retardation, Washington.

Jenkins, R., Rose, J. & Lovell, C. (1997) Staff stress and challenging behaviour. *Journal of Intellectual Disability Research,* **41**, 502–511.

Jukes. M. (1994) Development of the community nurse in learning disability: 1. *British Journal of Nursing,* **3**, 779–783.

Kerr, D. & Innes, M. (2000) *What is dementia. A booklet about dementia for adults who have a learning disability.* Scottish Down Syndrome Association, Edinburgh.

Kitwood, T. (1997) *Dementia Reconsidered. The Person Comes First.* Open University Press, Philadelphia.

Kitwood, T. & Bredin, K. (1992) *Person to Person.* Gale Centre Publications, Loughton, Essex.

McCallion, P. (1999) Maintaining communication. *Dementia, Aging, and Intellectual Disabilities* (eds M.P. Janicki & A.J. Dalton) pp. 261–277. Taylor & Francis, Philadelphia.

McIntyre, L.L., Blacher, J. & Baker, B.L. (2002) Behaviour/mental health problems in young adults with intellectual disability: the impact for families. *Journal of Intellectual Disability Research,* **46**, 239–249.

Moss, S. (1999) Mental health. Issues of access and quality of life. *Aging, Rights, and*

Quality of Life. Prospects for Older People with Developmental Disabilities (eds S. Herr & G. Weber) pp. 167–187. Paul H. Brookes, Baltimore, MD.

Nehring, W. (1994). A history of nursing in developmental disabilities in America. *A Life-span Approach to Nursing Care for Individuals with Developmental Disabilities* (eds S.P. Roth & J.S. Morse) pp.1–18. Paul Brookes, Baltimore.

Oliver, C. & Holland, A. J. (1986) Down's syndrome and Alzheimer's disease: a review. *Psychological Medicine*, **16**, 307–322.

Prasher, V.P. & Krishnan, V.H.R. (1993) Age of onset and duration of dementia in people with Down's syndrome: integration of 98 reported cases in the literature. *International Journal of Geriatric Psychiatry*, **8**, 915–922.

Royal College of Nursing (1993) *Guidelines for assessing mental health needs in old age*. Royal College of Nursing, London.

Thorpe, L.U. (1999) Psychiatric disorders. *Dementia, Aging, and Intellectual Disabilities* (eds M.P. Janicki & A.J. Dalton) pp. 221–231. Taylor & Francis, Philadelphia, PA.

Thorpe, L., Davidson, P. & Janicki, M. (2001) Healthy aging-adults with intellectual disabilities: biobehavioural issues. *Journal of Applied Research in Intellectual Disabilities*, **14**, 218–228.

Turner, S. & Moss, S.C. (1996) The health needs of adults with learning disabilities and the health of the nation strategy. *Journal of Intellectual Disability Research*, **40**, 438–450.

van Schronjenstein Lantman-deValk, H. (1998) *Health Problems in People with Intellectual Disability*. Unigraphic, Maastricht.

Wilkinson, H. & Janicki, M.P. (2002) The Edinburgh Principles with accompanying guidelines and recommendations. *Journal of Intellectual Disability Research*, **46**, 279–284.

Zerwekh, J. (1991) Tales from public health nursing true detectives. *American Journal of Nursing*, **91**, 30–36.

17

Future Directions and Challenges

Philip W. Davidson, Vee Prasher and Matthew P. Janicki

If we have succeeded in our goal, this book should have conveyed three important messages. Adults with lifelong intellectual disabilities (ID) represent a significant segment of adults with lifelong disabilities in the developed world. They represent an accessible population and one that is the focus of significant legislative activities and mandated services. They also represent a disadvantaged group of individuals with a broad range of co-morbid conditions and health needs. But what are we doing about responding to these messages?

The data reviewed in the varied chapters consistently point to the need for more research: research to improve our ability to characterize, recognize and treat mental and behavioral difficulties, research to ascertain best practices for community services and to prepare a competent workforce to staff it, and research to improve our ability to prevent behavioral and psychiatric morbidity.

Since 1990 governmental agencies have begun to recognize the need for more research on aging in the ID population. For example, in the US in 1989 the National Institute on Aging (NIA) of the US Department of Health and Human Services issued a program announcement (NIH (National Institutes of Health) Guide, 18 (19), 2 June 1989) calling for applications focused on adults with ID as they grow old. The announcement emphasized the need for research in five areas, including demography and epidemiology, adaptive functioning, social interactions and family support, intervention strategies, and service and care models. Few competitive grants addressing these issues have been funded. Moreover, the announcement addressed neither mental health-related studies nor fundamental biological research, in large part because few promising hypotheses were available at that time.

In the years since the NIA called for these proposals, the urgency for information about older adults with ID has intensified, and some new hypotheses may be emerging. A new look at research needs is in order. As we pointed out in Chapter 1, the need for information about the mental and behavioral disorders occurring in older persons with ID was one of the main findings of the WHO report on behavioral issues (Thorpe *et al.*, 2001, 2002). However, these materials summarized in only a general way the research issues facing this field, and have not proposed a research agenda.

In late 2001, the US Public Health Service sponsored two important meetings dealing with health or mental health issues in persons with ID. The first was a workshop on emotional and behavioral health sponsored by the NIH and co-sponsored by the Joseph P. Kennedy Jr Foundation. The second was the US Surgeon General's meeting on health disparities and intellectual disabilities. Both meetings dealt with important research questions but largely excluded discussion of mature adult and aging issues, especially those related to mental and behavioral difficulties.

A number of questions arising from our review of the field require more research before answers will be at hand. Many of these questions were also identified at the NIH-Joseph P. Kennedy Jr Foundation conference (NIH, 2001). For example, what are the real prevalence rates and natural histories of mental disorders in older persons with ID? There is as yet no consensus regarding the criteria that should be used to diagnose mental illness among persons with ID. Additionally, the genetic and biological bases of psychiatric or behavioral disorders in people with ID are not well understood, and we do not have good natural history data on the relative differences between behavioral phenotypes caused by lifelong social and environmental effects. These and other issues must be clarified before incidence or prevalence data can be taken seriously.

Once we have settled the issue of classification, life-span issues must be addressed. For instance, what is the influence of lifelong disability itself on behavioral or mental health? We have almost no data on the causes of changes in mental health status across the age span. What is known about risk factors for morbidity and functional decline on older adults with ID and when they arise during the lifespan? Most of the research on functional decline has been directed at appreciating the association between Down syndrome and dementia of the Alzheimer type (DAT). But only a fraction of older persons with ID fall into this category; indeed functional decline occurs in many, if not all, older people with or without ID who do not have DAT. Prevention or slowing of the progressive features of loss of function associated with aging would go a long way to increasing the likelihood that an older adult can age in place.

We must also begin to pay more attention to the interplay among the spirit, the mind and the body. We have seen more researchers beginning to investigate and understand the mechanisms that lie at the core of the frequently observed relationship between psychological and environmental states and health outcomes. Once thought impossible, there have been numerous demonstrations of the mutual influence of the nervous system (often referred to as the mind or brain) and the immune system, which in turn influences health and disease. Interest in these areas has been intense, and has been aided in part by increasingly sophisticated tools for demonstrating changes due to psychosocial factors. Few studies have examined the relationship of behavior and health status among aging persons with ID. Sulkes and Emmick in Chapter 6 have reviewed this literature, showing that there are ample data to suggest interplay between physical diseases and mental or behavioral disorders on persons with ID and that these associations may vary with age. Much more work is needed to flesh out the mechanisms that underpin such associations so that interventions and preventative activities may be devised. As we have noted in our own work (Davidson *et al.*, in press), the implications of these findings are that we must be suspect of the immediate presenting behaviors when conducting geriatric assessments and look for other than the obvious underlying causes, and that we must be alert that select conditions may present more as a function of age than as a function of lifelong disability.

Stress, and its effect on the immune system and health, has been a major challenge, both to define and to delineate specific causal relationships. The relationships among these variables are complex, and are mediated by many factors including sex, race, poverty, stressor characteristics (e.g. type, frequency and timing), support systems, availability of coping mechanisms, perceived control and vividness of imagery. In the research community, there has been a focus on specific diseases – cardiovascular disease, cancer, diabetes, gastrointestinal disorders – and the psychological contributions to the development, progression and/or remediation of these diseases. There has also been a focus on methods of responding to a variety of problems outside of Western medical tradition, some being distinctly psychological in origin, others borrowed from diverse cultures and traditions. Examples of these methods include support groups, biofeedback, hypnosis and self-hypnosis – particularly for pain management – progressive muscle relaxation and imagery – guided or otherwise – cognitive behavioral therapy, meditation, massage therapy, spiritual approaches, traditional Chinese medicine, T'ai Chi, chiropractic, and Ayurvedic medicine (Janicki *et al.*, 2002).

In the general mental health arena, more readily measurable but no less important contributors to mental and physical health include a range of recipient issues, such as:

■ *Seeking mental health care* – e.g. when do individuals self-identify as being troubled or disturbed? What are the characteristics of the individual and of the condition that may promote or discourage seeking appropriate mental health services? What theories, myths or personal fables exist that influence attitudes toward seeking care?
■ *Aspects of the therapist-client relationships* – e.g. which are the ones that facilitate or discourage appropriate interventions and mental health?

■ *Compliance factors* – e.g. what factors enhance compliance? Why do adults fail to comply?

It is striking, however, that little work has been done in these important biobehavioral health areas with aging adults with lifelong intellectual and developmental disabilities.

Many adults with intellectual disabilities have risk factors for poor health, such as much higher levels of poverty, lower levels of education, more obesity, less exercise, often low social support, as well as psychological barriers to seeking mental health care on the part of both the individual and service providers, and, for adults with physical disabilities, physical barriers. An illustration of how this may work is as follows. We know that poverty is associated with poor health. A closer examination suggests that low levels of social support, low educational levels and/or depression/anxiety often accompany poverty. Depression in turn has been found in numerous investigations to be associated with a number of health problems, cardiovascular disorders being among the most notable. The physiological mechanisms involved appear to include a higher proportion of sticky platelets, which in turn are associated with clotting and cardiovascular disorders (such as heart disease, stroke). Thus, it might be expected that reducing depression, perhaps by increasing social support or with antidepressants, might also reduce cardiovascular risk. Without specifically designing studies for individuals with disabilities, who may well have different reactions to both medications and to psychological interventions, the impact is unknown.

Given the above, we need to ask ourselves what are the important cultural, ethnic or racial influences on healthy aging and retention of behavioral or psychiatric health among older persons with ID? The WHO report (Thorpe *et al.*, 2001; 2002) identified the need to address multicultural issues by encouraging more cross-cultural research. While such studies are complex and difficult to finance and conduct, the data from them would go a long way toward identifying the influences of culture on prevalence, treatment and prevention of functional decline and the onset of mental or behavioral disorders. Correspondingly, comparative studies are needed to clarify concordance across cultures in rates of mental and behavioral disorders and treatment efficacy.

Answering these and many other questions through research will require more than the often-momentary enthusiasm generated by a conference. Indeed, we should define an international research agenda specific to aging and mental or behavioral health among adults with intellectual disabilities. The agenda should be comprehensive, with a focus on both basic and translational studies. It should be reasonable, identifying a consensus among scientists, practitioners, families and the persons affected by these disabilities. It should clearly state priorities. It should be related to theory and data from mainstream mental health, gerontologic and geriatric research and it should demand interdisciplinary participation from the aging and the ID sectors. And finally, it should be included in the portfolios of agencies and foundations supporting generic aging and mental health research. Philosophically and practically, our understanding of aging and mental or behavioral health in persons with ID is governed by general knowledge about aging, and about mental health; little will be learned if we isolate our research by adopting only an ID perspective.

References

Davidson, P.W., Janicki, M.P., Ladrigan, P., Houser, K., Henderson, C.M. & Cain, N.N. (in press) Association between behavior problems and health status in older adults with intellectual ability. *Journal of Aging and Mental Health.*

Janicki, M.P., Anderson, D., Davidson, P.W., Mughal, D.T., Braunschweig, C., Rimmer, J. & Draheim, C. (2002) An overview of three critical wellness issues affecting adults with intellectual disabilities: the mind, nutrition and exercise (eds T. Heller, M.P. Janicki, C. Gill & A. Factor). *Health Disparities and A Paradigm for Health Promotion: Report of the Invitational Symposium on Health, Aging, and Developmental Disabilities.* University of Illinois at Chicago, Department of Human Development and Disability, Chicago.

NIH (2001) National Institutes of Health workshop on emotional and behavioral health in persons with mental retardation/developmental disabilities: Research challenges and opportunities. http://drafty.ninds.nih.gov/news_and_events/emotional_behavioral_health_2001.htm.

Thorpe, L., Davidson, P., Janicki, M.P. & Working Group (2001) Healthy aging – adults with intellectual disabilities: biobehavioral issues. *Journal of Applied Research in Intellectual Disabilities*, **14**, 218–228.

Thorpe, L., Davidson, P. & Janicki, M.P. (2002) *Healthy Aging – Adults with Intellectual Disabilities: Summative Report* (WHO/MSD/HPS/MDP/00.3). World Health Organization, Geneva.

Index